I0814503

AFRICAN WOMEN – OF THE – ANCIENT WORLD

To my husband Ben, and my children.

AFRICAN WOMEN - OF THE - ANCIENT WORLD

Queens, Consorts, Warriors – Women

Katy Clark

First published in Great Britain in 2025 by
PEN AND SWORD HISTORY
An imprint of
Pen & Sword Books Ltd
Yorkshire – Philadelphia

ISBN 978 1 39903 527 9

A CIP catalogue record for this book is available from the British Library.

Typeset in Times New Roman 12/16 by
SJmagic DESIGN SERVICES, India.
Printed and bound in the UK by CPI Group (UK) Ltd, Croydon, CR0 4YY.

The Publisher's authorised representative in the EU for product safety is
Authorised Rep Compliance Ltd., Ground Floor, 71 Lower Baggot Street,
Dublin D02 P593, Ireland.
www.arccompliance.com

For a complete list of Pen & Sword titles please contact:
PEN & SWORD BOOKS LIMITED
George House, Units 12 & 13, Beevor Street, Off Pontefract Road,
Barnsley, South Yorkshire, S71 1HN, England
E-mail: enquiries@pen-and-sword.co.uk
Website: www.pen-and-sword.co.uk

or

PEN AND SWORD BOOKS
1950 Lawrence Rd, Havertown, PA 19083, USA
E-mail: uspen-and-sword@casematepublishers.com
Website: www.penandswordbooks.com

Contents

Introduction

When I was young, I could sit for hours with a book, happily soaking in its contents. It didn't matter what kind of book it was; I was happy sitting there in my own little corner, imagining the characters, places, and events that were taking place within those pages. So, to have the opportunity to write this book about these significant personalities is truly a thrill. Every adventure has a beginning, and mine started not too long ago. Before writing this book I was writing articles for *The Historian's Magazine*, based in the United Kingdom, which I am still actively writing for, and writing and publishing articles on many subjects of historical significance for several additional forums. The publisher discovered one of my articles, and now here I am with my own book dedicated to women's history and African history. Collective minds are essential to writing any text about critical historical characters as is carefully choosing these personalities to spotlight the rich cultural history and heritage that Africa claims. Ancient history often gets pushed to the back burner because it can feel so far removed for many; however, ancient history has a unique and captivating charm. Over the millennia of human existence, historical texts have shown the development and change of humanity through customs, cultures, and events. Ancient Africa holds a large piece of the long chronicle of humankind. This book features an all-female cast of prominent rulers from various parts of Africa over several centuries. These women existed outside the typical place in society where women were often placed. This book does not disrespect women in history who embraced a more traditionally domestic role, as they were leaders in their own way. The intent here is to celebrate a specific set of women who stepped outside of traditionalism to take on foreign threats and religious shifts, and become true champions of their people, whether it was perceived initially that way or not. As with any origin story, each of these queens has one too. Whether born into their prominent roles or placed there by a marital union, they were women and were treated as inferiors by some in their immediate spheres. However, the story doesn't end there. During the course of this book, they will appear chronologically. So, without further ado, I'd like to introduce these nine African women.

Queen Neithhotep ruled during the First Dynasty in Egypt. Her name is attributed to Neith, the goddess of war and hunting. Scholars initially believed she was a man; however, due to further research into her history after the discovery and deciphering of a clay seal impression, they have deduced that she was a woman, wife of King Narmer, and mother of Hor-Aha. She is arguably the first female monarch in history.

Hatshepsut (HAT-SHEP-SOOT) secured and expanded her nation's borders in Egypt during the 18th dynasty, somctime between 1478–1458 BC. She is known for her devotion to the gods, architectural advancements in ancient Egypt, and her extravagant jubilees, just to name a few. Although history has not always remembered her well, some of her redeeming qualities are being a competent decision-maker, educated, and for a time, being the High Priestess and God's wife of Amon. She was not supposed to inherit the throne, but two of her brothers died unexpectedly. Her royal seat was secured when her half-brother, Thutmose II, took Hatshepsut as his wife.

Queen Nefertiti is another queen reigning during the Eighteenth Dynasty in Egypt (1370–1330 BC), and historians have credited her reign alongside King Akhenaten as the wealthiest period in ancient Egyptian history. She broke religious tradition by suggesting a radical change in the polytheistic practices carved in stone, encouraging a more proto-monotheistic policy centred on worshipping the sun god, Aten. Her name was erased from the pages of history for many years by those who were ashamed of her legacy, mainly correlating to her reign alongside King Akhenaten's which instituted monotheism in ancient Egypt.

Queen Makeda of Sheba is first mentioned in the Hebrew sacred text, tied to Israelite King Solomon. Makeda was a tenth-century Ethiopian ruler considered to be a queen of great strength. She led a massive caravan to King Solomon's temple to resolve her curiosity about the king she had heard was endowed with great wisdom. Her history is tied to the Old Testament, an essential foundation of the present-day Ethiopian Orthodox Church. For centuries, her existence was mostly believed to be a legend until archaeological evidence of her ancient kingdom was uncovered in the ancient ruins of Jerusalem.

Amanirenas, the 'one-eyed' Queen of Kush, ruled from 40 BC to 10 BC, leading the Kushites against the Roman army in a battle that lasted from 25–22 BC. This military pursuit halted the Roman army from expanding southward. Knowledge of this ruler has long been obscure, but there is more to her than meets the eye. She is perhaps one of the most brazen of the queens discussed in this book. She showed defiance to any who would dare act as her ruler, and her insolence against the Roman Empire was on public display.

Shifting to the common era, Dihya Al-Kahina led an indigenous resistance to the Muslim conquest of the Maghreb in the region of Numidia, defeating Umayyad forces in the Battle of Meskiana from AD 695–700. She is mostly credited with defending North Africa from Arabian invasion.

Amina Sukhera of Zazzau is known as the 'Warrior Queen' during her 1576–1610 reign. She was born into royalty to King Nikatau and Queen Bakwa Turunku, and by the time she turned sixteen, she was gifted forty enslaved women, along with other luxuries common to royal status. She was intelligent and skilled in military strategy, leading a thirty-four-year campaign to expand Zazzau territory. She trained her warriors well and is celebrated in traditional Hausa praise songs.

Njinga of Matamba was a Southern African ruler of Ndongo from 1624–1663 and Matamba from 1631–1663, which is in present-day Northern Angola. She received political and military training during her childhood, which prepared her well when she was called upon to diffuse political crises as the Ambassador to the Portuguese Empire. Njinga also displayed resistance to foreign influence; her tactics turned brutal. She utilized her military training when she fought against the Portuguese slave trade.

Ranavalona I ruled from 1828–1861 during the Hova dynasty. She was known as the 'Mad Monarch of Madagascar' and 'Ranavalona the Cruel' during her reign. Scholars long believed her to be a tyrant and likely to have suffered from insanity; however, as more of her history is excavated, historians believe that she was trying to swell her empire and resist European foreign politics and colonialism in Africa. Whether she was insane or trying to progress her empire with limited European influence, her methods have been deemed cruel and inhumane.

These women are worth knowing, as well as the people they led. African history is as vibrant as the flags that wave over its many nations. Art, music and dance that originated in the ancient dynasties are still openly expressed today. The reader can expect to gain a deepened appreciation for African women's history through the extensive research displayed within these pages. For those who have not yet ventured toward this history, a new-found appreciation and delight are certain. These women may not seem to fit the roles they filled at first glance. History has a habit of remembering queens as ruling from palaces of stone, surrounded by ladies in waiting, security, servants, and any other luxury that comes to mind. But not these queens. Some of them may have had palaces, but many served their people in the trenches with their brilliant minds, bravery and blood on the battlefield. With sharp intelligence and swords drawn, whether literally or metaphorically, these nine African queens wrote their names in the pages of history, securing their legacies and the nations they ruled.

I love the analogy of sand, so you may see it referenced periodically throughout this book. Sand shifts, slides, blows in the wind, survives under the scorching sun, or settles beneath the weight of the sea, but it never disappears. The things that have been discovered after a shift in the sand is incredible. Secrets have been exhumed, ancient civilizations revived, and people rediscovered. Archaeologists, historians and scholars have collaborated to decipher the treasures that have been revealed, allowing our world the opportunity to celebrate the unearthed history, whether we hail from that part of the world or not. We have the opportunity to deepen our appreciation and knowledge of our own humanity and celebrate human history. The ancient African dynasties became the juggernauts of trade, rich in ivory, gold, incense, iron and livestock. Ancient Africans were the first to mine many of earth's precious materials, making them valuable trade partners worldwide, which also allowed for alliances to be forged and enforced in the event of foreign invasion.

From where I sit in my corner of the world, I'm going to spin the globe and turn over the sands in the hourglass of ancient Africa. A rich history awaits.

Chapter 1

Neithhotep: 'The Foremost of Women'

(NEETH-Hō-TEP)

First-dynasty Egypt is enticingly mysterious, which is part of its charm. Its ancient culture was founded on a developed religious structure that contained no formal sacred text. The stories are something out of a colourful fantasy dream. A wild cast of complex personalities, each with a unique story to tell and then woven together into a breathtaking tapestry that has beckoned the generations to its gates to experience a land unlike any other in this world. It's important to remember that the further one travels back through ancient history, the wider the gaps become. The world is never at a standstill. From the plates beneath the sea, to the mountainous glaciers of the Arctic and the sandy dunes in between, the earth shifts and bends.

This movement has resulted in monuments and even whole cities being buried over time. The longer something stays buried, the more difficult it is to find, and when it is, it is often missing important pieces to the puzzle that was once complete. However, ancient civilizations left clues ranging from imprints on small clay seals, paintings, and hieroglyphics, to massive tombs, called mastabas where the most ancient of Egyptian rulers were laid to rest. Throughout history, scholars, archaeologists and historians have collaborated to decipher the clues left behind and apply the knowledge to our modern world.

If one were to look at the world from a bird's-eye view in 3,000 BC, Africa would look quite different. Egypt was split into two parts, the upper and lower regions. It was not split based on geographic location, but rather by the current of the Nile River. This phenomenon is fascinating. The Nile River is the longest in the world, stretching for 4,132 miles (6,650km) with many prosperous cities sprouting next to its shores. It is one of the only bodies of water to flow north, meaning 'up' is 'downstream' eventually draining into the Mediterranean Sea. The Nile served as the primary water source for both regions and was essential to maintaining life in a part of the world that would otherwise have been consumed by drought.[1] Ancient Egypt had a unique landscape. It was surrounded by scorching sands and nourished by the waters of the Nile, making its inner cities well-fortified against invaders. The river waters supplied the land with rich black soil, making it agriculturally prosperous. Agriculture was the foundation of the economy in Egypt; its farms were plentiful in wheat and barley. Egyptian society was simplistic compared to the later dynasties. Civilization was primarily made up of simple farmers who tried to settle close to the river to produce crops and sell them in the ancient marketplaces.[2] Those who didn't farm mined valuable minerals to sell or trade for other goods. The Nile was the 'lifeblood' for farmers, which made up the greater population of those living in ancient Egypt. Spanning out, beyond the civilization that hugged the Nile, were a sequence of oases, surrounded by a seemingly endless terrain of mountains of sand.

Ancient Egypt was undergoing massive transformations. During the pre-dynastic era, through the First Dynasty, Egypt had not yet erected the impressive monuments that we attribute to it today. Monuments such as the Great Sphinx and the Great Pyramids did not yet exist. Trade was increasing due to the valuable materials excavated by miners such as precious stones, copper, turquoise and gold. Religious foundations were laid and building projects such as monuments, tombs and mastabas, which were the precursors to the pyramids and temples, were underway.[3] Military campaigns were launched against Nubia, Libya, and Sinai, resulting in greater wealth and expanded territory. The north and south regions were identified by their crowns which was a representation that held significance as the chain of events unfolded. The White Crown of Northern Egypt (*Hedjet)* is a tall, cone-like shape with a bulbous tip and is associated with the god Osiris.[4] On the front of the crown is a creature symbolizing the goddess Nekhbet and her protection over Upper Egypt. The Red Crown of Lower Egypt (*Deshret*) is the royal headdress of the goddess Neith (also Net, Neit, Nit).[5] It is bright red and has a thin black coil that overhangs from the front. Several small statues depict this ancient goddess adorned with this crown. The two crowns combined are called *Pschent*, and it is shown in ancient hieroglyphics that depict the conquering of Lower Egypt during the First Dynasty.

The two regions followed a polytheistic religious foundation, meaning a belief system that adhered to the worshipping of many gods, which also means that no god was all-powerful or all-knowing. Each had a designated duty with correlating attributes that were believed to aid in the individual lives of the people and the world around them. While all the gods and goddesses were respected and worshipped, there were a select few who held prominence among the royals, priests and priestesses. Sais, in Lower Egypt, was believed to be the birthplace of Neith.[6] She is one of the oldest deities in Egyptian religion, alongside Nekhbet who is associated with the town Nekheb in Upper Egypt. Nekhbet was considered the protector of royal children, making her an important goddess among the imperial family in the Upper region. Ancient art shows Nekhbet wearing the *Hedjet* of Upper Egypt alongside her counterpart Wedjet who is wearing the *Deshret* of Lower Egypt. The merging of Upper and Lower Egypt was significant. The painted artwork and representations etched in stone beautifully show the combining of the two regions. Several artifacts show the two goddesses together, representing their regions with a single crown, and bestowing the combined crowns (*Pschent*) on the Egyptian king, symbolizing unification.[7]

The River Nile may have been the lifeblood of Egypt's agricultural economy, but religion gave its people societal structure and order. The religious origins are a collection of stories tracing back to a divine family. Religion in ancient Egypt is among the many facets that offer insight into the early dynasties. Myths about the ancient deities were written to give them personalities, duties, geographic associations, and relational connections tracing back to an origin story. However, their divinity was not entirely comprehended. Even after centuries of study, Egyptian religion remains complex. Some gods and goddesses are depicted in human form, while others are animalistic. Most intriguing are those that are a human-animal hybrid. Their polytheistic beliefs infiltrated every facet of life, and every element had a deity that ruled over it. According to Egyptian mythology origins, the creation myth of Heliopolis describes a vast watery darkness, until a mound of fertile soil was brought to life through the goddess Neith.[8] She began the institution of childbirth, believed in a structured world order, and watched over the souls of those who died. Weaving is a characteristic attributed to Neith; she was believed to produce the burial dress wrappings for those who had passed on, preparing them for the afterlife. She is one of the few deities who was divinely involved in a human's life from the first breath through to the final passage to the afterlife, even watching over the canopic jars holding the removed organs from the departed human body.[9] As one of the oldest deities, this mother goddess is credited with the inception of creation, keeper of the balance of life, and the mediator between heated disputes among the gods. She was worshipped from the early Predynastic period through the beginning of Roman rule.

According to mythological origin stories, Neith gave birth to Atum (The Complete One also known as Re) and Sobek (the crocodile god). She created Apep (the great serpent) and enemy of Re by spitting into the waters of Nun. The myth continues, alluding to a sudden burst of life from Atum to create a male-female pair, Geb (god of the earth) and Nut (god of the sky). The two mated, birthing four gods: Osiris (god of the dead/lord of the underworld), Isis (goddess of healing and magic and sister-wife of Osiris), Seth (god of chaos, desert and storms) and Nephthys (goddess of the air, Mistress of the House, and sister-wife of Seth). This was the foundation of brother-sister unions.[10]

According to mythology, the earth's inhabitants were chaotic, uncultured and barbaric. The birth of Osiris was praised, with many believing that the deity would end the savage ways of the people, that a strong religious foundation would take root. Before long he was the god-king of Egypt. Subsequently, his brother Seth developed a deep-rooted jealousy that grew into an incurable hatred toward Osiris.

Osiris was married to Isis, though Nephthys was attracted to Osiris. Betraying her marriage to Seth, she disguised herself to look like Isis and seduced Osiris. His seed fulfilled her longing, and she became pregnant with Osiris' child, Anubis (god of funerary practices and protector of graves). While Osiris was away on a journey, his brother Seth conspired against him by devising a plot to murder the favoured god. He fashioned a chest that would fit Osiris perfectly. Seth made it into a game, proclaiming that the one who fitted inside the chest perfectly would be the winner. When Osiris climbed inside, one of Seth's co-conspirators closed the lid, trapping Osiris inside. Osiris was unable to free himself, succumbing to the confines of his tomb, his brother's malice tightening around his airways like a serpent. The chest was disposed of in the Nile where it drifted out to the Mediterranean Sea. It bobbed along with the dead Osiris inside until it reached its journey's end, in the roots of a tree in Byblos. The tree was eventually cut and fashioned into a pillar for the palace in

Byblos. The goddess Neith hovered close to Osiris' body, adhering to her protective role over the dead.[11]

Since Isis was the goddess of magic, she disguised herself as a swallow, aiding her in gaining access to the palace to retrieve the chest. She returned to the Nile Delta, hiding the chest in the marshes. Unfortunately, Seth was out hunting in that area and found Isis attempting to hide Osiris in the marsh. When Isis left the boggy hiding place, Seth opened the chest and hacked his brother's body into fourteen pieces and scattered them over a vast area, all except the penis, which he threw into the Nile where it was devoured by a fish.[12] All Isis' magic and rituals did not bring Osiris back from the dead. The only thing left to do was gather his body and prepare him for burial.[13]

It was essential for the body parts to be intact for the spirit to be a part of the afterlife. Isis searched high and low, gathering the body parts of Osiris to make him whole again. Since his penis had been devoured by the river creature, she fashioned an artificial penis so that he would be complete, qualifying him for a proper burial through traditional mummification at Abydos. Osiris became the god of the dead. His place as Lord of the Underworld was secured, as well as his immense significance in the lives of the ancient Egyptians.[14]

There are of course variations to this myth. The Greek playwright Plutarch describes the death of Osiris as him being defeated by his brother Seth, falling on his side on the riverbank at *Nedjet*. Plutarch also proposed a different version of what happened to Osiris' penis, asserting that it was removed and buried in Memphis. In Plutarch's version, Osiris and Isis' son Horus was not conceived before Osiris' death. She is described in the playwright's version as morphing into a sparrow and hovering steadily over her husband's arousal, magically becoming impregnated by him with their son Horus (god of healing, protection, and kingship). Nearing the end of this origin story, Neith was consulted to mediate between Horus and his uncle, Seth. Believing in maintaining harmony in the world, Neith favoured

Horus, who defeated his uncle, reclaiming his right to rule and restoring order throughout the land of Egypt. His eyes were said to be the sun and the moon, watching over the world. He had the ability to fly to Re and return to those who needed relief from fear and doubt. Horus was a highly revered deity, favoured by Re and praised by the ancient people.[15]

Horus is depicted on many tombs of the ancient pharaohs, illuminating their prominent stance in society, and their hierarchal rank, and has led researchers to the graves of these rulers and their stories that beg to be told. Two of which are Narmer, also known as Menes, who ruled Upper Egypt and his wife hailing from Lower Egypt, Neithhotep.

Narmer was a man of unquenchable ambition. He is most commonly believed to be the son of Ka, also known as King Scorpion, who was a fierce warrior and dominant ruler. Ka, also known as Sekhem Ka, may be one of the earliest-known proto-dynastic rulers, reigning over Thinis in Egypt's Upper region.[16] One of the most significant finds dating back to the predynastic period is the scorpion mace head. The artifact is a bowl-shaped jar, portraying a man bearing the crown of Upper Egypt and a scorpion in front of him. In this scene, several of what appear to be birds are hung by the neck, signifying people who had been conquered by a warrior king.[17] The mace head was found by archaeologists James Quibell and Frederick Green during an archaeological dig in 1897–1898.[18] Since these two significant artifacts were found during the same dig, and in an area relative to each other, it is suggested that Pharaoh Narmer was the Scorpion King, not his predecessor Ka. This is continuously argued among Egyptologists today.

Whether Narmer was the son of this fearless warrior or the Scorpion King himself, he was the embodiment of the progressive and conquering traditions long embedded in the dynastic heritage of Egypt. The basic physical characteristics of Narmer are not well known. However, what is lacking in the knowledge of physical attributes is made up for in understanding who he was as a conqueror and ruler. He disapproved of Egypt being divided. Any nation that is divided is seen as an easy target for foreign invaders to attack, pillage, destroy, and ultimately dissolve the independent nation and absorb it into another, or wipe it off the face of the earth entirely. Narmer realized that a unified Egypt would be stronger and would increase his land title and wealth. However, he wanted to maintain peace with those he intended to rule. If Egypt was to become one nation, he would have a strong military front due to the increase in soldiers but also due to the men having knowledge of their regions of origin. This would prove to be most useful when preparing for possible invasion from the surrounding nations' armies and withstanding the land. He was an effective military strategist and he set his sights on Lower Egypt.

Conquests in pursuit of greater wealth and expanded territory is a tale as old as time, and it fits the narrative of Narmer's military campaign to unify Egypt. Narmer, the ruler of the Upper Kingdom, desired to expand his lands and make Egypt a single nation. The suspected motive was unity and peace between the two regions. While this may be so, there is reason to believe Narmer achieved this by force and most likely through several campaigns. Egypt was divided, each region having its own ruler. This structure had existed for many years, so it is unlikely that the southern kingdom was conquered in a one-and-done deal.[19] Conquering the opposite region gave him pharaonic power, which meant that he was not only the uncontested ruler over Egypt, but also highly favoured among the gods. Unifying Egypt meant that he restored peace throughout the land, even if by force. This would have been believed to have given him high favour from Horus, who is also accredited in Egyptian mythology as a conqueror of chaos and bringer of peace. One of the most telling artifacts from the First Dynasty is the Narmer Palette. The carving on the palette shows Narmer wearing the crown of upper Egypt while wielding a club and clutching the hair of one of his subdued subjects.

Horus is shown perched overhead, which is interpreted as Narmer's conquest being watched over and blessed by the ancient deity. The opposing side shows a bull trampling over its enemies, with two people appearing to hide in fear from the mighty conqueror.[20] Narmer was victorious in his pursuit to unify Egypt. He is later shown to be wearing the crown of the Upper Kingdom inside the red crown of the Lower Kingdom. This is a definitive symbol of the conjoining of the two regions. Which brings us to Lower Egypt, the birthplace of Egypt's first known female ruler, Neithhotep.

Who was Neithhotep? The simple explanation is that she was the daughter of the conquered Lower Egyptian king, and the wife of pharaoh Narmer, named for the goddess Neith. However, there is so much more to her. It just took some digging. When her tomb was found she was believed to be a man due to the size of the mastaba and other distinctions that would have been bestowed exclusively on male rulers. Originally from Sais, believed to be her birthplace, her name has some added significance since it is at Sais that the goddess Neith is said to have first risen to religious prominence. She was a highly revered deity. Neith was the goddess of creation, warfare, and weaving, and is believed to be one of the most ancient Egyptian deities.[21] As the goddess of warfare, she was also known as the master of the bow and arrow. She was the goddess kings turned their prayers to when discussing military campaigns and the threat of homeland peace and security. The name 'Neith' is attributed to contentedness. It is also shown by several artifacts that Neith wore the red crown of Lower Egypt, which remained an enduring symbol of the region's devotion to its religious origins until military conquests marched through demanding a unified Egypt.[22]

It is unknown how Neithhotep felt about her union with Narmer. Did she favour her union with the victorious king? Was she a negotiating piece or perhaps a prize of war? These questions remain shrouded in mystery. However, she embraced her role as royal regent over Egypt. The roles of the king were vastly different to those of a regent. In many cases the royal regent served as a substitute leader if the reigning pharaoh was too young to rule, or if the pharaoh was stricken with poor physical or mental health. Pharaohs in ancient Egypt held a unique status, not only among their people but among their gods as well. As king, Narmer would have had a bridge between his human self and the deities. The pharaoh was seen almost as godlike and was assumed to have their favour. According to Lorna Oakes' and Lucia Gahlin's encyclopaedia of ancient Egypt, 'The king could be regarded as a god, or as somewhere between the divine and mortal world, or as a mere human being. It is safe to say, however, that the concept of kingship – the office, rather than the man himself – was considered divine. It was felt that the king could relate to the gods in a way that none of his subjects would have been able to, which must have enhanced the nature of kingship and inspired respect, if not awe, in the people.'[23]

As queen consort, Neithhotep's primary duty was to support her husband and king in his military campaigns, and in religious, social and economic reform. Per ancient portrayals, Narmer's reign was divinely looked over and protected. It was successful, and most notably, the city of Memphis was established as the original capital of Egypt; it was a prosperous city and served as the beginning of urbanization in Egypt. However, his reign ended abruptly and violently after a hippopotamus attack.[24] The beast, weighing up to five tons, and although herbivorous, did not hesitate to charge and attack. Despite their weight, they are fast swimmers and can conceal themselves underwater, just keeping their beady eyes above the surface. A hippopotamus will attack as an army of one or part of a herd. In addition to their weight, they are known for having exceptionally flexible jaws, being able to open their mouths wide, and using their powerful jaws to trap their victim in their massive, bone-crushing teeth. Once the victim is thus trapped, hippopotamuses will pull their detainee under the water, thrashing and stomping their victim to death. It is not out of the realm of possibility that King Narmer suffered a similar end to this description. Upon his untimely demise, Neithhotep was thrust into the role of leader over Egypt and protector of the dynasty.

Her son, Hor-Aha was not yet mature enough to lead, so it is widely accepted that Neithhotep ruled as king of Egypt until her son came of age. It's paramount to acknowledge the importance of Neithhotep's reign. Scholars previously confined her to a 'queen consort' role.[25] That, however, does not endow the capabilities essential to dynastic ruling decisions that would affect the future of the kingdom, nor would it have influenced the rising and shifting culture emerging from Egypt, further suggesting that she was far more prominent a ruler than a queen consort. Neithhotep guided Egypt through the passing of its ruler by solidifying its culture, religious foundations, agriculture and trading practices, and military guard. All her efforts contributed to creating the pathways to the legacy of the dynasty and the ones succeeding it.

After the passing of Narmer, Neithhotep invested her time in preparing her young son to rule the kingdom she would eventually leave to him. She provided him with thorough military training, and religious instruction, and instilled a reverence for Egypt's many deities. Due to the absence of his father and royal influence, Hor-Aha's mother would have assumed that role naturally, acutely aware that her instruction directly impacted the future security of Egypt. Considering what scholars know about Neithhotep, she successfully prepared her son for the monumental task of assuming the throne over the dynasty.[26] Even though Egyptian thinking was more progressive regarding the status of women, she would have certainly had to prove herself in a still deep-rooted patriarchal system. She found herself at the centre of Egyptian society, a benevolent ruler, and a sustainer of the dynasty. Neithhotep undoubtedly understood the immense weight of her responsibilities. From what is written about this first queen, she embraced the many changes and confronted the responsibilities in her life with contentedness and courage. As a female ruler, Neithhotep held fast to every ounce of strength with both hands, while surrounded by a male-dominated system – royally, politically and socially. She was the keeper of ancient traditions and assumed the responsibility of training her son in military strategies, concepts of war and trade, fortifying the kingdom's boundaries, and ensuring the survival of the dynasty and those that succeeded long after her rule. Considering the centuries of enduring traditions that have been so carefully preserved on the many surviving monuments, her reign was a massive success. Archaeologists have proven this by discovering her successful dig at the Wasabi Desert, which uncovered large amounts of gold and precious stones.[27] This site increased the dynasty's wealth and created more trade opportunities with the surrounding nations. Some of the greatest discoveries relating to her legacy are the inscriptions found at the Wadi Ameyra location in the Sinai Desert. Archaeologists have discovered that Neithhotep ordered the expedition to mine precious materials such as turquoise and copper from that region and to gather food items.[28] A queen consort would not have had the authority to order such a task. This is a fantastic example of how she increased the wealth of her dynasty and made Egypt a valuable trade partner among foreign neighbours.

During Neithhotep's reign many ancient customs were either implemented or sustained as established traditions and ceremonies. She helped instil a reverence for the gods and goddesses by taking part in daily rituals, offerings, and sacrifices. What can be tangibly understood is the impact the religious cohesiveness had on the masses who served the deities through festivals and structures built in their honour. Temples erected for the gods were not regularly used for congregating. Entrance to these structures was strictly limited to priests and priestesses, who were only permitted inside the temples to perform rituals. Only during festivals would the people congregate at the outermost areas of the temples. Human sacrifice became common practice, especially among royals when a pharaoh passed on to the afterlife. It was not uncommon for people to willingly offer themselves as a sacrifice, hoping to continue to serve their king in the next life.

In addition to her success in expanding Egypt's wealth and resources, she ensured that the roots of religious practices ran deep. There is strength in a name, and Neithhotep undoubtedly felt the strength in hers. She strongly believed in religious foundations and strived to keep worship at the heart of Egypt's civilization. In ancient Egypt an annual festival was held in praise and worship of Neith, called the Festival of Lamps (also known as the Feast of Lamps).[29] The festival commenced each year on the thirteenth day of the third month. Saucers of salt and oil were brought to the sacred temple as an offering. The light of the lamps burned through the night. Delicious food, dancing and music were enjoyed in abundance. The festival had a special significance that surpassed all other indulgences. It was believed that the veil between the heavens and the earth was parted during this festival, allowing those living to see and speak with loved ones who had passed into the afterlife. The Festival of Lamps is still practised today in Egypt; however, its focus has shifted to the goddess Isis.

Her name carried immense representation throughout her life, it was equally significant when she died. Exploring the symbolism associated with Neithhotep and the goddess Neith, her burial arrangements offer insight into the impact she had on the female rulers who came after her.

The resting place of Neithhotep was discovered by French archaeologist Jacques de Morgan in 1897.[30] His experience led him to believe that the buried royal was a man. Due to the limited artifacts that have survived from the First Dynasty, it is unknown how long her reign endured. The tomb is an impressive size, embellished with markings that would indicate the tomb was built for a male ruler. However, one distinct characteristic punctured a hole in his initial theory. Inside her tomb is a *serekh*, which is a decorative feature that holds substantial significance. As previously mentioned, Horus was a supreme deity. The depiction of this highly respected god on the *serekh* meant that the Egyptian king had a likeness with the god himself. Horus appears at the top, indicating that the name is attributed to a royal. A *serekh* was placed in tombs of male rulers, except hers bore a pair of crossed arrows above a crest honouring her name, which is incredibly noteworthy.[31] This is the symbol of the goddess Neith. 'She was revered as the mistress of the bow … ruler of the arrows'. Neithhotep's mastaba dwarfed her pharaoh husband's. Narmer's tomb was two small pits dug in the earth with minimal ceremonial items, which was the traditional practice when he passed into the afterlife. While Narmer's tomb is particularly modest, his queen's was a massive structure. It is believed that her son and successor Hor-Aha ordered the construction of Neithhotep's mastaba to be a symbol of his devotion to her and promise that the world would know how significant she was, not only in her own right but in Egyptian history.[32] Her efforts as regent and queen were focused on preserving religious foundations and continuing the construction of sacred temples and statues that had gained a lot of forward momentum during Pharaoh Narmer's reign.

Despite the efforts to build an enduring and high-standing tomb that would catch the eye of distant travellers as they trekked across the desert, it was constructed of mudbricks, making it impossible for the structure to withstand the elements throughout the centuries. It was not until subsequent dynasties that the great pyramids, made of more durable materials, were constructed. In its time, a mastaba such as Neithhotep's would have been a sight to behold. Inside, several significant items have been recovered from her tomb. Clay bowls, seal impressions, and ivory tags bearing her name were found, along with beads, charms or protective devices called amulets, and jewellery made from ivory, semi-precious stones, and shells.[33] Her tomb is known as the Great Tomb of Naqada, meaning Gold City, appropriately named since the area is known for its gold mines.[34]

Neithhotep's legacy and impact are beautifully carved and painted along the walls of history. Her leadership paved the way for the dynastic rulers who came after her, especially women. Her story is one of endurance and embracing change for the good of her people and out of respect for her own legacy. She helped solidify the religious foundations that remained at the core of ancient Egyptian society and culture, ensured the future of the dynasty through the training of her young son into the maturity of a king, increased Egypt's wealth, and most importantly, demonstrated that a woman can rise to perform at a high rank. A woman could become queen, despite being the daughter of a defeated king. She could rise above the confines of a patriarchal system which is perhaps why she is called 'the foremost of women'.

European fascination with ancient Egypt is traced as far back as the Greek historians Herodotus and Strabo. Herodotus wrote of the things he saw and what was spoken to him by the Egyptian priests.[35] Over time, Egypt became a focus of religious and military conquests, including the pursuits of Napoleon Bonaparte who recruited skilled mathematicians, scientists, and astronomers.[36] Visitors to ancient Egypt have greatly increased over the centuries. Early Egyptologists spent many years studying the remains and deciphering the hieroglyphics left behind by this civilization. Conquests turned into excavations for knowledge, recognition, and treasure. Countless digs have been performed, producing many items of intrinsic and historical value. Like other disciplines, archaeological excavation methods have improved. Unfortunately, the early years of discovery were unkind to the history that lay beneath the sands.

Archaeologist Émile Clément Amélineau was harsh with his findings. He was only interested in artifacts that were intact and valuable so that he could sell them. If they were broken, fragmented, or lacking in any way, the items were discarded or broken. He also did not extend generosity to his workers. His hired help was underappreciated and underpaid, and unfortunately, they succumbed to the temptation of thievery.[37] Archaeologist François Auguste Ferdinand Mariette had similar sentiments when it came to artifacts discovered in ancient Egyptian sites. His methods were destructive, to say the least. He employed the use of dynamite to break apart the structures he intended to excavate.[38] This undoubtedly irreparably destroyed what could have been deciphered from the structure itself, as well as the items inside the tombs.

Another archaeologist, Sir William Matthew Flinders Petrie, was enthralled with Egypt. The Father of Modern Egyptology, as he was appropriately nicknamed, performed his archaeological digs with far more care.[39] He is credited with finding a bandaged arm in the tomb of King Djer (c. 3000 BC). He brought this fascinating artifact to a museum, but the assistant curator, who only saw value in items such as gold, precious stones, and jewellery, failed to see the significance of this item, and threw it away. Had he kept the bandaged arm, the early methods of mummification could have been more thoroughly studied. The archaeological methods and mindsets of that time share some responsibility for why there are gaps in this history.[40]

There is far less known about Neithhotep than about the queens that came after her, such as Hatshepsut, Nefertiti and Cleopatra. Much of the predynastic period was destroyed or thrown out; a primary contributor to why much of Neithhotep's early background is lost. There are a few interpretations presented in books and articles that suggest an array of possibilities about her and what her duties in Egypt might have been. Early archaeologists believed her identity to be that of King Teti, relating to the royal line of Ramesses the Great. Egyptologists have since refuted those claims, pointing to the clay seals that were found in the tomb of Queen Meritneith, which lists the names of pharaohs from Narmer to Den. The clay fragments also define the First Dynasty as being ruled by Narmer, not Hor-Aha or Djer as earlier archaeological interpretations suggested.[41] Other interpretations include that she was the wife of Hor-Aha, not Narmer, as well as the suggestion that Narmer and Hor-Aha were the same person.[42] These interpretations are not supported by the more recent and in-depth analysis of the artifacts found in the massive *mastaba* of Neithhotep in Naqada. Items in other royal Egyptian tombs, such as ivory tags bearing her name, heavily support the more widely accepted conclusion that she was indeed the wife of Narmer and mother of Hor-Aha. Her origins and connections to the great kings of the era continue to be researched and debated, which is necessary considering the long chronicle Egyptian history boasts.

Predynastic and First Dynasty Egypt has undeniable gaps that beg to be filled with accurate data. When looking out on the vast horizons of history, there are parts that have remained shrouded in mist and fog. As we shine a light on this unventured terrain, discoveries of great fortune are found, while at other times, the more that is illuminated, the deeper the fog reveals itself to be, and further exploration is necessary. Without the efforts of the collaborative minds invested in the search for the past, a huge piece of history and culture would be lost, and less would be known about this early dynastic queen who ruled Egypt in her own right. Unified efforts have allowed historians to give this piece of history back to its people, and the world. Knowing about personalities like Neithhotep, the world can hold fast to and celebrate part of its cultural vibrance.

The public has the opportunity to enjoy Egypt's magnificence. The ancient sites that have endured the constant tossing of the sands can be taken in through the senses whether at a museum or venturing to the great land of Egypt to gaze upon its history firsthand. Items such as the clay jar seals that bear her name and ivory pieces are now on display at the Metropolitan Museum in New York. Museums worldwide have countless collections from the Old Kingdom in Egypt on display for public viewing, scholarly research, and cultural celebration. Perhaps as archaeologists continue to dig deeper and decipher more of the inscriptions that have been unearthed or washed up onto the beaches after centuries of wandering, more will be known and understood about this queen who might have remained lost to us.

Chapter 2

Hatshepsut: 'God's Wife of Amun'

(HAT-SHEP-SOOT)

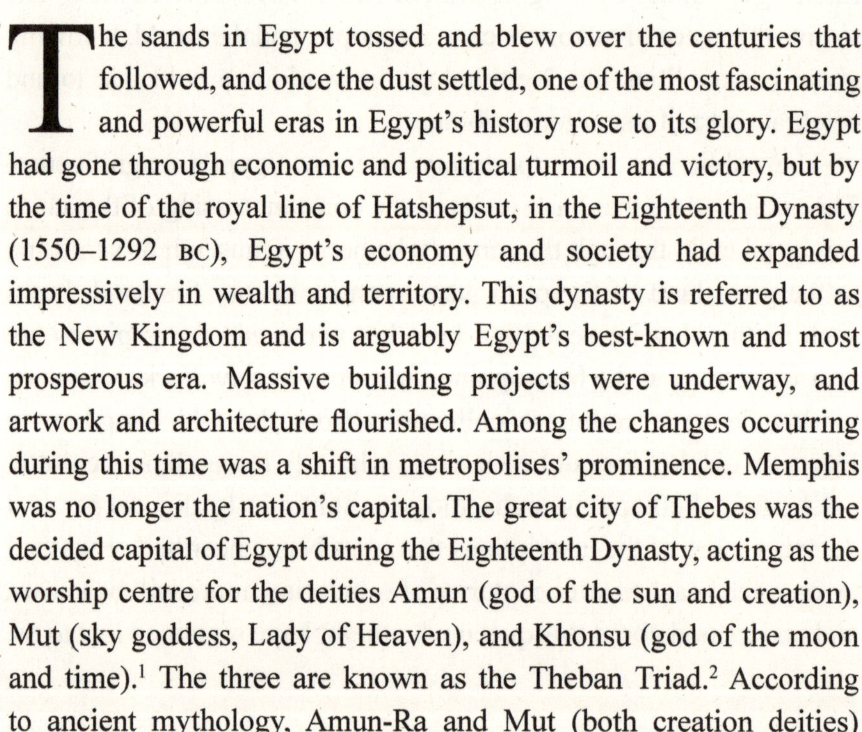

The sands in Egypt tossed and blew over the centuries that followed, and once the dust settled, one of the most fascinating and powerful eras in Egypt's history rose to its glory. Egypt had gone through economic and political turmoil and victory, but by the time of the royal line of Hatshepsut, in the Eighteenth Dynasty (1550–1292 BC), Egypt's economy and society had expanded impressively in wealth and territory. This dynasty is referred to as the New Kingdom and is arguably Egypt's best-known and most prosperous era. Massive building projects were underway, and artwork and architecture flourished. Among the changes occurring during this time was a shift in metropolises' prominence. Memphis was no longer the nation's capital. The great city of Thebes was the decided capital of Egypt during the Eighteenth Dynasty, acting as the worship centre for the deities Amun (god of the sun and creation), Mut (sky goddess, Lady of Heaven), and Khonsu (god of the moon and time).[1] The three are known as the Theban Triad.[2] According to ancient mythology, Amun-Ra and Mut (both creation deities) produced their son, Khonsu. During the Old Kingdom, Khonsu was depicted as terrifying and hostile with an unquenchable bloodthirst. It was believed that he rallied the deceased pharaohs to take part in feasting on other gods and goddesses.[3] By doing so, the kings would absorb the powers and authority of the gods. This belief was even recorded in stone known as the Cannibal Hymn.[4] This text is believed to have been engraved in the pyramid of Pharaoh Unis during the fifth dynasty. However, by the beginning of the New Kingdom, the beliefs attributed to Khonsu were a drastic contrast. Instead of being a bloodthirsty and sadistic cannibal who lured unsuspecting deities to his feasts, he was now believed to be a benevolent and youthful god, acting as a pathfinder for those who were lost and seeking direction.[5] He was even attributed with illuminating the moon that hung in the night sky. Thebes proudly displayed the glory of Egypt. Beautiful temples made of stone, and embellished with artwork, stood proud, reaching toward the skies. The Temple of Karnak, which means fortified village, was used to worship the god Amun Ra.[6] Despite being known as the god of the sun and creation, he was said to come from humble beginnings but eventually rose to be one of the most prominent deities during the New Kingdom.[7] To the south of this temple resides the temple of Mut (wife of Amun) and within her temple lies the temple of their son, Khonsu. Her temple resides in the city of Luxor (what was ancient Thebes).[8] It is surrounded by a crescent-shaped lake known as the Sacred Lake.[9] The Temple of Khonsu was a small but complete sanctuary. Its construction was originally begun by Ramesses II but was not completed until later in the Eighteenth Dynasty.[10] Many additional temples were erected for other gods and goddesses, which are sprinkled around Thebes. In its original glory, the Temple of Karnak was over 50,000 square metres and displayed 5,000 statues of Amun Ra.[11] The great temple had over 80,000 slaves, servants, and priests.[12] The city's construction was funded by the vast wealth acquired during numerous military successes over the surrounding lands and kingdoms. Much of the expansion was the result of military conquests, such as the conquering of the Hyksos and expelling them from the Nile River Delta.[13] King Ahmose drove the Hyksos to the eastern border of Egypt and into Palestine. Riches were gathered and either kept for royalty or given to treasuries dedicated to the gods, particularly Amon Ra, who had become the most worshipped and revered god during the Eighteenth Dynasty.

Pharaoh Ahmose is largely credited as the founding father of the Eighteenth Dynasty, using strong military campaigns to unite the nation of Egypt after years of discord.[14] He was born into the royal family in Thebes and catapulted to the throne at the age of ten, which is young to be handed the responsibility of ruling a kingdom, however, it was not uncommon.[15] Surrounded by royal viziers and regents, he undoubtedly had enough support to give him the guidance needed until he came of age. Between the Sixteenth and Seventeenth Dynasties Egypt coexisted with the kingdom of Hyksos, which had Palestinian origins.[16] Desiring a unified Egypt, Ahmose led his army against the Hyksos army, disbanding them and solidifying a more stable and prosperous reign for his heir, Amenhotep I. This conquering is depicted in ancient artwork, showing Ahmose gripping the head and hair of a subdued Nubian in one hand, and clutching a ceremonial axe in another, posed to sever the head of his conquered enemy.[17] Not only did Amenhotep seize a favourable start to his reign, he also successfully expanded Egypt's territory by initiating wars in Nubia (what is now modern-day Sudan) and conquering the Nubians.[18] This land was heavily coveted by the Egyptians and became a place of intrinsic interest for the Greeks and Romans during the subsequent centuries. Resources such as gold, other precious metals, ivory, timber, a wealth of livestock, and slaves were in high demand. Seizing this area expanded Egypt's wealth and resources, both agriculturally and socially, making them the conquering juggernauts of that time.[19] Even with all the gold and resources available at his fingertips, the reigning king did not secure what Egypt ultimately needed: a successor to take over when Amenhotep died. Amenhotep failed to secure an heir within the royal bloodline, so his general, Thutmose I, succeeded him to the throne.[20] He was the third ruler during the Eighteenth Dynasty. He was a great warrior-king, leading his armies in multiple conquests, most notably his dominance over Nubia during his second year as pharaoh. He led his unmatched massacre in Nubia to the Euphrates River in Carchemish (present-day Syria) and continued to Hyksos.[21] After reducing the enemy to ash his army arrived at Thebes, proudly displaying the corpse of the Nubian chief, who had been tortured and mutilated in his final moments.[22] The conquered people were publicly executed. With the enemy's army removed from Thutmose's path, the riches of Nubia were there for the Egyptian dynasty's taking. The army dug their hands deep into rich gold deposits and filled their satchels and wagons. Shortly after his military success, civil unrest and defiance reared its head in the Land of Kush, a kingdom in Nubia along the Nile Valley which is now located in modern-day Sudan and southern Egypt. The Kushites were planning an uprising against Thutmose and his equal in aggression, Queen Ahmose (also known as Ahmes).[23] There was only one solution evident to the royal pair: total, merciless annihilation. Pharaoh's army once again returned with riches confiscated from their defeated foe. Some of the riches were given to the gods as an offering of thanks and worship for a successful campaign. Thutmose I married his sister, Ahmes, who gave birth to several potential royal heirs. It is this bloodline that led to the reign of Hatshepsut.[24]

Hatshepsut's existence was believed to be divinely orchestrated. Her conception and birth are part of a mythical narrative. According to mythology, Amon-Re (Amun-Ra), god of the sun and arguably the most powerful of ancient Egyptian gods, fell in love with Hatshepsut's mother, Ahmes.[25] Unable to resist her beauty he left his home in the sky to lie with her. She awoke from a deep sleep, sensing his presence and smelling his scent. Desiring to express her devotion to the god, she offered her heart and body and satisfied him.

After several encounters (whether at different times or during this one night), Ahmes became pregnant with Egypt's future queen. Her name, Hatshepsut, means 'she of noble bearing'. The conception of Hatshepsut is depicted through ancient art. Amun-Ra is seated in the bedchamber with Ahmes, their knees are intertwined, and their bodies are held erect by two fertility goddesses. This symbolizes their sexual union.[26] Following this picture is Heket, the goddess of childbirth, who is attending the creation of Hatshepsut, kneeling before the potter's wheel of Khnum, god of procreation. She is holding an ankh in her hand, which is the symbol of life. Next, Hatshepsut is presented to Amun-Ra, who is seen holding the ankh in his right hand. He is pleased with the results of his creation.[27] Finally, Queen Ahmes is depicted being led by the hand of Khnum and Heket. It was exceedingly uncommon for women to be shown as pregnant in ancient art, however, if one looks closely, the slightest bump can be observed in the queen's midsection.[28] This artistic representation symbolizes the divine guidance she received during her pregnancy all the way to childbirth. Ancient women often gave birth in a crouching position while standing on birthing mudbricks.[29] The infant mortality rate was high so any divine assistance during pregnancy and childbirth was coveted, especially from the goddess Taweret (The Great One), who is depicted as a hippopotamus with a crocodile's tail. Small statues show her sitting on her hind legs, with a protruding belly and engorged breasts. She is often seen holding the ankh or tyet-amulet, which also symbolizes life. Her protection of the unborn extended to all infant life, not only the royals.[30]

Royal heirs that were believed to have been conceived through the seed of a god or goddess were immediately placed in high standing among the royal family and Egypt's loyal subjects. Whether or not Hatshepsut was the product of a sexual encounter between her mother and Amon-Ra, she was a member of a royal bloodline and a close-knit family. When Hatshepsut was born, it was as if her whole world had been planned for her. She was the daughter of the king and sister of young boys who would presumably continue the dynasty. She was her father's pride and joy. At just ten years of age, she was named High Priestess and was given the name 'god's Wife of Amun'.[31] This title was prestigious, and Hatshepsut undoubtedly felt the immense responsibility she bore. Women who had social elitist status or the privilege of being born or married into such a status could become a temple priestess. As High Priestess (*hemet netjer*, meaning servant of god),[32] her duties were numerous and were often carried out in seclusion. Only the high priest or priestess was permitted access to the innermost parts of the temples where worship commenced. She kneeled before the statues of deities. She burned incense, recited sacred prayers, sang hymns, danced, and played instruments. Harps, tambourines, and clappers were the favoured instruments for worshipping gods.[33] Another responsibility Hatshepsut would have had was to engage in funerary rituals. In addition to solemn songs and prayers for the deceased, she would have been cast to play the role of a deity in a re-enactment performance of the death of Osiris.[34] The role would have either been that of the ancient goddesses Isis or Nephthys. This practice was performed in honour of the deceased and served as a reminder of the religious foundations laid during the Old Kingdom. As 'god's Wife of Amun', her duties went far beyond hymns, prayers, and the burning of incense. A primary characteristic of a high priestess was purity. For as long as she kept her title and duties as a priestess, she was to remain celibate, but beautiful and pleasing to Amun-Ra. Hatshepsut, in her beauty and purity, remained sexually arousing, serving as an object for masturbation by the great deity, enabling Amun to continue his re-creation and the renewal of his power.[35] Her physical purity ensured an unsoiled experience for Amun. He could renew himself without physically damaging her virginity. Hatshepsut undoubtedly had a highly developed maturity for she understood and respected the position she had been bestowed.[36] Despite her youthfulness, she was the mother of the religious community. She had access to the dynasty's abundant wealth and was given charge over large estates and many people.[37]

Hatshepsut's brothers Amenmose and Wadjmose were both strong boys, greatly favoured by their father. The eldest son was to be the next royal to sit on the throne of Egypt, however, both brothers met an untimely death. It is unknown what the exact cause of the two princes' demise was. Possibilities include illness, accident, or an animal attack. The loss was crushing to Pharaoh Thutmose I. In his grief, he had large memorial stone structures built in their honour.[38]

Hatshepsut's husband, Thutmose II, was born to Thutmose I's second wife, Mutnofret (Mut the Beautiful). Some scholars believe that she may have been the mother of Thutmose I's sons Amenmose and Wadjmose, however, this theory remains inconclusive. Solidifying her enduring royal status, the young Hatshepsut married Thutmose II around the age of twelve years, ending her reign as High Priestess. It is unknown how old he was when he married Hatshepsut, however, it is believed that he died young; much younger than the age considered for full male maturity, typically in a person's forties. Marrying young was a common practice at that time, particularly among royal families. Her husband was a sickly and frail boy and was undoubtedly a last resort regarding the continuation of the royal line.[39] His older half-brothers were much better suited to assume the throne, but he remained the only viable option as a male heir.

After ten years on the throne, Thutmose I passed away. Like his sons' deaths before him, it is not recorded what he died of; it is believed that he died a mature man.[40] The passing of her father altered Hatshepsut's security in the plan that had been devised for her. Not only did her father's and brothers' departure leave a gaping hole in the future of the dynasty, but it left a void for Hatshepsut as well. She had to briefly rely on her title of 'the king's daughter' until she could secure her royal status through marriage to her half-brother, Thutmose II, and successfully produce a male heir to continue her familial lineage.[41] Moreover, Thutmose II needed his marriage to Hatshepsut to legitimize his own right to rule.[42]

Hatshepsut and Thutmose II were similar in age, and while they were the rulers of the dynasty, they were still young enough to be closely watched and advised in all they did. Queen Ahmes served as regent until Thutmose II was old enough to rule on his own.[43] As regent, Ahmes would have seen to it that the royal pair were prepared to spend many nights together in constant pursuit of pregnancy. Since they were such a young couple, about twelve and thirteen years old, their wedding night would most likely have been the opposite of a private affair. It was vital that a male heir was conceived. This means that Hatshepsut's and Thutmose II's sexual encounters were not only observed, but coached, making sure she received his seed just right.[44] The consummation of their marital union was believed to be successful when she became pregnant, however, she did not bear a son. She gave birth to a girl named Nefrure.[45] If Hatshepsut bore other children, it is not recorded. Babies who were stillborn or miscarried were not remembered in name or memorialized in any way.[46] Hatshepsut failed to produce a male heir, so Thutmose II took another wife, Isis, into his bedchamber, impregnating her successfully with a son, Thutmose III.[47]

Thutmose II did not sit on the throne for long, possibly a decade. Information regarding his reign is scarce, especially in comparison to his father's and his own son's reign. This could in part be due to him dying at a young age, at least much younger than the standard of maturity. An event during his reign that is documented is his success in halting a revolt in Nubia, a territory belonging to Egypt's southern region. However, this victory did not solely belong to the young king as it was most likely Ahmes who ordered the Egyptian army to Kush.[48] Hostilities in Nubia were nothing new. Battles fought for land, power, and dominance is a tale as old as time, and by the time this young king assumed the throne, Egypt had gone through many periods of social, economic, and military turmoil.

Like his father and half-brothers, the cause of Thutmose II's death is not conclusive. What is known is that his body was often covered in lesions and raised pustules. This would most likely have been caused by a virus, fungal, or bacterial infection in the skin.[49] His body was covered in painful puss-filled boils. When his mummy was discovered, his skin still bore the scars of the physical affliction he suffered.[50] Archaeologists and scholars surmise that he had an enlarged heart as well, and experienced shortness of breath and arrhythmias: an irregular heart rhythm.[51] Illness, whether acute or chronic, could certainly have been the cause of the young king's passing.

Once again, Hatshepsut said goodbye to a brother, only this time it was to her husband as well. The new king of Egypt had been chosen, but the challenge of ensuring the infant would survive to adolescence loomed. Infant mortality rates were staggeringly high. Diseases and conditions such as tuberculosis, malaria, leprosy, and diarrhoea – causing deadly dehydration – were often too much for an infant's immune system to battle. In addition to infectious diseases, parasites from contaminated food and water were often fatal. Infants and toddlers in ancient Egypt were also easy targets for dangerous wildlife such as snakes, scorpions, crocodiles, and other predatory animals. Some infants died from malnutrition or birth defects. For Hatshepsut, keeping the boy-king alive and raising him to maturity was a nerve-wracking responsibility. Until Thutmose III was old enough to rule, Hatshepsut was given the task of being his regent.

Early scholars interpreted her rise to the throne as an ambitious power move, asserting that she somehow knew how to manipulate the system. One reason for this mindset is that she quickly assumed responsibility for a boy who was not her son, acting as his regent for seven years before declaring herself the uncontested king.[52] It was not customary for a female royal to assume such a role. Perhaps those around her were immediately suspicious of her intentions, while others may have believed that Hatshepsut was merely doing what needed to be done in securing the royal line. If Thutmose III did not survive to adulthood, the royal line of Hatshepsut's father would not endure. However, her ambitions were not the only deciding element to her becoming king. Hatshepsut had a clear vision for Egypt, and she maintained an immense confidence in herself to realise her visions of expansion, foreign trade, vast wealth, and a strong military defence. She was proud of her lineage and the dynasty her father had built and left to her and Thutmose II to rule. She fully intended to keep a firm grasp on her father's legacy and build onto what he left behind. In addition to this, Hatshepsut believed she was divinely appointed to be a great pharaoh.[53]

According to ancient texts, mainly in Thebes, the royal oracle interceded on Hatshepsut's behalf before Amun-Ra. The oracle declared to Hatshepsut the will of the creator gods for the crown to be bestowed on her. Hatshepsut also believed her father petitioned the gods on her behalf for her to sit on the throne. Her official declaration of moving from regent to co-ruler over Egypt would have ruffled some feathers. However, with the oracle's blessing, she took her place of authority with her chin up and shoulders square in physical defiance of any opposition hurled her way.

Despite being surrounded and engulfed in a patriarchal system, Hatshepsut knew how to play the game. She consistently reminded those around her whose daughter she was. Hatshepsut was the daughter, wife, sister, and stepmother of a king. She decorated her monuments with images of her father and scripts memorializing him. By doing so, she reiterated to all, from the elite to the commoner, the authority she was born with and had married into.

Determined to represent herself as the powerful and capable ruler she believed she was, she ordered the construction of stone structures to bear her image, but with a difference. She wanted to be portrayed as masculine. Statues bore the face of Hatshepsut, adorned with a long beard – a symbol of royalty. Her delicate, feminine frame was reshaped with broad shoulders and a masculine build.[54] This was not an attempt to hide or redefine her femininity, but rather a strategic plan to show her people, and foreign powers, that she was more than capable of ruling the dynasty, even if she was a woman. To say she proved her point is an understatement. Her rule was a massive success. Growth in Egypt occurred under her watch, beginning with building projects such as monuments, temples, and tombs. These monuments include massive obelisks, the temple complex in Luxor, and her mortuary temple at Deir el-Bahri which is considered to be her greatest architectural achievement.[55]

Her mortuary temple lies across three terraces. The lowest level has barges to bring her obelisks from Aswan to Karnak. The middle section has her divine birth painted on the walls. At the entrance of the uppermost level stands statues of Osiris and Hatshepsut. This level also hosts vaulted chambers and a sacred court dedicated to her and her father, as well as Amun Ra and Re-Horakhty. On the south side, a chapel stands dedicated to the goddess Hathor and Anubis. The southern colonnade shows Hatshepsut's successful expedition to Punt. She proved herself an incredibly savvy trading and bargaining partner. The exact location of Punt is unknown, but scholars believe it resided somewhere on the Horn of Africa. She returned to Thebes with fragrant incense – very valuable to a High Priestess – gold, ivory, panther and leopard skins, as well as live wildcats, apes, and giraffes. She also returned with a healthy stock of ebony, ivory, frankincense, myrrh, cinnamon wood, and people from the land of Punt, who would most likely find themselves labourers and servants to the Egyptian royalty.[56] Hatshepsut transported trees, non-native to Egypt such as the myrrh and frankincense trees, and successfully transplanted them by transporting the trees in baskets filled with Punt's rich soil, being careful to keep the trees' roots undamaged. Hatshepsut is also partially credited (along with Nefertiti) with a revolutionary facial aesthetic, eyeliner.[57] It was discovered that ground frankincense produces resin. Once the resin is extracted it can be used as eyeliner.

In addition to her excellently keen eye for trade and increasing the dynasty's wealth, she was a prolific builder. She had two pink granite obelisks erected, one in her honour and the other to Amun-Ra.[58] These celebrated her jubilee, sixteen years into her reign as pharaoh. An obelisk is a tall stone pillar with a rectangular or square cross-section, often with a pyramidal top. Her obelisk still stands near the Temple of Amon in Karnak, however the other has since toppled into a heap of cracked and crumbled stone. While she was indeed a trailblazer for females to rule successfully after her, this did not sit well with those who favoured the patriarchal system. Ancient Egyptian society was built on tradition, and tradition demands that kings be men. Despite the male-dominated frame of mind, she served as an inspiration to Thutmose III, despite early scholars' belief that he felt animosity toward her. There is nothing recorded that supports this claim definitively. In fact, he had a comfortable and safe life under her rule. She ensured that the young king had extensive military training, learning from the best commanders in the army. Even though he was not her son, she wanted his reign to be successful. The continuation of her lineage in future dynasties was undoubtedly a primary motivator.

Her influence over Thutmose III proved itself when he grew to be a man. Hatshepsut appointed him supreme military commander of the empire.[59] He led several successful campaigns, most notably his conquering of the city Megiddo, a city near Canaan.[60] It was located in what is now modern-day northwest Israel overlooking the Valley of Jezreel, which some also consider ancient Palestine. The land was an agricultural gold mine with rich, fertile soil and thousands of healthy livestock. He was quick to mobilize his army, knowing that by the time they arrived at the city the opposing army would have increased in numbers and support from Canaan and Kadesh. The army of Canaan and Kadesh may not have had the same reverence for Thutmose III as they did for Hatshepsut, and they, unfortunately, underestimated him. Her successful reputation spread swiftly throughout the land by the time this battle commenced. While Thutmose III sacked Megiddo, his stepmother lay dying. Thutmose III marched forward with close to 15,000 men. The Egyptians' enemy was terrified of the army charging toward them. They abandoned their chariots of gold and silver. Thutmose III's army plundered the battlefield, filling their arms with all the spoils they could carry; however, this gave the enemy the opportunity to retreat to Megiddo, a well-supplied fortress. Thutmose III and his army had to wait about eight months for the fortress to run out of supplies, forcing the inhabitants to emerge from the safety of its impenetrable walls.[61] The Egyptian army ravaged the city, taking thousands of livestock, mostly cows and horses. Children were taken as slaves to be raised in Egypt. Thutmose III did not order the execution of the city's high officials. Instead, he appointed trusted men who had remained loyal to him. The people of Megiddo were taken back to Egypt to live the rest of their lives as unpaid labourers. During his reign, he conquered 300 cities.[62]

One of the events related to kingship is the Heb sed Jubilee. Traditionally, this celebration would take place during the thirtieth year of a pharaoh's reign.[63] However, a pharaoh could choose to hold this celebration at other times. Hatshepsut is one of the pharaohs who chose to celebrate outside of the conventional timeframe.[64] The jubilee resembles a royal coronation and symbolizes the pharaoh's renewed commitment to the people. The king dressed in a short kilt with an animal tail at the back, most commonly resembling a lion's tail.[65] During the celebration the pharaoh's strength was tested to show agility, even pharaohs who were advancing in age were required to undergo this show of might. Rejuvenating rituals were performed for the king's benefit, hoping there was still some energy left to continue ruling.[66] Hatshepsut was able to bask in the merriment and praise held in her honour at least once before her body began to give way to age and illness.

Near the end of her life, Hatshepsut had aged to approximately her late forties or fifty, which was considered a long life. She may not have known what was ailing her, but she was acutely aware of the pain she felt down to her bones. Her body became brittle and fatigued before ultimately succumbing to incurable illness in 1458 BC When her mummy was discovered in 2007 her bones revealed the painful truth, she had suffered from bone cancer.[67] Some scholars believe she may have had diabetes as well.[68] This is quite possible since the royal diet was high in sugar from a steady consumption of rich fruits and honey. The discovery of Hatshepsut's mummy employed other academic disciplines to aid in piecing together how the famed king died. A jar was found containing a salve. Scientists confirmed that it was not a perfume, but rather a cream made with palm and apple nutmeg oil. In addition to the oils, flacon was present, which would have been used to treat chronic skin conditions such as eczema and psoriasis.[69] Creosote, asphalt, and benzo(a)pyrene – a lethal carcinogenic found in coal, tar, and tobacco smoke – were also found. Scholars surmise that Hatshepsut likely suffered from a skin condition such as eczema or psoriasis and regularly exposed herself to the harmful ingredients to find some relief, even if only temporary. Unfortunately, the carcinogenic salve was most likely the primary cause for her developing debilitating bone cancer.

Preparing for the afterlife was paramount. It was a sacred practice, instilled by the goddess Isis when her husband-brother Osiris was murdered.[70] The mummification process was arduous and performed by a priest with a careful hand, and undoubtedly a strong stomach. The entire process lasted seventy days. The first step was to remove the internal organs as they rapidly decay, except the heart. Ancient Egyptians believed the heart encapsulated the true being of a person. An incision was made in the abdomen, which would release gases that naturally build up after death. The priest would carefully reach his hand inside the abdominal cavity, slowly removing the intestines, then reaching further to retrieve the liver and stomach, followed by the lungs. The brain was removed with a hooked instrument in small portions through the nostrils to ensure facial damage did not occur. The removal of the brain was one of the most time-consuming tasks of mummification. The organs were stored separately in canopic jars, which are buried with the person. Next, the body was prepared for drying. Natron, a type of salt, was the preferred element since it had excellent drying properties. Once the body was completely dried out, it was thoroughly washed to remove any residual natron. The body was filled with aromatic spices and resins such as myrrh and cassia. It was wrapped in hundreds of yards of linen; a warm resin was applied between several layers. Sometimes each toe was individually wrapped. Once wrapping was complete, the mummy was ready for final interment into the tomb.[71] The only way a person's soul could be permitted into the afterlife was by preserving the body. While it is recorded that commoners could undergo mummification, it is not mentioned as a regular practice outside of royalty.

She remained shrouded in secrecy for centuries because the hieroglyphics recording her name, accomplishments, and reign had been destroyed. It was once widely believed that Thutmose III went to great lengths to erase her legacy from history, but again, this theory is not supported. The erasure of her name remains a mystery. A tomb bearing her name was first discovered in 1822 after hieroglyphics were decoded on the walls of Deir el-Bahri, which means Northern Monastery.[72] The tomb was built by her royal vizier, the high priest of Amun, Hapuseneb. The location is KV20 in the Valley of the Kings.[73] However, when her sarcophagus was opened, archaeologists were shocked and puzzled to find it empty. Fascinatingly, Hatshepsut had three tombs prepared.[74] One of her tombs was cut in a remote valley west of the Valley of the Kings while she was queen regent during her husband Thutmose II's reign. Her second tomb was cut at the foot of the cliffs in the eastern corner of the Valley of the Kings. Some scholars believe this tomb was designated for her father, Thutmose I to reside in. The original plan was to have a passage cut to the burial chamber, that would reside beneath the sanctuary of the queen's temple. Reasons for her ordering the construction of multiple burial chambers vary, and none of them are conclusive. It's possible that she had them built based on her status at the time, especially since life expectancy was low and uncertain. The Valley of the Kings is an impressive landmark. Within the massive hills of sand-smothered rock, over sixty tombs of Egypt's pharaohs are encased. The inner walls display the stories of a pharaoh's life, beautifully told in colour and exquisite detail.[75] Deep shafts and pillared chambers are built within, however, thieves somehow still managed to slither themselves down the deep shafts and endlessly long corridors, stealing from wealthy dead pharaohs. Hatshepsut's tomb is the longest. It resides 215 metres from the entrance and 100 metres down into the rock.

In addition to her tomb, the tomb of Senenmut was discovered at her temple.[76] Senenmut was Hatshepsut's most supportive force in her life. He was a man of humble origins who made his way up the ladder of royal association, becoming a respected man of status with the pharaoh. He was born to Ramose – a man of whom little is known other than that he was 'revered' – and Hatnefer, often referred to as the 'lady of the house', a title given to a woman of modest means and no role of societal honour. She was given charge of the affairs in the home and raising her family. It is likely that Senenmut's service to the royal family began with Thutmosis II. Scholars believe he may have acted as a tutor for Hatshepsut's daughter, Nefrure, among his other duties performed for the pharaoh.[77] Senenmut was appointed to oversee the construction of her obelisks in Aswan, as well as other architectural feats, much like a foreman. Hieroglyphics never depict him as married, however, his relationship with Hatshepsut remains mysterious and is debated among scholars and historians. First, his loyalty to her was unfailing and unmatched by any other in her sphere of influence. He was dedicated to every cause, project, trading venture, and ritual held in her honour. Hatshepsut's name is repeatedly declared on the walls of his monuments. Senenmut was skilled and intelligent. He was a scientist, astronomer, and artist.[78] He may also have been her protector, making it difficult for him to abstain from emotional involvement with her, even though Hatshepsut was the pharaoh.

She did not have the authority to choose a husband. Her gender barred her from such choices. She was expected to remain celibate as she no longer had a husband. This vow of celibacy was called into question when archaeologists decoded the artwork on the tapestry found in Senenmut's burial chamber. The artwork displays the queen facing toward a dark-skinned man. She is holding a chalice and wearing a wig. This, alongside the writings on the wall, has led scholars to believe that not only were the two secret lovers, but they produced a child together.[79] The tapestry is on display at the Cairo Museum. If Hatshepsut did bear Senenmut's child, it became one of the most mysterious royal cover-ups in Egyptian history. A mummy, discovered in the Valley of the Kings, was once believed to possibly be the child of Hatshepsut and Senenmut.[80]

The way Hatshepsut is remembered in history has not been consistent, and had it not been for the unexpected discovery of her mummy in 2007, the conclusions drawn by scholars may have cast an unfavourable light on her legacy. It's possible that someone sought to eradicate the collective memory of Hatshepsut by scratching her images out of the stone and tapestries and demolishing some of her statues. Fortunately, they failed. It was once believed that Hatshepsut was an underhanded and devious woman, hungry for power, usurping the throne of Egypt with force. This interpretation paints a dark picture of a woman. But was she a wicked woman of selfish ambition as once thought? Recent research leads down a brighter path, and a new understanding pushes the shadows back to illuminate the truth of one of Egypt's most successful rulers. She used her pharaonic power to usher in change, embrace and sustain foreign resources, and prepare her stepson to fight for the good of the dynasty, maintain

Egypt's wealth, and ensure its continued expansion. She ensured he was well-equipped in his military training so that he would be an uncontested warrior and leader of the Egyptian army.

Hatshepsut rose to power when the country was basking in economic, agricultural, social, and financial prosperity and stability. She developed trade routes and trade partnerships in foreign lands, increased Egypt's wealth, and ushered in a new era of architectural achievements. Trees, exotic animals, and livestock that were not native to her lands were successfully migrated and sustained. The Eighteenth Dynasty is a crown jewel in Egypt's rich history, and Hatshepsut was instrumental in making Egypt one of the leading global powers.

Chapter 3

Nefertiti: 'A Beautiful Woman Has Come' (NEH-FUR-TEE-TEE)

Drifting through the years, and further down the Nile, the story of the Eighteenth Dynasty of Egypt found itself pulled by a rogue current. After Hatshepsut's reign, Egypt went through growing pains once again. These were not necessarily negative. Thutmose III left a legacy as the fiercest warrior of the Eighteenth Dynasty, increasing Egypt's wealth and resources substantially. By the end of his rule, Egypt was an undefeated military power. His successor, Thutmose IV maintained successful commercial relationships with Syria, Crete, Phoenicia, and the Aegean Islands.

Egypt already had an abundance of gold, so that was no longer the resource sought after. What Egypt lacked was silver. Having such amicable trading alliances allowed the Egyptians to gather more than silver. Under Thutmose IV, textiles were imported, inspiring elaborate and decorative ceiling patterns.[1] Egypt's temple aesthetics became as pertinent as the foundations they were laid upon. Foreign influence is depicted in the royal tombs.

Amenhotep III seceded Thutmose IV after the king's death. Once again, Egypt engaged in battle with the Kushites. The Kushite army was defeated and another victory was added to Egypt's impressive history of military dominance. Additionally, Egypt secured an ally, Asia. Former foes, this national cooperation stabilized with the marriage of Amenhotep III to Princess Gilukhepa, a minor wife to the young pharaoh.[2] Scholars believe Amenhotep III was ten years old when he married the princess from Mitanni, an Indo-Iranian empire and one of the world's significant powers, residing in western Asia. Like many marriages in ancient times, they were arranged for political and royal advantage. It was seldom that the concept of love was a present element in marriages, especially among those who married as children. His marriage to Gilukhepa was purely diplomatic and used as a means of securing an ally for Egypt.[3] The fate of Princess Gilukhepa is not known and knowledge of her is scarce. Amenhotep III's reign was successful. He celebrated three Heb sed jubilees and was highly revered as a divine son of Amun. His conception is another that is entwined in ancient Egyptian mythology. According to the myth, the god Amun took on the form of his father, Thutmose IV, and lay with his mother, Mutemwiya, impregnating her.[4] His rule is respected for perpetuating the ancient traditions and religious foundations set by the Old Kingdom and upholding a prosperous economy. Under his reign, mortuary temples, never ceasing in impressive advancement, were built for him. This royal line led to the birth of Egypt's most controversial king, Akhenaten.

For many years, Thebes was the established capital and religious centre. However, during the reign of Nefertiti and her husband, Akhenaten, traditions and familiar customs were uprooted and relocated. Egyptians reluctantly embraced the many changes imposed by the pharaoh and his wife and accomplice in every endeavour.

This chronicle of Egypt's history is complex and filled with several theories, and none disappoint in their theatrics. The people navigated through daunting changes in just about everything, coming face to face with the unfamiliar. For a millennium, the legacy of Nefertiti was buried, seemingly by intention, but as the sands shifted, a massive gap in Egypt's history was filled with scholarly treasures, an absolute gold mine of discoveries. Welcome to the pharaonic reign that truly stands alone. The reign of Nefertiti, Egypt's most beautiful woman.

The lineage of Nefertiti has long been debated among Egyptologists. For many years, it was believed that she was a Mitanni princess, however, more recent scholars stand firm stating she was not foreign but was indeed an Egyptian herself.[5] It is not definitively known who her parents were, however, one theory stands out among the rest, linking her to the royal Egyptian family as the daughter of Ay and the niece of Queen Tiye.[6] Queen Tiye is the Great Royal Wife of Amenhotep III and the mother of Amenhotep IV, better known as Akhenaten, making him and Nefertiti cousins, not brother and sister, or even half-siblings.[7]

Queen Tiye's origins and historical record are obscure, much like Nefertiti's. However, Tiye's impact on Egypt has been documented and she undoubtedly made a profound impression on Nefertiti. She had a strong personality and was quite shrewd. Tiye was a force to be reckoned with. She set a precedence of strength and voiced her politics openly with foreign diplomats. This outspoken behaviour would have been shunned or even punished in other cultures, but ancient Egyptian women held far more status and utilized freedoms that were void in other cultures. The leaders of foreign nations respected Queen Tiye for her confidence, not only in herself but in a room of elite leaders who were undoubtedly men. Her political value is referenced in the Amarna letters, which consisted of several hundred clay tablets.[8] The tablets were a series of correspondence between the rulers of Egypt, Assyria, Babylonia, Hittite, and Mitanni, offering an abundance of insight into international diplomacy. The clay tablets were discovered in 1887, at a complex in what is now known as the 'Central City' of Amarna, which was an isolated location during the reign of Akhenaten.[9] Queen Tiye freely conversed with these foreign rulers as her husband's co-diplomat. Perhaps one of the most profound influences Tiye had on her son and her niece was the obvious equality in a partnership she shared with her husband, Amenhotep III. This partnership is depicted on a stone statue of the pharaoh and queen side-by-side at equal height.[10] Statues bearing the image of a queen were often smaller in scale than that of a pharaoh, even if only slightly. Amenhotep IV adopted this co-ruling mindset with his wife, Nefertiti. Together, the two built an empire unlike any other seen in Egypt before.

Amenhotep IV had a natural drive for power, which was not entirely motivated by selfish ambitions for power, but rather a desire to thrive and reach the heights of wealth, land, and military power, and maintain its established place as a major world authority. If he were to see his lofty visions come to fruition, he needed his beautiful queen to do more than support him in private conversations. He needed Nefertiti to use her influence inside and outside the walls of their palace. Their ideas for a reconstruction of the foundations of Egyptian traditions were built on and required an unbreakable, united front if they were going to succeed.

Egyptian pharaohs leave unique legacies behind, however, Amenhotep IV's legacy is somewhat tainted. The ancient Egyptians prided themselves on their long-enduring honour of traditions, especially religious customs. Amenhotep IV and Nefertiti cut and unravelled the tapestry of their foundations, leaving their people in disbelief, uncertainty, and concern. The power couple began a massive disassembling of the religious structure in Egypt by removing all gods and goddesses from places of worship and proclaimed that the people would only worship 'the one true god, Aten', also known as 'Aton'.[11] This did not sit well with the people or the palace personnel. Not only were they having their customs stripped from them (which altered all aspects of daily life), but the people undoubtedly felt a sense of anxiety over abandoning the gods they believed still held divine power and authority over them.[12] Perhaps the people feared dire consequences for their betrayal. However, the pharaoh was also an absolute authority and was believed to be endowed with god-like sovereignty too. The pharaoh's word was absolute, so the changes ordered by Amenhotep IV were enforced in song and stone. The reign of Akhenaten began.

Amenhotep IV married Nefertiti about four years into his reign. He changed his name to Akhenaten, which means, 'beneficial to Aton'.[13] Despite some concerns regarding the many changes being imposed, they introduced numerous fresh architectural and artistic feats. The backbone of the new art form was an artisan and master sculptor named Bek. He was the son of Men, another skilled carver and Bek served as an apprentice under his father where he acquired his skills in artistic expression and realistic representations.[14] He carefully followed the instructions given to him by Akhenaten, including the granite monuments for the mansion of Benben used by Queen Nefertiti, which was her own private sanctuary, serving as a priestess to Aton.

In addition to this being a place of worship, the Hwt-Benben, which means 'Mansion of the Benben', was the location of solar rituals, and was once believed to be connected to the earth's beginnings.[15] Ancient Egyptian mythology offers another creation story described as darkness and chaos being the only measure of existence until it was broken when the Benben stone arose out of a primordial hill.[16] Another myth suggests that it was the landing place for Atum where he began his work of creation. The Benben is now an architectural term for the top stone of a pyramid.

The Amarna art style gained prominence during Akhenaten and Nefertiti's reign. During previous dynasties, people (especially royals) were artistically depicted in their ideal forms. The Amarna style turns from idealism to portray a more realistic representation of a person, including physical flaws and defects.[17] Humans are portrayed with pronounced physical features, slanted eyes, hanging jaws, slouched shoulders, large hips, skinny legs, slender necks, and elongated skulls. Akhenaten may have ordered this portrayal due to his documented physical defects, which were most likely caused by a pituitary condition. He is also depicted as having an elongated head and a long jaw. There are several reasons for this portrayal of the king's appearance, however, it is possible that Akhenaten suffered from a condition called craniosynostosis, a condition that causes cranial deformities.[18] This art form also gave a pronounced detail to fingers, toes, ear lobes, and wrinkles, which was something less distinguishable in earlier ancient Egyptian art. It is possible that Akhenaten wished to design a new art form that gave attention to physical defects either to normalize his appearance as he may have felt inadequate in his less-than-perfect physical form or to preserve the conditions of his carnal state for future understanding.[19] Since Akhenaten's mummy is yet to be found, scholars can only hypothesize about his possible medical conditions based on sculptures and artwork preserved on the walls of archaeological sites.

Even more illuminating is the way the royal family is illustrated. Akhenaten and Nefertiti are shown as doting and loving, giving their daughters kisses and holding them in their laps, displaying a far more intimate context of the portrait of marriage and family.[20] This is something that had been excluded in earlier artwork. The mural is a lovely representation of the maternal and paternal relationship within the royal family who had just begun to grow their young household.

Amarna art was mostly centred on the religious shift imposed by Akhenaten. Thebes had been the religious centre in Egypt, but the location of worship was moved to Tell el-Amarna where new temples were built, such as Re-Harakhte and the precinct of the god Amun at Karnak. Aton was no longer depicted as anthropomorphic as in earlier artworks. He is portrayed in his natural state as a sun disk, showering light and warmth on the earth's inhabitants below.[21] Akhenaten believed that his reign was favoured and blessed by the sun god, which is seen in artwork showing the pharaoh standing under the shining disk, sunbathing in the favour of Aten. The artwork also shows the peripheral surroundings of river valleys, deserts, common citizens, birds, and animals. In contrast to the previous methods of worship, Aten was praised out in the open instead of exclusively within the dark and secluded temple chambers. Religious ceremonies were singularly focused on Aten. Pharaoh Akhenaten even included monotheistic celebrations at his royal jubilee. Amarna art can give an illustration of elaborate beauty or the distortion of the human form.

During his reign, Akhenaten moved the capital city of worship to Amarna on the east bank of the Nile River. It was a beautiful landscape that basked in the lush soils fed by the river. The bright sun reflected off the endless white sands, making it attractive to Akhenaten to designate this location as the new religious capital. The fresh location also acted as a separation from Thebes and the polytheistic religion that Akhenaten and Nefertiti no longer adhered to. The architectural plans for the new worship temples were exquisite. King Akhenaten required that the temples be built with haste so as not to delay the establishment of the Aten cult. The religious reformation, including the new art form, has become known as the Amarna Revolution. Initially, the Great Temple of Aten was built with mud bricks, which ensured the structure would be built quickly. However, this caused several issues with the temple's foundations, leading to many deep cracks in the walls and floors, which was also not aesthetically pleasing. The mudbrick was replaced gradually with limestone.[22] The temple was massive (750 x 2,400 feet), the largest temple in the new city.[23] The complex had additional temples built named 'House of Rejoicing' and 'Gem Aten', meaning 'Aten is Found'.[24] The use of talatat limestone bricks correlated with Akhenaten's reign since it was widely used in the construction of temples during his rule. The painted art expressed throughout the temple walls is a beautiful representation of the natural world and the abundant favour Aten placed on the royal family. One art piece, in particular, shows Nefertiti outdoors with two of her young daughters, with the great sun disk's rays reaching down toward them, casting a depiction of light and blessing. Also, Nefertiti is painted without her husband, Akhenaten, which is significant as it shows autonomy.[25] Women believed to be of significance and high status would have been depicted in such a way. The many art pieces illustrate an intimate side of the royal couple. Not intimate in the context of marital relations but rather an emotional intimacy, rooted in the strong bonds of family. She was not only a pillar of strength in their home, she was the backbone he needed if his aspirations for the new religious centre were going to succeed.

The Great Temple differed dramatically from previous places of worship. It was completely open-air and had no roof, contrasting greatly with the heavy stone slabs used as roofs on other temples.[26] Places of worship were filled with light and warmth. It was intentionally designed this way as King Akhenaten desired worship to be direct, with nothing acting as a barrier between praises and the god Aten. Hymns were sung with abundant rejoicing, reaching toward the skies, and echoing off the stone walls with beautiful percussion.

The Great Hymn, also known as the Aten Hymn, was written by Akhenaten himself during the Amarna period and is considered one of the most relevant religious literary texts of the Eighteenth Dynasty.[27] It is one of the longest hymns written to Aten and is a testament to Akhenaten's devotion to the deity, despite the criticism he received. It is a poetic piece with some of the primary themes of this hymn describing the land of Egypt as being abundantly blessed by Aten as well as the strong connection between the sun deity and Pharaoh Akhenaten. The Great Hymn was discovered at the Akhetaten (Amarna) ruins. On the west wall of the tomb of Ay, the hymn was inscribed on thirteen columns of hieroglyphics. Unfortunately, it has been vandalized and damaged, however much of it remains intact enough to be deciphered. Many offerings were presented, such as flowers, perfumes, incense, food, drink, meat, and vegetables.[28] Worship was no longer a secluded experience but became a public community act. Inside the sanctuary were 722 offering tables where Nefertiti practised much of her praise to Aten, as well as 900 tables around the sacred temple area as well.[29] Ceremonies could last from the first light seen perching on the distant horizon until the great sun disk sank into the deep blue pools of dusk. King Akhenaten and Queen Nefertiti officiated these ceremonies as priests, Akhenaten serving as the intermediary between the god Aten and the people. This temporarily eliminated the religious need for a priesthood. Commoners most likely continued the old worship practices; however, the noble class would have had to adopt the new methods of worship.

Throughout the dynasties of ancient Egypt, mythology has been a present, consistent theme among the many changes each dynasty endured. Akhenaten and Nefertiti were well-versed in the ancient stories. Many scholars perceive and interpret Akhenaten's motives for the religious shift, suggesting that he felt he was above the old traditions and could change things on a whim simply because it was his will as the reigning pharaoh.[30] However, a deeper look at the origin story of Aten (also known as Atum) paints a more elaborate picture of why Akhenaten and Nefertiti adopted a monotheistic religion, and it intertwines with ancient mythology.

Surrounded by darkness, the god Aten sat upon a benben (mound), alone in his existence. Feeling a creative urge, he spat a thick substance out into the cosmos, bringing twins Shu and Tefnut into existence. Aten charged Shu with governing the air and wind.[31] Shu's twin sister, Tefnut became the goddess of moisture. The two became a mated, marital pair. Their union of air, wind, and moisture gave birth to Geb (god of the earth) and Nut (goddess of the sky). Their father Shu was responsible for keeping them (earth and sky) from touching as this would protect the balanced circle of life.

When Akhenaten and Nefertiti adopted the monotheistic religious stance, they had statues built with themselves as Shu and Tefnut, suggesting they were divinely appointed and favoured by Aten. Despite the mythological origin story, the reigning power couple openly rejected the belief in the existence of other gods and goddesses, feeling that Aten alone was deserving of praise since he was the god of creation.

Akhenaten and Nefertiti's marital relations produced six daughters: Meritaten, Meketaten, Neferneferure-tasherit, Neferneferure, Setepenre, and Ankhesenpaaten (later known as Ankhesenamun).[32] Despite the pharaoh and his queen having a seemingly strong and stable marriage, their relationship was not monogamous; most, if not all Egyptian royal relationships were polygamous. Akhenaten had another wife, Kiya. Information about this second wife is scarce but what is known is that she began her role as the pharaoh's wife in high standing due to fruitful vineyards and economic savviness. Kiya ended up disgraced, despite being considered 'beloved' by her pharaoh husband. However, the events leading up to her disgrace are even less known. She may have been the product of Nefertiti's insecurity over another royal wife garnering favour and affection from her husband. With Kiya as a 'beloved' wife, Nefertiti may have felt that her influence over Egypt was challenged and wanted to eliminate the competition.[33] Most records of her have been erased or destroyed. One of the most important connections Kiya had to the royal family has survived, and that is her likelihood of being the mother of one of the most famous pharaohs in Egyptian history, Tutankhamun. During the period of their multi-god abandonment, Akhenaten and Nefertiti endured immense heartbreak. Two of their daughters, Setepenre and Neferneferuaten 'The Younger' passed away.[34] At this time in Egypt, plague was on the rise, sparing few that came in contact with the deadly illness. It is believed that at this time, former Egyptian queen Tiye also passed away from the plague. Not long after, the couple's daughter Meketaten died giving birth to her father Akhenaten's child.[35] She is estimated to have been fourteen years old. As if this was not enough to bear, Egypt lost much of its northern territories to Syria. This massive heartbreak and military failure became the driving force of Akhenaten's mission to change the religious foundations and give fierce worship to Aten in the hopes that the ill will that had befallen him and his family would be lifted.[36] If the pharaoh ever felt he needed divine forgiveness, it would have been during his moments of tremendous loss. He ordered the immediate removal of all obelisks and statues of the other ancient gods and goddesses, and their names scratched out of the stone. Even the word 'gods' was ordered to be carved out so that the concept of polytheism in ancient Egypt would be permanently erased.[37] This angered many, especially those in the noble ranks, but the order was carried out as the pharaoh demanded. Akhenaten ordered bountiful offerings to be made to Aten for the means of building the temples and religious complex and statues in Amarna, with no regard to the cost or replenishment of the rich stores Egypt had boasted of for centuries. Akhenaten brought Egypt to bankruptcy.[38]

The cause of Akhenaten's demise is not definitively known. When he passed away, the worship city of Akhetaten (Amarna) did not survive. Temples and statues were dismantled and destroyed in an effort to erase the legacy of his reign and revert to the polytheistic religion and customs. The subsequent dynastic rulers viewed Akhenaten as a heretical pharaoh and strived tirelessly to re-establish the old traditions. The religious capital was moved back to Thebes and the revenue that had been directed to maintain the Aten cult was reverted to investing in the old religious traditions.[39] King Tutankhamun was one of the later pharaohs to publicly condemn the religion enforced by his father and stepmother.

After twelve years as Egypt's queen, Nefertiti's name ceases to be mentioned. Scholars at first surmised that she had died, however, more recent scholarship believes she performed more heightened royal duties under a new name. Abandoning her birthname of Nefertiti, she became known as Ankhkheperure Neferneferuaten, meaning 'Manifestations of Re Are Alive.'[40] It is believed that under this new name, she became co-king alongside her husband, Akhenaten. The continuous name changes continue to perplex historians; however, the knowledge of this name change opens another door to the complexity of Nefertiti's reign. Her name supposedly changed again to Smenkhkare to continue her administration.[41] For many years, the assertion that Smenkhkare was Nefertiti was widely rejected. Images, though rare, show the individual Smenkhkare dressed in a masculine kilt and reference the royal wife, Meritaten. Adding to this twisted family tale, the belief that she was indeed the same individual with a new name gained relevance and credibility because Akhenaten married his daughter, Meritaten. Since Akhenaten was deceased, someone had to assume the masculine role of royal leadership, allowing Meritaten to continue her role as 'Great Royal Wife', Nefertiti (as Smenkhkare) may have adopted a masculine role. If she had embraced this male alter-ego, it would have catapulted Meritaten's status to the proud position, of 'Great Royal Wife'.[42] Many disputed this claim since Nefertiti was a woman, making the name 'Great Royal Wife' an absurd assertion, especially since a union such as this would not have a physical consummation of marital union, which partially legitimized royal marriages with the hope of producing viable heirs to the throne.[43] Additionally, this claim also allows for an additional theory of family lineage. Since Akhenaten married his daughter, Maritaten, it is possible that his daughter-wife is the actual mother of Tutankhamun. This genealogical theory holds more weight since it aligns more closely with the timeline in which Tutankhamun became king at the age of eight. Nefertiti's daughter Ankhesenamun married her half-brother, the young Tutankhamun, and was likely appointed as royal regent to the boy-king since he did not have one upon his ascension to the throne.[44] This would have given Nefertiti an abundance of opportunity to build influence into the royal pair and instil in them the desire to continue the task of restoring religious stability and peace, hoping to end the discord that had been woven into the legacy of Akhenaten.

When Akhenaten passed away, he left behind a dismal and unflattering legacy, and Egypt in a confused and financially bankrupt state. As the reigning king, Nefertiti was the target of the disdain of the people and the subject of every whispered gossip regarding her deceased husband's crazed attempts to erase the deep-rooted religious traditions and customs that were truly beloved by the people. Nefertiti felt the sting of the people's anger and distrust, but with grace, she began to build the nation up, one brick after another. She was the one who abandoned the city of Akhetaten (Amarna) as the religious capital, hoping for reconciliation with the people.[45] This was a monumental task. The people of ancient Egypt were deeply religious and devoted to their gods. If peace was going to be an outcome, her every step had to be calculated and patient. Restoration between Nefertiti and the people was not complete during her lifetime, despite her best efforts.

Adding to the confusion of the timeline of the Eighteenth Dynasty, the royal line became less definitive and posed more questions than answers. Nefertiti ruled as pharaoh after the king's demise, most likely taking her place as king sometime between twelve and eighteen months after Akhenaten passed. Her time as reigning pharaoh was brief; most scholars estimate her reign was a mere four years. One of the first tasks Nefertiti (Neferneferuaten) undertook was re-establishing polytheism and mending the broken relationships between Egyptian royalty and the people. The deconstruction of the temples at Amarna was a positive first step toward reconciliation and conforming again to the old religion and its corresponding customs and traditions.

Instead of being able to heavily focus on expanding Egypt's territories and build back the tremendous wealth that had been spent on the Aten cult, Nefertiti had the weighted task of undoing the religious and financial harm strapped to what was left of her reign. Nevertheless, she embraced this task with grace and respect for her people. She reinstated the sacred statues of Khonsu (god of the moon), Amun (god of the sun and king of all gods), Mut (mother goddess/mother of all creation), Nefertum (god of healing), and Sakhmet (goddess of war and the destroyer of Re's enemies) at Thebes and Memphis.[46] The presence of the deities' structures provided a sense of normalcy, and the people undoubtedly began to feel at peace, knowing their reigning pharaoh was invested in the people. Piece by piece, she began to heal the wounds inflicted on the stone temples of the old religion and ensured the inner sanctuaries were filled with hymns again.

Nefertiti recruited help from her successor, Tutankhamun, and her daughter Ankhesenamun. Nefertiti relied on future generations to rebuild the great nation of Egypt and restore it to its former glory, expanding in wealth and land. She utilized what influence she had on the young Tutankhamun. Even at a young age, the boy-king was a fierce supporter of the ancient polytheistic traditions and abhorred the Aten cult enforced by Akhenaten during the Amarna Revolution.

The life of Nefertiti is in no short supply of mystery. The changing of her name and the possible whereabouts of her mummified remains continues to be a fierce debate among Egyptologists. When the city of Amarna was abandoned, it's possible her body was disposed of. Other members were interred at Amarna, however, three were moved to the Valley of the Kings.[47] One of these is Smenkhkare, for whom there is a wide debate regarding true identity. Were Smenkhkare and Nefertiti the same person? Some scholars believe so, but others are not so sure, believing that Smenkhkare was a man, not the beautiful Nefertiti. It is believed that three of the royal princesses born of Akhenaten and Nefertiti were buried at Amarna. If they were, their bodies would have since been moved to an unknown location.

The tomb of KV55 in the Valley of the Kings does not disappoint though. The mummy of Queen Tiye is one of the most fascinating findings of human remains discovered in Egypt. She was found with another female mummy and one of an adolescent male laying between them.[48] Their tomb had been an unfortunate target of a robbery. The young boy has yet to be identified, but Egyptologists were able to surmise that he was a youth due to his short stature and lock of hair on one side of his skull, called, 'the side lock of youth'. It is possible that this mummy was Thutmose, son of Tiye and Amenhotep III, who died during adolescence. The mummy of Queen Tiye had long, wavy locks of hair, still holding fast to its rich auburn colour despite the many years that had passed and the sand and dirt that had become her tomb. Hair analysis ultimately led to her identity.[49] Interestingly, King Tutankhamun was buried with a lock of Tiye's hair, and most genealogical experts believe her to be the grandmother of Tutankhamun.[50] Queen Tiye underwent traditional mummification, and for the most part, her body is well-preserved. She had significant damage to her chest, which likely occurred during the robbery of her tomb. Egyptologists firmly believe the young woman buried with her is Tiye and Amenhotep III's daughter, referred to as 'The Younger Lady'.[51] Her name remains anonymous; however, DNA testing confirms she is the mother of King Tutankhamun. Amenhotep III and Tiye had six daughters. Until more archaeological discoveries are made or the mummies of the other five daughters are discovered, the identity of 'The Younger Lady' may remain elusive.

There has been speculation for over a century about where the tomb and mummy of Nefertiti is located. It was previously believed that 'The Younger Lady' was Nefertiti, but this theory has not gained archaeological or scholarly support, especially since the definitive DNA conclusions of 'The Younger Lady'.[52] Significant efforts were performed to erase Nefertiti's name from the record. There was such disdain for the royal legacy of Akhenaten and Nefertiti that the succeeding pharaohs were ashamed of this era in Egypt's history. Her name and legacy were shoved underground, buried beneath the sands; her name and face were carved out of any monument that saw the light of day. One of the most effective ways to ensure the erasure of her name and Akhenaten's was to tear down the monuments of their sacred city and reuse the materials for newly constructed temples, as well as maintain or add to existing structures. For many years, their existence was concealed, and their roles in the dynasty became a secret. When it came to Nefertiti, the Egyptian royalty fell silent. That is until her name was resurrected in 1912.[53]

Since the mummy of Nefertiti is yet to be found, the artwork about her, and that portion of the Eighteenth Dynasty are the next best thing. Knowledge of the Amarna period was held captive in obscurity until an excavation at Amarna was held by German archaeologists in 1912. They found many valuable artifacts that are worthy of display, however, it's what was found in two separate rooms of the Amarna House that became an archaeologist's dream discovery: the busts of Akhenaten and Nefertiti. The busts are two pieces of craftsmanship by the great Egyptian sculptor, Thutmose.

Nefertiti's bust is among some of the most well-known art pieces of the eighteenth dynasty. It is made up of limestone at its core with painted stucco layers. It is beautifully symmetrical; however, the left eye is missing the details of the iris. The quart's iris was either lost or was never added to the eye, to begin with. The bust has an elongated blue crown with horizontal bands wrapping around it. The cobra has been broken off the front of the crown. This bust has been a portrayal of the ultimate aspirations of regal beauty and has been coveted since its discovery on 6 December 1912.

German archaeologist Ludwig Borchardt led his archaeological team to the discovery and decided to add the busts to Germany's impressive collection of art instead of gifting them to the Cairo Museum.[54] Intrigued by their discovery, they intended to travel back to Amarna in 1914, but with the Great War raging, they were prevented from going back. The bust of Nefertiti was a coveted piece that came from a period in Egypt's history that truly stands alone in its religious reformation, architecture, and artistic expression. By the onset of the Second World War, news of the bust that portrayed the ultimate aspiration of regal beauty had spread to the masses. In 1929, Egyptian officials had attempted to organize a trade for other works of art in the hopes that the bust of Nefertiti would be returned to Egypt, but Germany refused.[55]

In 1933, Hermann Wilhelm Göring, Minister-President of Prussia advised the bust to be returned to Egypt.[56] The arrangement was intended to be temporary and was a decision with political and military motives behind it. The sixteenth anniversary of Fuad I of Egypt's ascension to the position of the sultan and ultimately king was an upcoming event, and the bust of Nefertiti was intended to act as a celebratory display piece. The motive was to enforce an alliance between Germany and Egypt. The plan was thwarted by Germany's charismatic dictator, Adolf Hitler, who openly opposed sharing the beautiful queen in March 1934. Hitler was mesmerized by the beauty of Nefertiti and the architectural quality that had endured for many centuries, refusing to allow Germany to part with it.[57] He intended to make the bust an attraction at Ägyptisches Museum.

The Second World War began its assault when Germany invaded Poland in 1939. Nefertiti's bust was packed into a crate and prepared for evacuation. Many crates filled with stolen art were loaded onto German military trucks and dispersed between several mines. The crate holding Nefertiti's bust was buried deep within a salt mine, along with hundreds of other valuable art pieces. When American troops arrived at the mine, they discovered her bust, along with Germany's gold and silver reserves.[58] The mine was liberated of the artwork by American troops.

Egypt learned of the busts' whereabouts and attempted talks with Dwight D. Eisenhower regarding the return of Nefertiti's bust to Egypt. These talks were unsuccessful as American authorities resolved that the art piece legally belonged to Germany.[59] However, it was not safe to return any artwork while the war raged. Museums were unfortunate structural casualties, and by the war's end, several museums lay destroyed in piles of rubble and ash. The bust was placed in a storage unit in West Berlin. Finally, in 1967, it was put on display again at Ägyptisches Museum until 2005.[60] The beautiful Neues Museum that lay in ruins, destroyed by war, was rebuilt, and restored, surpassing its former glory. Construction was completed in 2009. To this day, the famous bust of Nefertiti is proudly displayed in Berlin.

The legacy of Nefertiti is complex and inconsistent. Some extend high praises for her devotion to her husband, Akhenaten, and their innovation in architectural and artistic feats, while others condemn the power duo for betraying ancient traditions and plummeting the nation into debt and religious insecurity. There is disdain for their committed dismantling of a religious system that had endured for thousands of years before them. Love her or hate her, Nefertiti was a woman of profound influence, in her lifetime and centuries beyond the grave.

The queens of Egypt mentioned here were innovators, paving the way for foreign trade routes, bringing with them the lush treasures of other lands, and aiding the enrichment of their kingdoms. They engaged in essential discussions with the elite males within their sphere of influence. Despite having rights as women that would not have been enjoyed women living in other world nations, they still had to navigate a patriarchal system that was solidly set in place. Their stories have a relatable lure. As mothers, they lost children. We will never know the sound of their wails or the aching of their hearts. But we can grasp a great deal of their human experiences through their beautiful expressions in the art and architecture that survives them. They were the pillars of strength for their families. They were shrewd negotiators, intelligent trade partners, wise military strategists, and fiercely supportive marital partners.

Egypt is truly mesmerizing, as were the women who took charge of their nation, guiding their people through war and uncertainty, and into prosperity. Egypt claims a proud and vibrant history, steeped in tradition and culture. Now our compass takes south, where the Nile River becomes the Blue Nile. A place that boasts a diverse climate and landscape. The sands disperse to make room for the lush greens of Ethiopia.

Chapter 4

Makeda: 'Queen of Sheba'

[MA-KEH-DA]

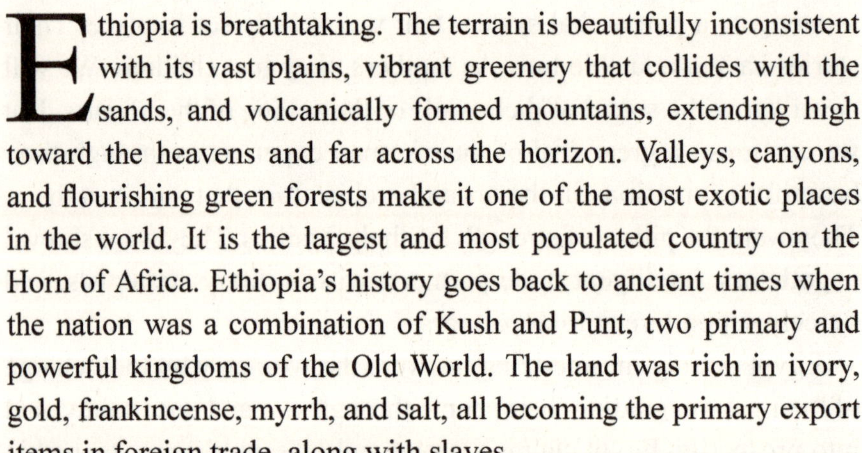

Ethiopia is breathtaking. The terrain is beautifully inconsistent with its vast plains, vibrant greenery that collides with the sands, and volcanically formed mountains, extending high toward the heavens and far across the horizon. Valleys, canyons, and flourishing green forests make it one of the most exotic places in the world. It is the largest and most populated country on the Horn of Africa. Ethiopia's history goes back to ancient times when the nation was a combination of Kush and Punt, two primary and powerful kingdoms of the Old World. The land was rich in ivory, gold, frankincense, myrrh, and salt, all becoming the primary export items in foreign trade, along with slaves.

Ethiopia is powered by an abundant water source, the Blue Nile. Originating in Lake Tana, the river travels south and then west across Ethiopia until it finds its way north, flowing towards the Mediterranean Sea.[1] The river loops across northwest Ethiopia, plunging through valleys and canyons into Sudan. It is only in this passage that it is called the Blue Nile. During the Ethiopian winters, very little rain falls, causing the river to dry, but when the Indian Ocean releases moisture from its relentless waves, cool air fills the highlands, mixing with the rising moisture and causing torrential rainfall, giving way to rushing waters. The river current gets so high that the waters become almost black.[2] The Sudanese word for black is the same for blue, giving the river its name, Blue Nile. It is the lifeblood of this region, providing hospitable conditions for healthy agricultural growth. The Blue Nile is also considered by many Ethiopians as holy; it is believed to be the Gihon River that flowed out of the Garden of Eden.

Just as attractive as its land are Ethiopia's people. A vibrant culture is on display through the avenues of music, colourful clothing, body and face paint, dances, and foods. Music is integrated into the culture, and a unique blend of instruments creates sounds one can't help but sway to. The Masinko is a single-stringed instrument that resembles a fiddle. It is made with horsehair which is pulled tight against a bamboo rod or stick and a piece of hide. The player rubs the bow against the string to produce its sound. The Krar is a lyre made with five strings and a bowl-shaped resonator for carrying its sound. (It is also known as the devil's lyre.) The Bengana is a six-stringed harp, traditionally played for spiritual purposes. The Washint is a flute made of bamboo consisting of four to six holes. The Kabero is a drum made from animal hide. It is worn with a strap over one shoulder. While it is double headed, it is most commonly played by thumping only one side.[3]

Dance has been a form of worship, celebration, and expression for countless generations. Each region has specific dances unique to its culture, in fact, there are over 150 exclusive dance movements in Ethiopia depending on the region. The Tigrayans opt for mesmerizingly smooth, circular motions that involve their shoulders and necks to achieve the movements. The Amharas use their upper bodies and necks when they dance. The Oromas people engage their whole bodies, which also involves several jumping movements. Gurages have a more acrobatic style, which involves whole-body coordination. Lastly, the Welayita, Kenbata, Sidama, and Dawro people are recognized for their belly dances. Each dance is rhythmic and quick-paced.[4]

Food is also a chief component of Ethiopian culture. Several savoury dishes consisting of meat, lentils, and blended spices are all staples of a traditional diet. Ethiopian foods have an exotic taste and aroma due to the blend of spices, which include cinnamon, cardamom, ginger, and sacred basil (also called holy basil which has a sweet aroma, contrasting to regular basil which has a spicy fragrance and bold taste). These spices are combined to make a dish called Berbere. Other spices used are turmeric, mitmita, and chili powder. Kitfo is a common meal made of raw beef and chili powder, while Tibs are small pieces of meat sauteed with rosemary twigs and commonly served with lentils.[5] Ethiopian culture, including its music, dances, body and face painting and food is sure to leave one's senses seduced. The religious and cultural history is just as enthralling. There are three primary religions in Ethiopia: Judaism, Christianity, and Islam. However, other religions are present. The kingdom of Sheba is traced far back to biblical times under the reign of King Solomon who personified its grand entrance on the stage of ancient history.

Since Sheba's origin nation is so highly debated, it is important to explore another geographic possibility: Ancient Arabia.[6] To the northeast of Ethiopia, across the Red Sea, the large land mass of Arabia resides. Arabia is surrounded on each side by four bodies of water. The southern region borders the Indian Ocean, and the southeast connects to the Gulf of Aden. To the east lies the Persian Gulf, and to the west is the Red Sea. The northern region reaches the Mediterranean Sea. These waters provided the primary food source for the ancient people, mostly consisting of saltwater fish.[7] These bodies of water made trade successful with the surrounding regions of Egypt, Greece, Rome, Babylon, Persia, and Assyria. Ancient Arabia was the cradle of trade, its exports being spices and silks.[8] During ancient times, the land was richer in vegetation due to heavier rainfalls. The land has drastically changed, hosting vast sandy deserts and mountains. The people were made up of multiple tribes who were fiercely devoted to each other. While this was beneficial in a micro-social sphere, the nation as a whole did not represent unity. Each group had exclusivity at its core. The concept of community was kept at a distance. Arabia (now present-day Yemen) is believed to be the birth place of Islam in 570AD/CE,[9] now the dominant religion of the land.

The ancient kingdom of Sheba (also called Saba) played an important role in trade, architectural feats, and foreign cooperation. The definitive location of this kingdom and the differing opinions are worth exploring in more detail. Some scholars believe the kingdom was located in Yemen near the southwestern corner of the Arabian Peninsula. However, the *Kebra Nagast* places Sheba in Ethiopia.[10] Regardless of where this ancient city resided, there is no question of its importance in African history. Valuable resources flowed from this land like the proverbial milk and honey. Sheba was known as 'Green Country'.[11] Trade routes in Sheba were innovative and were known as 'incense' or 'spice' routes.[12] Sheba was rich in frankincense and myrrh. Sap was extracted from the trees and stored, becoming some of the most coveted exports in the surrounding lands.

Access to the Qari Port in India was beneficial. It was a long trek lasting 1,200 miles, taking sixty-five days to travel one way.[13] The route was constantly traversed, and it was worth the journey. The trade gave each cooperating region access to valuable resources, building foreign alliances, and strengthening the economy.

Sheba's agricultural economy was healthy and thriving, to the point of requiring constant tending by the local farmers who had green fingers for growing and maintaining such bountiful crops. An additional benefit was the irrigation provided by the Marib Dam.[14] Some of the crops produced were wheat, dates, millet (which is a type of cereal grain), grapes, and barley. Most of the grapes were pressed, fermented, and turned into wine, which was another export distributed from Sheba. This kingdom also boasted impressive architecture, primarily as large stone structures, some embellished with written texts. These texts mainly consisted of the accounts of military campaigns, royal proclamations, and the list of the reigns of kings.[15] Walls were not beautifully painted with scenes of royal life or events, greatly differing from their Egyptian neighbours. The greatest temple in Sheba was Mahram Bilquis, located near the capital Marib, present-day Yemen. Mahram Bilqis is also known as the Temple of Awwan, meaning, 'Sanctuary of the Queen of Sheba'.[16] Having religious significance, the temple served as the worship centre and a sanctuary of refuge. In addition to buildings and temples were stunning statues of alabaster stone and metalwork. Much of their inspiration came from Greece and Rome.

Religion resembled that of the Mesopotamian residents, embracing polytheistic religious beliefs. A few of the highest deities were Ea (god of wisdom and magic), Anu (god of the heavens), Almaka (god of the moon), Shamsh (Almaka's daughter and goddess of the sun), and Enlil (god of the earth, storms, wind, and fate).[17] In addition, there were thousands of astral and minor gods. Like other ancient cultures, religion was integrated into political decisions, backing military campaigns, and farming. The land of Sheba embraced similar religious beliefs. However, Sheba included three dominant monotheistic world religions: Christianity, Judaism, and Islam. In fact, the kingdom of Sheba is mentioned in the Bible, Torah, and Qur'an, as well as its cooperative partner in trade, Israel, under the reign of King Solomon.

Religious texts are filled with men and women, most having a checkered past. The ancient scribes wrote of kings and the commoners in their shining glory, and in contrast with all their faults. King Solomon is among the chronicle of Israel's kings. Most of what is known of King Solomon is recorded in the Bible, specifically in the first eleven chapters of 1 Kings and the first nine chapters of 2 Chronicles. His father was King David of the tribe of Judah and was born from the womb of Bathsheba, a beautiful woman who was arguably the most beloved of David's wives.

According to religious text, when King David was nearing death, Bathsheba petitioned on Solomon's behalf to have him crowned as king of Israel, even though he was not the firstborn.[18] Solomon had several older brothers who would have been in line for the throne according to birth right.

Through the efforts of Bathsheba, the prophet Nathan, and divine sovereign influence (as the Biblical scriptures describe), Solomon was crowned king. His reign has become known as the Golden Age of Israel and boasts monumental successes. He secured alliances with Tyre, Egypt, Moab, and Arabia.[19] Most notably, his construction of the Great Temple of God in Jerusalem is among his greatest feats. This temple is widely believed to have held the holy grail of Jewish and Christian history: the Ark of the Covenant. Upon the temple's completion, King Solomon hosted an extravagant celebration. He ordered the sacrifice of 22,000 oxen and 120,000 sheep.[20] The temple is extraordinarily significant as it is believed that God's presence resided inside it, specifically, the chamber on the far western end, called The Holy of Holies. This chamber was built with specific measurements, thirty feet in length, width, and height (ancient measurements state 20 cubits for length, width, and height). Only the chief priest had access to the holy chamber. The temple also had several side rooms and a lavish courtyard that could be accessed by priests and commoners. This temple was later destroyed, and its treasures were plundered by the Babylonians led by King Nebuchadnezzar II in 586 BC. However, after King Cyrus of Persia defeated the Babylonians in 538 BC, he extended an offer to the exiled Jews to return to Jerusalem to rebuild the temple. Construction of the new temple was completed in 515 BC.

King Solomon is most markedly renowned for his wisdom. Those who witnessed his rule were left in awe, particularly regarding conflict resolution. Perhaps one of the most famous incidents is documented in the biblical book 1 Kings 3:16-28.

'Now two prostitutes came to the king and stood before him. One of them said, "Pardon me, my lord. This woman and I live in the same house, and I had a baby while she was there with me. The third day after my child was born, this woman also had a baby. We were alone; there was no one in the house but the two of us. During the night this woman's son died because she lay on him. So she got up in the middle of the night and took my son from my side while I, your servant was asleep. She put him by her breast and put her dead son by my breast. The next morning, I got up to nurse my son and he was dead! But when I looked at him closely in the morning light, I saw that it wasn't the son I had borne." The other woman said, "No! The living one is my son; the dead one is yours." But the first one insisted, "No! The dead one is yours; the living one is mine." And so they argued before the king. The king said, "This one says, 'My son is alive and your son is dead,' while that one says, 'No! Your son is dead and mine is alive'." Then the king said, "Bring me a sword." So, they brought a sword for the king. He then gave the order: "Cut the living child in two and give half to one and half to the other." The woman whose son was alive was deeply moved out of love for her son and said to the king, "Please, my lord, give her the living baby! Don't kill him!" But the other said, "Neither I nor you shall have him. Cut him in two!" Then the king gave his ruling: "Give the living baby to the first woman. Do not kill him; she is his mother." When all Israel heard the verdict the king had given, they held the king in awe, because they saw that he had wisdom from God to administer justice.'[21]

Those that bore witness to the quarrel between the two women and Solomon's subsequent ruling had to have left the court with slack-jaw expressions and the hairs raised on their arms. Word of his wisdom spread to distant lands until it reached the ears of Makeda, Queen of Sheba. Intrigued by the stories she heard about the man endowed with a divine gift of wisdom (as it was Solomon who asked God for this gift), Makeda prepared to trek the long journey to Jerusalem to witness his wisdom in action for herself. However, this was not the only reason for her visit. Queen Makeda's meeting with Solomon was also politically and economically motivated. He needed her country's goods, resources, and access to trade routes. Reciprocating in cooperation, and maybe some generosity, King Solomon allowed Makeda access to the Palestinian and Mediterranean ports, enhancing trade for the land of Sheba. The queen brought with her an impressive 120 talents of gold to gift King Solomon. This sum of gold equates to 3,600,000 US dollars today.[22] Makeda's trip to Jerusalem is believed to have made an impact on Solomon's country as well as her own.

Makeda's journey to Jerusalem was undoubtedly long and arduous. She was a queen who did not travel lightly, considering the abundance of treasures she brought along with her. Her material entourage included gold, silver, wood native to her lands, exotic spices, precious stones, and 800 donkeys, mules, and camels.[23] Among the heavy caravan trailing behind her, her inquisitive mind carried a list of riddles to test Jerusalem's wise king.

She was greeted into Solomon's temple, and, given his proclivity for extravagance and luxury, his presence and her surroundings were nothing short of overwhelming, even for her as a woman of exorbitant wealth. The celebration of her arrival was filled with music, dancing, and frivolity. Musicians and singers were invited to lend their talents to this grand jubilee. Masinkos, krars, and kaberos were in full crescendo, and maintained their stamina into the early hours of the day. Jesters served as entertainment to the invited masses. Makeda's and Solomon's initial reactions to each other are not recorded, but their subsequent interactions were cordial. Makeda was a true vision of a woman. Solomon undoubtedly did not let her beauty go unnoticed.[24]

Sheba's queen was curious to see what made King Solomon stand out among so many other rulers. She tested the king with a series of riddles, which are not specified in any text, however, folklore embellishes this tale, providing riddles to display Solomon's wisdom. According to folklore, Makeda tested Solomon asking him to tell a boy from a girl as the pair looked alike and to reveal which flower was real and which one was artificial. King Solomon replied that the girl would catch an apple in the lap of her dress and that a bee would only be drawn to the real flower.[25] His wisdom left the queen in awe and admiration. Her visit to Jerusalem lasted for six months, and during this time, she witnessed his striving for wise jurisdiction in all matters concerning his people and his land. When Makeda boarded her chariot for the long journey home, Solomon had 6,000 chariots brimming with extravagant gifts.[26] In addition to her being royalty, several theories have been discussed among scholars of what really prompted such lavish treasures gifted to her by King Solomon. Some may surmise that he was simply returning the generosity she bestowed upon him when she arrived in his lands, however, it seems the motive may be far more involved than that. She was a woman who displayed strength, competency, wealth, and an exotic beauty that Solomon may not have previously encountered. At least, not to the same calibre as the Queen of Sheba.

There are several paintings and artworks that depict Makeda, most of which show a woman with smooth, ebony skin void of blemish. She is embellished with a crown of gold and what looks to be embroidered fabric with intricate designs of gold. She is dressed in fine clothing and jewellery, displaying her extravagant wealth.[27] The texts written about Makeda of Sheba are somewhat inconclusive and highly debated. However, there are several stories to explore that are fascinating, dramatic, and poetic. Her impact on African culture and society is a result of her explorations, experiences, and personal connections she made along each foot of her travels. Considering how influential she was on a continent the size of Africa is no less than astounding. Her name is attached to religious texts and folklore.

The *Kebra Nagast* is a great place to open the curtains on the dramatic legend of Makeda: The Queen of Sheba.

There is myth, mystery and legend regarding Makeda of Sheba. In addition to her name appearing in religious texts, she is also found in other literature, such as the *Kebra Nagast*, which is considered by some to be a sacred text itself. By translation, the name means Glory of the Kings, and more closely resembles a collection of legends with Queen Makeda and King Solomon acting as its central theme. It was written during the fourteenth century in Ethiopia in the language of Ge'ez by a writer named Nebure Id Ishaq of Axum. In his written combination of myth, folklore, and mysticism, Nebure expands on Makeda's trip to Jerusalem, drawing special attention to the supposed attraction between the Sabaean queen and King Solomon. While in Jerusalem, Makeda was well provided for. Her seat at the table was in no short supply of meats, honey, wine, and delicious sweets.[28] It is believed that during her time absorbing Solomon's counsel, Makeda denounced her worship of the sun and embraced a new belief in the God of Israel, bringing the Judeo-Christian faith back to Ethiopia.

Of the many tales that surround her name, sexual seduction remains a peak interest. As legend tells it, the night before Queen Makeda's departure from Jerusalem, King Solomon threw a lavish feast. His finest wines were served, and meals were strongly spiced during preparation. Not wanting to turn away anything the king presented to her, she submitted to his offerings of food, drink, and song until her senses were intoxicated with indulgence.

The night was late, so Solomon invited Makeda to share his chambers. He was enticed by her beauty but made her promise not to touch anything of value to him. Makeda gave Solomon her word. Before lying down to sleep, the king ordered one of his guards to put a carafe (pitcher) of fresh water within Makeda's reach. Makeda awoke, her pallet as dry as sand from the heavily spiced foods she had eaten. She kept her eyes on Solomon for a long time, and when she was convinced he was in a deep sleep, she reached for the pitcher and let the water quench her lips and tongue in sweet relief. Only pretending to be asleep, Solomon opened his eyes, his arm striking out and grasping her arm like a serpent. He chastised Makeda for breaking her vow, reminding her that water was more precious and valuable than material riches. Admitting her guilt, she submitted her most sacred parts to Solomon in sexual oneness.[29] However, it is believed that Makeda had longed for this union from the beginning. It is written that their sexual union produced a child, a baby boy named Menelik. Makeda left Jerusalem, taking a part of Solomon within her womb back to the Horn of Africa.[30]

The legendary kingdom of Sheba is almost as elusive as its queen. For centuries, the kingdom was buried under close to twenty feet of sand until the 1950s when excavation teams and archaeologists uncovered four mighty pillars, which were just the tip of the iceberg. As the digs continued, a large part of the city was unearthed, revealing towers of stone bearing ancient Sabaean script detailing every intricate part of life within the folds of the kingdom. Standing over 2,000 feet, were two towers, one to the north and one to the south, towering over desert lands bearing deep and winding grooves. This was once the great irrigation system that supplied Sheba with a reliable water source that nourished the land around it. A great dam called the Marib Dam was formed, providing the north and south oases, known as the 'Land of Two Paradises' with fresh, rushing water. This land of paradise was surrounded by grasses and tall trees with massive green canopies. Today, it is a sharp contrast to its ancient portrait. The land is a vast desert where life seems scarce, and water even scarcer. It is believed that the dam was destroyed by a massive earthquake, or heavy rainfall occurred, damaging it beyond all repair.[31] With the dam destroyed, essential irrigation was halted, choking out the green life surrounding its receding shores. Over time, the land of Sheba became the dry, sandy, and desolate landscape it is today. Much of the Marib ruins remain buried under the sand, but there may come a day when precious remnants of her reign will emerge again.

Menelik I was brought up under Queen Makeda's supervision and guidance. Information about his early life is limited, most records of him record his life from his twenties onward. Solomon heard that he had indeed borne a son with the beautiful Makeda and his heart was filled with joy.[32] Consistent with her conversion, Makeda brought her son up in the Jewish faith.

Solomon implored Menelik to remain in Jerusalem, but his son desired to return to Ethiopia. There is a myth that King Solomon gifted a replica of the Ark of the Covenant to Menelik, however, as legend tells it, Menelik switched the two, bringing the real Ark back with him.[33] Others say Menelik was unable to transport the real ark due to the supernatural powers protecting it. Upon the death of Queen Makeda, King Solomon crowned Menelik I emperor of Ethiopia. This secured the expansion of the Solomonic dynasty in Africa, which lasted for more than 3,000 years. There is a large Jewish population living in Ethiopia. This is due to Solomon sending thousands of Israelites to Ethiopia, securing a fertile breeding ground for the Jewish population.[34] Menelik I's reign lasted from 954 to 930 BC.

Makeda's relevance is far-reaching in African culture. The question of her origins is widely debated and continues to perplex archaeologists. Much of Queen Makeda's memory survives in oral tales that have endured for thousands of years. According to the Yemenis, Makeda appeared out of the sand dunes of Marib. The *Kebra Nagast* offers a colourful and exciting narrative describing her origins. Some of the information is repeated with its own flare from the tales.

Makeda was brought up in a family of serpent and dragon worshippers.[35] One day, in her youth, her parents offered her flesh to their serpent god along with milk and sweet beer. She was tied to the top of a tree to await her fate. In a fit of salty tears, one fell on the seven saints who had gathered below her. Curious, the saints inquired if her being was spirit or human. She advised of her humanity and the cruel ending planned for her by her parents. The dragon-serpent approached to claim his offering. He was seized by the seven saints, his blood spattering. Some of his blood landed on Makeda's heel. Her heel became like that of a donkey. Makeda was an outcast in the village due to the unsightly and deformed appearance of her foot. She heard rumours of King Solomon and his medical skills and planned to travel to see the king in the hopes he could restore her foot. Once she stepped on the threshold of the palace, her deformed foot was restored to its natural shape.[36] The legend continues in similar tones to other accounts with the queen breaking her promise and drinking the fresh water left within her reach. However, the *Kebra Nagast* offers an extension to this tale. Not only did King Solomon impregnate Makeda of Sheba, but another woman as well, although her name is not mentioned. In fact, this tale describes both women getting out of bed at the same time to drink the water, they were discovered by King Solomon, and he took them both to his bed.

Before he sent both women away, he gave them each a silver staff and a ring. He instructed them that if a girl was born, to give her the staff and present his daughter to him, and in the same way, he instructed her to give his son the ring and return the boy to him.[37] Makeda and the other woman both bore sons. When they came of age (sometime in their early twenties), each son was given a silver ring and sent to King Solomon as requested. Upon hearing of his two sons' imminent arrival, he devised a plan to test their wisdom, or lack thereof. He dressed himself in beggar's clothes and had a palace friend dress in his royal robes. The friend, dressed in the king's finest, took a seat on the throne and awaited the two young heirs. King Solomon played this game of deceitful dress-up for three years, forcing his sons to wait until he agreed to meet with them. After three years, King Solomon arranged to meet his sons. The son of the other woman immediately approached the man on the throne, grasped his hand, and paid homage, believing him to be the king and his father. Menelik, son of Makeda, did not see any likeness of this man in himself. His eyes searched the whole room thoroughly, until his gaze met the man in rags whose features strongly matched his own. Menelik knelt before the true king in reverence. King Solomon was overjoyed, declaring, 'My true son!'[38] He acknowledged the other man as his son but deemed him a fool.[39]

The people of Israel were displeased with King Solomon for allowing his son Menelik to have almost a kingly status and expressed their disdain publicly, stating that they would not be ruled by two kings.[40] King Solomon decided that it was favourable to send Menelik back to Ethiopia to appease his people and swell his kingdom there under the rule of his son. He declared Menelik I King of Ethiopia. By this time, according to historical records, Makeda of Sheba had passed away, making a clear path for Menelik to rule the nation, along with the blessing and proclamation of his father.[41]

Modern-day scholars have deemed the *Kebra Nagast* as Ethiopian folklore since there is little evidence to support the claims of the fourteenth-century text. Archaeologists have continued to search for the Queen of Sheba, most notably beginning in the early 1950s by archaeologist Wendell Phillips. Phillips' excavation only lasted a year, ending in 1952, drastically limiting the amount of finds that could have been unearthed. Just when the anthropologic world thought a breakthrough was in sight, digs were halted.[42] Sheba went back under a heavy cloak of sand and time, failing to break through the barrier of myth and legend.

The concept that Jerusalem had historical ties to Sheba was seen as controversial. However, when the Ophel excavations commenced, led by Dr. Eilet Mazar in 2012, a major discovery occurred in the ancient ruins of King Solomon's temple in Jerusalem. A clay pottery jar containing remnants of incense and inscribed with Sabaean text was found.[43] It was discovered in an area believed to be where King Solomon conducted his administrative actions. This piece of archaeological treasure puts a firm link in the historical chain connecting Israel and the Kingdom of Sheba. Excavations of this site have recommenced in recent years, led by the Institute of Archaeology at Hebrew University and the Armstrong Institute of

Biblical Archaeology. The primary focus will be the Second Temple Period structures as well as the subterranean drainage tunnels. As archaeologists work tirelessly through these ancient foundations in Jerusalem, more of Makeda's famed visit to King Solomon may be unearthed.

The ruins of Marib are believed to be part of the ancient kingdom of Sheba. The Temple of Bilqis (meaning Sanctuary of the Queen of Sheba), also known as Barran Temple, was home to the moon goddess Almaqa. The script chiselled on the walls also mentions Dhat Hameem (god of the sun) and Athter (goddess of blossoms). There are six columns of stone and a sacred courtyard enclosed by a brick wall. On the western end, five towers still stand, overlooking the mysterious city of ruins. The main temple gate stands to the north. The route to these ruins is guarded by Yemeni military personnel. The Temple of Bilqis is considered the largest pre-Islamic temple in Yemen.[44]

Military involvement complicates how extensive excavations can be conducted inside the ancient ruins of Sheba. The mixture of folklore, myth, and religious texts creates a swirling blend of historical truth and fiction which makes for a colourful story but can be a bit dizzying as well. Archaeologists have yet to find any structures that bear the queen's image, but scholars are hopeful that future digs will reveal concrete truths about Queen Makeda, the ancient land of Sheba, and shed more light on her trip to Jerusalem that is steeped in the truth, separating from the folklore that has engulfed her name throughout history. Her story is elusive, but historians have not closed the book on her chapter yet. Southern Arabia and Ethiopia both claim to have ancestral ties to Makeda. Based on archaeological findings, the ancient kingdom of Sheba resides in what is now southern Arabia, however, if Makeda had a son with King Solomon who was sent to Ethiopia to rule, that region of Africa also has reasons to lay claim to the queen's origins.[45] The frankincense that she brought with her as a gift to King Solomon is only found in two parts of the world, Ethiopia is one of them. Some have claimed to be descendants of Makeda due to having ancestral ties to Menelik I. Many support this claim due to the large Ethiopian Jewish population that exists in the present day. Many Ethiopians credit the Sabaean queen with instituting Judeo-Christianity in Africa.

Our compass now shifts back to the northwest, following the great Nile River to the vast terrain of mountainous sand dunes where water is scarce. The era that is ushered in next is nothing short of inspiring, where queens take their nation by the reigns, leading their countrymen in ferocious battles against the strongest military powers and nations known on earth at that time. The Kingdom of Kush was surrounded by world giants such as Egypt and the Roman Empire. To say they fought bravely to stave off the enemy would be a grave understatement. Welcome to the land of desert storms, where the Blue Nile and White Nile weave their way through the east.

Chapter 5

Amanirenas: 'The Cycloptic Queen'

(AH-MON-E-RAIN-ES)

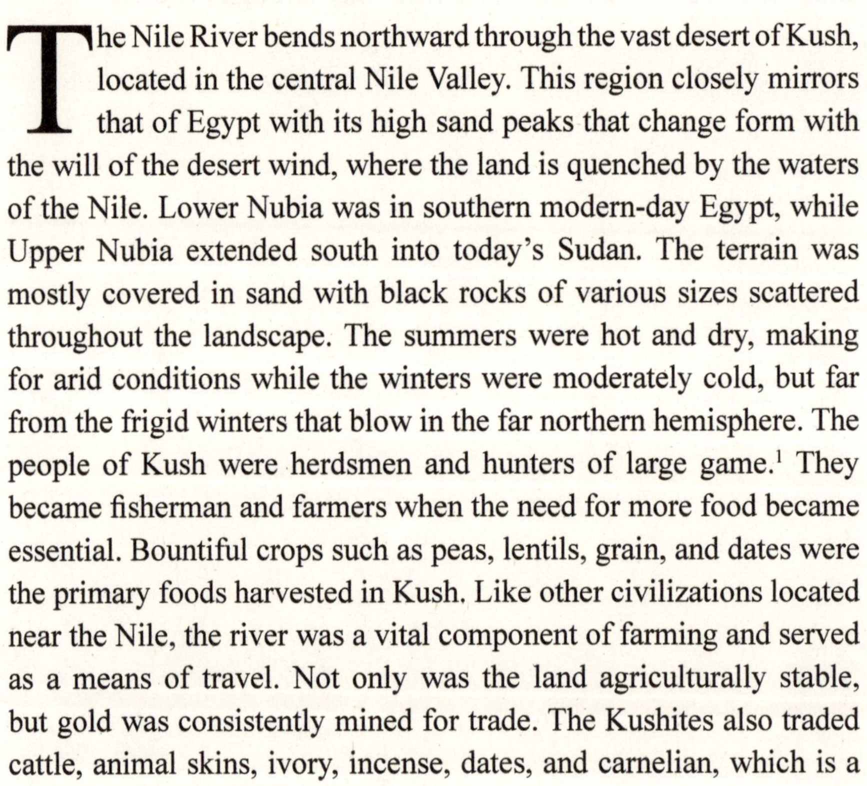

The Nile River bends northward through the vast desert of Kush, located in the central Nile Valley. This region closely mirrors that of Egypt with its high sand peaks that change form with the will of the desert wind, where the land is quenched by the waters of the Nile. Lower Nubia was in southern modern-day Egypt, while Upper Nubia extended south into today's Sudan. The terrain was mostly covered in sand with black rocks of various sizes scattered throughout the landscape. The summers were hot and dry, making for arid conditions while the winters were moderately cold, but far from the frigid winters that blow in the far northern hemisphere. The people of Kush were herdsmen and hunters of large game.[1] They became fisherman and farmers when the need for more food became essential. Bountiful crops such as peas, lentils, grain, and dates were the primary foods harvested in Kush. Like other civilizations located near the Nile, the river was a vital component of farming and served as a means of travel. Not only was the land agriculturally stable, but gold was consistently mined for trade. The Kushites also traded cattle, animal skins, ivory, incense, dates, and carnelian, which is a red or titan stone, known as the 'stone of kings'.[2] Egypt was their main trade partner and exchanged their goods for grain, wine, beer, and oils. Kush often bartered with Egypt for corn, bronze, and cloth.[3] Much of Kush's history was discovered in ancient Egyptian records, highlighting that the land of Nubia was known as Kush for at least 2,000 years.

Nubia was a transit region, making it ideal for trade, especially being a border region with Egypt. Since the land was abundantly rich in gold, ivory, and ebony, Kush was a desirable trading affiliate.[4] However, this also made it the target of potential aggression from neighbouring powers including Egypt and Sudan who sought to invade Kush and Nubia and plunder the precious resources from its ground and streams. Nubia was fiercely contested for these precious metals, exotic animals, and slaves, and the conflict over it endured for many years.

The beauty and value of Kush did not only come out of the earth but were crafted by the skilled hands of its people. The Kushites were known for their beautiful ceramics. Some of the most beautiful pottery to emerge from this era in ancient history was from Kush.[5] Pottery vessels were made entirely by hand. Ceramics were decorated with intricate designs, rich colours, varying shapes and sizes; many had a metallic appearance.[6] Some artwork resembled that of their Egyptian neighbours and embodied a Hellenistic influence. Art that depicted humanity included exquisite detail, especially in facial features, much like that of the Amarna period in ancient Egypt. The cartouche of the female ruler, Arnekhamani, is seen on the *Aegis of Isis*.[7] This piece resembles the goddess Isis, a prominent and beloved deity in ancient Nubian culture. The eyes are large and almond shaped. The collar is broad and exaggerated in size, however, there is a hole in the centre of the forehead where the *uraeus* would have extended from her headdress, signifying that the woman of this art piece was a goddess.[8]

A fierce foe of ancient Kush was the Roman Empire. Caesar Augustus seized control over Egypt from Cleopatra VII and

Mark Antony, establishing Egypt as a Roman providence. This changed the economic relationship between Egypt and Nubia. The trading of gold and other riches greatly diminished, and the Nubian kingdom did not find favour in, or pay homage to the rapidly growing Roman Empire. The Roman army was highly strategic and calculated. Their presence in battle was menacing and intimidated many armies that had once prided themselves as military juggernauts, only to turn and flee like whipped dogs. One reason the Roman army was successful in war was because of its battle formations and vast weaponry. They often used the 'tortoise' marching technique where the exposed men at the front and sides interlocked their large shields and the rows of men behind held theirs aloft creating an impenetrable barrier of shields. This formation closely resembled a tortoise shell.[9] The shield placement helped protect the men from the opposing army's advances, and more importantly, from the arrows of archers firing from a distance. The shield was a protective tool in the vast weaponry used by the Romans. In fact, the Romans had several deadly weapons at their disposal.

Swords were perhaps the most common. Historian Marilee Hanson brilliantly defines several ancient Roman weapons in her work, which is published on the English History website. The gladius was a short, two-sided sword, approximately forty to sixty centimetres in length. The inner blade was made of a softer steel and was covered by a hard steel on the outer blade. This sword was worn on a Roman soldier's right hip and was designed for close-quarters combat. The spatha is a longer sword, approximately one metre in length, and was designed to deliver powerful, mortal wounds. The pugio is a dagger about fifteen to thirty centimetres long and five centimetres broad. This weapon was easy to conceal, making it an offensive tool for inflicting harm during hand-to-hand fighting. The hasta was a non-conspicuous weapon. It was a spear, reaching almost two metres, the tip of which was made of iron. The pilum was a lightweight javelin about seven feet long with an iron spike fixed to the top of the wooden shaft. The average weight of a pilum was four pounds, making it easy to throw and penetrate shields and armour. Plumbatas were lead-weight darts that could be thrown up to thirty metres. These were useful when attempting to wound an enemy before close combat. The onager was a sling that held stones for hurling. Stone-throwing was used as a deterrent to take the advancing army's attention off the intended main assault. Finally, the ballista and the scorpio catapults, the former launched heavy darts called bolts.[10]

The body armour was designed to make it difficult for the enemy to penetrate. Its hardened leather was used for vests, like today's gilet, which were reinforced with metal plates. A heavy woollen tunic was also worn, covering a Roman soldier to his knees. The helmet was domed and made of brass, bronze, or iron. The neck guard on the back provided an extra measure of protection. The shields the Roman army employed were just as strategic as their marching tactics. Of semi-cylindrical design, the shield was so long it covered from chin to thigh, adding an essential layer of defence. It was made of light wood with metal surrounding its edges, complete with a bronze handle welded to the shield's interior.[11]

An army's success in battle depended in part on a sound strategy. The Roman army had excellent military strategists who not only ensured the army was well equipped with effective battle tools, but also trained the army in battle formations. The phalanx formation involved soldiers standing side by side in ranks, three feet between each row of soldiers. If a man was killed, he was replaced by the man behind him. The shields were also used to push the enemy back. The Roman army was separated into four groups. The *Velites* were made up of inexperienced soldiers positioned at the front. This group was responsible for the early attacks at the onset of battle. The *Hastati* threw javelins from behind the *Velites* and drew their swords in preparation for the advancing enemy's army. The *Principes* were spearmen and skilled swordsmen, considered the best soldiers in the

Roman army. By the time the *Principes* entered the battle, the enemy had been exhausted by the prior attacks and then had to fight the most experienced and skilled soldiers. The *Triarii* was the last group to go forward if the *Principes* were unsuccessful for any reason.[12] If the enemy army decided to retreat, Roman cavalry advanced and pursued the retreating army, running the fleeing soldiers down. This division was skilled at breaking down walls and even used special cranes that allowed groups of Roman soldiers to scale the enemy's defensive walls.

The Romans built a dominant empire through conquering lands, plundering their enemy's resources, and precious materials, and taking the foreign people as slaves. Their impressive conquering feats include Egypt, Greece, and Turkey, making them the leading military force surrounding the Mediterranean at the time.

The Kushite army brought their own skills and weaponry to the battlefield. Ancient Kush and Nubia were known as the 'Land of the Bow', making their weapon of choice the bow and arrow, known as the *Ta-Seti*.[13] The Kushites were exceptional archers with impeccable accuracy regarding aim and distance. The wails of dying men followed soon after their arrows were loosed, raining a shower of iron spikes into the flesh of their enemy. The Kushite army did not utilize nearly the quantity of weapons as the Romans; however, the vibration of their bows would have been a fearful sound, even for the most menacing of armies. Swords were also used for close-quarter fighting, along with axes, pikes, and shields made of ox hide.[14] The Kushite army was not dressed in elaborate armour, leaving their flesh far more exposed to devastating injury. However, the lack of weight gave them agility and speed. Their limbs were free to move swiftly and wield their weapons with less interference. This would also have heightened their sense of vulnerability and self-protection, which is a valuable trait in warfare. Their victories in warfare are etched in stone; so too are their losses. Just like all other military powers throughout the course of time, the bell of victory fell silent. Battles are won and lost by all, and the Kushite army was no exception. They had many valuable resources and were surrounded by dominant world powers like Egypt and Persia. They were conquered by Egypt in 1504 BC under the rule of Pharaoh Thutmose I.[15] The capital Kerma was destroyed, leading to the subsequent Egyptian sovereignty over Nubia. However, in 727 BC, the Kushite army invaded Egypt under the Kushite king, Piye, occupying the city of Thebes and the Delta Valley.[16] They ruled this part of Egypt until 656 BC when Nubia withdrew to their own lands, realizing that an inevitable defeat was before them at the hands of the powerful Assyrian army. Victory and loss in warfare went back and forth like a tennis match for centuries between the land of Kush and its surrounding nations.

The Kingdom of Kush has an established history of employing strong female rulers who instituted policies, led their army into battle, and rehabilitated the land and the people once the fighting was over. Many cultures around the world saw no leadership potential or value in women, but Kush was not among those nations. A chronicle of highly capable women exists depicting victories for their people, nations, the treasures that they plundered, and the subsequent respect they commanded, even from nations that wielded more power, authority, and wealth. The women of power in the land of Kush were depicted as voluptuous, but also violent. They had the beautiful curves of a woman's body (believed to be an attractive trait among many cultures), but they could be menacing and deliver savage punishments to their aggressors. The kingdom was driven by women, and between 50 BC and AD 40 (approximately ninety years), three women consecutively ruled over Kush, Amanirenas, Amanishakheto, and Amanitore. Among the greatest and most revered of these warrior women of Kush, was Amanirenas, the cycloptic queen.

Amanirenas' origins are somewhat sketchy, despite the famous conquests she is known for during her reign. She was born in 57 BC; however, the identity of her parents remains a mystery. When she gained status through her marriage to King Teriteqas of Kush,

Amanirenas forged her name into history. It was upon the untimely death of King Teriteqas that Amanirenas rose to power (about five years into the Roman occupation of Nubia) and led her people through a merciless campaign against the great and powerful Roman army. She was given the title of 'Qore' and 'Kandake' which shows that she ruled independently as queen.[17] Her palace was vast and had several brick-vaulted rooms lined with gold leaf.[18] She also had an impressive warehouse that held an abundance of gold and ivory tusks, a primary export of ancient Kush.[19] Queen Amanirenas was a lion among her people. She embraced the authority bestowed on her and wielded it with strength and uncompromising resolve. Her leadership may have been underestimated by enemies she met in battle, but their false assumptions were quickly remedied when they came face to face with a woman who was described by the Greek historian, Strabo, as a 'masculine woman with one eye destroyed'.[20] She was a staunch opposer of the growing and militant Roman Empire, and she did not hide her defiance. In a cunning and arguably antagonistic move, Queen Amanirenas sent Julius Caesar a bundle of golden arrows with a message. If he wanted peace with the Nubian nation, then the arrows were a gift of foreign friendship, if not, she advised that he and his army would need them.[21] This was a brazen act by the queen and no doubt caused her enemy's eyebrows to rise in surprise and offence.

Meanwhile, in occupied Roman territory, Caesar appointed a poet and soldier, Gaius Cornelius Gallus as his prefect. Cornelius invaded Nubia, laying claim to Philae, and had his achievements engraved on erected stone structures, displaying his intense egocentrism.[22] His victories were written in Latin, Greek, and Egyptian hieroglyphics. He imposed high taxes on traders in Nubia and Kush. This did not sit well with the Roman Empire as he was openly glorifying himself, not the emperor. Cornelius instigated malicious gossip against Caesar Augustus, so as punishment, he was disenfranchised, with orders to have him publicly disgraced and exiled. Rather than face this humiliation, before the decree was ratified, Cornelius committed suicide.[23]

A new prefect was appointed, named Aelius Gallus, who was commanded to lead the military expedition to Arabia. His command extended over 15,000 troops in Egypt; some of the soldiers were transferred to the army from other lands.[24] Amanirenas saw this as an opportunity to challenge the Roman army. Tension between the two powers was about to froth into a full boil. The Romans had encroached on Nubian lands and enforced high taxes on the Meroitic people. Believing the Kushite and Nubian people to be in a more subjugated attitude, the Roman army temporarily withdrew the majority of its forces to pursue other conquests planned in Arabia. This was an opportune time to form a military strategy with the element of surprise at the centre of her plans. Amanirenas stalked the Roman army, watching for weaknesses weighed against advantages, and observed Augustus' lack of ability to keep track of his own army and growing empire.[25] When she deemed the opportunity ripe, she commanded her 30,000 troops to attack the Roman-occupied cities of Aswan, Elephantine, and Philae. As claimed by Strabo, her army plundered these cities and took many Romans as slaves.[26] The statues of Caesar were toppled and trampled. One was decapitated with the strong swing of a Kushite sword. She and her army retreated to El-Dakkeh (meaning 'mound of rubble').[27] Petronius demanded that Amanirenas and her army return the plundered loot taken from the Roman army. She refused, which greatly angered the new prefect. Petronius ordered his infantry of 10,000 men to charge the queen at her royal residence. He captured the area which is now Qasr Ibrim and established a fort for his men. Archaeologists discovered Roman garrisons and artillery during a dig in the 1990s. In an act of defiance against the Roman Empire and a display of her dominance on the battlefield, Amanirenas took the severed statue head and buried it under the steps of the temple dedicated to the worship of Amun,[28] allowing her and her people to trample the head of Caesar

Augustus every day. This obviously angered the Roman Empire, particularly Caesar Augustus. Eight hundred cavalry and over 10,000 Roman infantrymen were deployed to go head-to-head with the Kushite army.[29] The latter was severely underestimated by the Romans, believing that since the King of Kush, Teritiqus, was dead either through illness or battle injury, the army did not have an efficient or militarily skilled leader. They were sorely mistaken.

One day, under the scorching heat of the ancient sun, her war skills were tested to the limit, and her physical form was altered forever as she faced a Roman soldier in battle. Sand shifted beneath the soles of swift sandals, and dust billowed and blanketed her enemy in a blinding, dense haze. The sounds of steel blades pierced the air and the heavy breathing of her enemy was her guide to continue her attack with accuracy and precision. Ultimately, the attack left her face scarred and disfigured by three slashes across her cheek. Her eye was irreparably damaged, rendering her blind in one eye. When the fighting ceased, Amanirenas went back to her camp, face stinging and stiff from the dried blood that stained it. She nursed her wounds and when the pain settled, her vengeance was rekindled. The ferocity of her appearance was a physical display of her resilience and defiance. The grit that flowed through her veins was as tough as a Roman's leather tunic, and her enemy was about to know that full well. The preparations for war commenced on both sides. The Roman army set its sight on Meroe, the capital of Kush.

Although it outnumbered the Romans three to one, Amanirenas' army, assembled in Pselchis, was driven to retreat, and many were taken prisoner. Among the prisoners were the queen's generals. Petronius had them extensively questioned, but they were cunning, telling him that the Kushite army had retreated to Napata, the ancient capital and site of sacred temples. In fact, Napata had been abandoned by the rulers hundreds of years earlier.[30] This led the Romans on a wild goose chase to a city that was over 300 miles from where Amanirenas' army really was. In his fury, Petronius burned

Napata to the ground and travelled to Cyrene. Amanirenas retaliated in what is described as a barbaric counterattack. Her son was killed during this military engagement.

She continued to face off with the Romans. Cannon shooting hundreds of darts pierced the flesh of anyone in their path; they could reach up to several hundred yards. This made a frontal assault by the Kushite army impossible. She ordered her army to surround the Romans in a relentless attempt to trap them in a hilltop city. What resulted was a four-year military campaign that left hundreds of thousands lying dead on the sand, weighed down further by a massive financial cost, but ultimately resulting in victory for Kush, and sealing Amanirenas' legacy as the fierce warrior queen she is known as today. Caesar signed a treaty stating that he would remove his army from Kushite lands and would not encroach on natural resources such as ivory, gold, and iron.[31]

Caesar prepared to go to Europe for negotiations, inviting Amanirenas to negotiate her terms as well. She opted to stay in her country, appointing one of her diplomats to go in her stead. Her emissaries successfully negotiated the withdrawal of Roman troops from the second Cataract to the Egyptian border, and the cancellation of the high tax imposed on Meroe.[32] This showed other world leaders her autonomy, independence, and supremacy, which was a notable breaking of gender barriers. She had a trusted few in her sphere of influence that would negotiate in her favour. Those who spoke for her certainly knew better than to double-cross her. In 21 BC, Caesar declared Kush to be a sovereign nation. Amanirenas never paid homage or tribute to Rome and her remaining eleven years as the Queen of Kush were known as 'The Golden Age'.[33]

Ancient Nubia is home to several archaeological finds that have yet to be understood. However, scholars have studied them, hoping to eventually decipher the ancient Meroitic script. The Temple of Amun (not to be confused with the Theban temple in Karnak in Egypt) is among the fantastic discoveries. The area is an impressive vastness of land, covering over sixty kilometres of the Nile Valley. Located in the ancient capital Napata in the Nubian kingdom, downstream from the fourth Cataract of the Nile (present-day Sudan) and surrounded by seemingly endless sand, this temple stood from 750 BC to 590 BC. This site features the ruins of several temples and the Hill of Barkol, which is believed to be a holy mountain, and the royal seat of the god Amun. This hill is also called Jebel Barkal, meaning 'Pure Mountain', as it was referred to by the ancient Egyptians.[34] When the capital was moved to Meroe, Napata continued to be a city for hosting royal coronations and remained a sacred cemetery. Napata was the official royal burial site of Kushite princes and other citizens of either royal or significant stature.

Perhaps the most telling of the ancient Kushite royalty is the depiction of its female rulers and their legends of victory. Another temple with a vibrant story to tell is the Temple of Meroe, also known as 'The Lion Temple' located in Naga in the Nubian kingdom.[35] It was dedicated to the Kushite god Apedemak, who bears a strong resemblance to the African lion. This lion is carved into one of the most well-known art depictions of Kushite victory. Engraved into the stone is a later successor of Queen Amanirenas, Queen Amanitore. She is depicted as strong and almost barbaric, gripping the hair of her subdued enemies, and wielding her weapon of choice to swing the final death blow.[36] Apedemak in the form of the lion is crouched between her legs, taking swipes with sharp claws at the prisoners grasped by the queen.[37] On the opposite wall, Queen Amanitore's husband, King Natakamani is depicted in a similar stance with the lion crouched between his legs as well.[38] Flying overhead is a vulture, resembling the god Nekhbet, while the falcon flies over the queen, resembling the god Horus.[39] What is so striking about this artistic representation of warfare is its resemblance to the Narmer pallet.

The art on the temple walls in Kush also strongly mirrors that of the pre-Amarna period in ancient Egypt. The art dominantly shows the profile of the human form; however, a striking difference is the way women are illustrated. The Kushite women, particularly of royalty, are shown as voluptuous, fierce, and powerful. There is an autonomy shown in the artwork that was not seen in Ancient Egyptian art until the Amarna period under the rule of King Akhenaten and Queen Nefertiti. Religious concepts can be seen in the art of Kush, however, the Kushites had a blend of Egyptian and Nubian gods.

Not all the art found at Meroe originated in Kush. As mentioned before, the bronze head of Caesar Augustus was buried under the temple steps at Meroe, and later became known as the 'Meroe head' since it was discovered there in December 1910, below the temple ruins, by British archaeologist John Garstang. Keeping with ancient Greek fashion, the head represents the 'ideal' physical appearance of a man. It was made of bronze and weighed seventeen kilograms. The bronze has since morphed over the ages into a teal green. The eyes are made of calcite, which is a polymorph of calcium carbonate and a component of limestone, which was commonly found throughout northwestern Africa. The bronze head of Caesar is impeccably well preserved due to it lying face down in the sand, protected from the hot, dry conditions that battered the earth above it. This piece is now housed at the British Museum.[40]

Among the impressive treasures buried in the sands of Meroe is the Hamadab Stela. The slab is made of sandstone with forty-five rows of ancient Meroitic script. The language is yet to be fully deciphered. Amanirenas is mentioned, along with religious deities. Archaeologists are still striving to decode the ancient text as they hope it will clarify the finer points of the war between the armies of Amanirenas and Caesar Augustus. The outcome of the battle at Napata continues to be debated among scholars, historians, and archaeologists. However, the deciphered oral and text accounts of Kush's battles with the Roman army remain in overwhelming favour of Kushite victory.[41]

Some scholars believe that the collapse of Kush was the result of the rivalry with the Aksum kingdom in northern Ethiopia over traded goods. Several events contributed to the fall of these ancient kingdoms. Fifty years after the death of Caesar Augustus, Emperor Nero planned to lead an expedition deep into Africa in pursuit of finding the source of the Nile River, however, that was not his only intention. He also set his sights on the city of Meroe, plotting to invade and attempt to dominate the land of Kush, refusing to submit to previous defeat. His plans were cut short when he committed suicide, which was followed by a bloody civil war.[42]

For many years, the Roman Empire was a leading world power politically, architecturally, and militarily. Eventually, the weight of the empire's own success became too much to sustain. It gained countless riches and goods from plundering sacked cities, dragging their spoils back home. The confiscated resources only benefited the nobility, so the rich got richer, while the poor remained chained to their situation. This led to a social crisis and an urban uprising. With a weakened social structure prone to uprising, a foreign enemy became a threat to the empire's future security. Among their enemies was the ferocious group, the Visigoths.

The Visigoths were a division of the Goths, located in the northeastern European region. They were a Germanic people who at one time fought alongside the Roman army.[43] One of their most menacing and courageous warriors was a man named Alaric, the first king of the Visigoths. Since his efforts in the Roman army were so successful in the sacking of several kingdoms, Alaric naturally assumed that his contributions would be rewarded by the Roman Emperor through a promotion in the army and all the wealth and title that went along with it. He clearly assumed too much, as no such promotion or reward was given. Alaric was infuriated and his pride was deeply wounded. He did not have the support of the Roman Empire as he thought, and his people began to feel the separation from the leading mother of nations through starvation. Alaric rallied his troops and began his trek on the road to Rome. If he was not going to be given a promotion within the Roman army, he was going to utilize all his knowledge of Roman military strategies to defeat the army he had once paid homage to. Alaric's army did not have the capability of breaching the city's well-fortified walls, so they lay siege to the city of Rome, blocking shipments of grain and other goods, effectively starving the inhabitants inside.[44] The population was weakened, giving Alaric and his army the advantage over the debilitated city. Rome was ravaged by the Visigoths, leaving it reeling in despair, soaked in blood and shrouded in ash.

The Roman Empire's expenditure on war, defending its own land, and upholding a lavish lifestyle, took a fatal financial toll. There weren't enough financial resources available to advance the city's infrastructure, support its people, and continue to pour into the military coffers. In addition, the Roman government allowed corruption to sink its teeth into the financial, political, and social veins of the Empire, ultimately bleeding the faith of the people dry. Roman citizens no longer trusted their government. The army began to fill with foreign soldiers who did not feel an allegiance to the Empire and was stretched far too thin to adequately defend Rome's more immediate borders.

A solution was inspired and implemented by Emperor Diocletian, and while it was meant to be temporary, it resulted in a permanent arrangement until the Empire fell. Rome was split into two regions, the Western region (at Milan) and the Eastern region (at Constantinople).[45] Although temporary, the governing powers bickered over military aid and resources. Rome would never recover from the split. The fall of Rome was a perfect storm of over-stretched resources, corruption, slave deficits, and foreign invasion, all exacerbated by a world power that had quite frankly been poisoned by its own pride. Like so many ancient empires, the empires of Kush and Rome ended. Many historians believe that Kush was eventually absorbed into the Roman Empire, ultimately ending with the dissolution of both.[46]

The Kingdom of Kush in the land of Nubia faded into the shifting sands of history, but its legacy of fearless women being elevated to positions of power over its people and on the battlefield has remained a vibrant chapter in Africa's history. Amanirenas is among the most prominent women in ancient Nubian history, captivating historians throughout the ages, including the ancient Greek philosopher, Strabo, who enjoyed travelling and soaking in his antiquated surroundings, documenting his findings of some of the earliest civilizations that still have plenty to offer from the halls of the ancient world. Strabo travelled extensively to Kush, Rome, Tuscany, Asia Minor, and Ethiopia, studying countries and the exciting people of each region.[47] He was a prominent historian during the reign of the Roman emperor, Augustus. He described Amanirenas as 'a masculine woman with one eye destroyed' in his text *Geographical Sketches*.[48] He also described the account of Petronias' army marching to Napata to destroy the great city. Some historians have queried this event due to the distance between Napata and Meroe, questioning his army's ability to march the long distance under the scorching temperatures.[49] Scholars are still working to decode and interpret the Meroitic language and until then much of the history of the Meroe people is yet to be discovered.

Despite the large gaps in the Meroitic language, Amanirenas is no longer hidden within the deep folds of Kush's sand and toppled stones. Thanks to the surviving texts that have endured over the centuries, the stories and legends connected to women such as Amanirenas can continue to educate the world about ancient places, the people who lived there, the rivers that sustained life, and the cooperation and conflict between cultures and nations. Amanirenas stands out among the ancient queens for her uncompromising spirit and wise negotiation skills that benefitted her people. She was not afraid to wield the weight of her sword and soak it in the blood of her enemies if freedom was guiding its sharpened point. Her legacy paved the way for the women ruling after her to continue to lead with a comparable spirit and pride. Two succeeding Kandake, Amanishakheto and Amanitore, became known as warrior queens of Nubia, undoubtedly inheriting the fierce legacy of Queen Amanirenas before them.[50]

Stelae and monuments bearing the image of these queens still stand today, and while weathered from the harsh desert elements, their image is immediately recognized, and their names are among the few in the Meroitic language that have been decoded.

Our compass now takes a dramatic shift to the northwest, leaving the vast terrain of sand dunes behind, and leading toward North Africa in what is now present-day Algeria, bordering the Mediterranean Sea. The theatrical narrative of war, religious unrest, and cultural vibrancy continues as time ticks on, and we cross from the ancient into the modern era.

❦ Chapter 6 ❦

Dahia al Kahina: 'The Jewish Sorceress'

[DAY-UH AL KA-HEE-NAH]

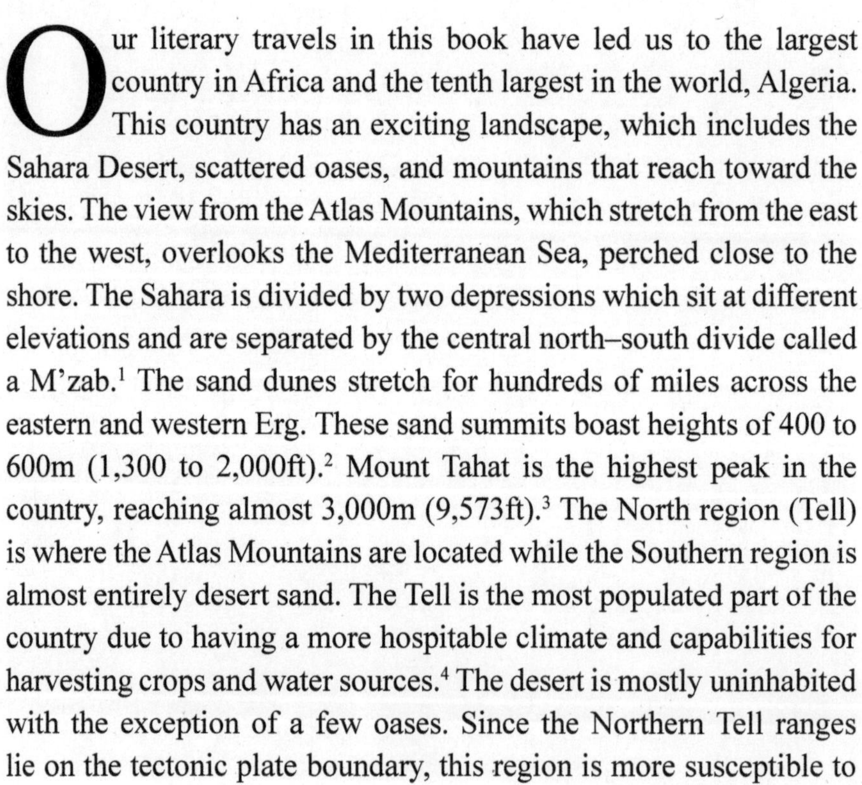

Our literary travels in this book have led us to the largest country in Africa and the tenth largest in the world, Algeria. This country has an exciting landscape, which includes the Sahara Desert, scattered oases, and mountains that reach toward the skies. The view from the Atlas Mountains, which stretch from the east to the west, overlooks the Mediterranean Sea, perched close to the shore. The Sahara is divided by two depressions which sit at different elevations and are separated by the central north–south divide called a M'zab.[1] The sand dunes stretch for hundreds of miles across the eastern and western Erg. These sand summits boast heights of 400 to 600m (1,300 to 2,000ft).[2] Mount Tahat is the highest peak in the country, reaching almost 3,000m (9,573ft).[3] The North region (Tell) is where the Atlas Mountains are located while the Southern region is almost entirely desert sand. The Tell is the most populated part of the country due to having a more hospitable climate and capabilities for harvesting crops and water sources.[4] The desert is mostly uninhabited with the exception of a few oases. Since the Northern Tell ranges lie on the tectonic plate boundary, this region is more susceptible to earthquakes.[5] The North and South regions are separated by the High Plateau where some of the agricultural abundance is grown such as barley, wheat, and oats.[6] The Western region is where tobacco, olives, dates, millet, corn, rye, sorghum, and rice are grown.[7] Algeria also has an impressive high-grade iron deposit. In addition, it is a leading trader in the export of petroleum and natural gas. In the desert, grasses such as the Esparto, commonly called, 'Spanish grass' grow in great quantities. The grass is widely used to make baskets, ropes, sandals, and mats.[8] Spiny shrubs, jujube trees, acacia, and tamarisk call the desert their home.

While the Algerian landscape is mostly mountains and desolate wilderness, the land also consists of forestry. Of its total land area of 238 million hectares, 2.5 million (0.9 per cent) are forest.[9] The forests have a variety of Juniper, Cedar, Oak, as well as related oaks such as Corn and Holm. Shrubs of rosemary, thyme, lavender, laurel, sage, and garse can be harvested as flavours for Algerian foods and natural remedies.[10]

There is a variety of wildlife as well. Wild bore, macaque, mouflon, and barbary deer roam the grasslands.[11] Small rivers and streams attract the winged wildlife in the animal kingdom such as storks and vibrant flamingos. Across the Sahara, gazelle, jackals, hyenas, fennecs, and desert hares graze and scurry.[12] The desert is also home to species of scorpion. While Algerian wildlife is an exciting aspect of the country, the people and culture are what give its history its depth. Many Algerians are Arab, and most citizens are descendants of ancient Amazigh tribes.

Several languages are spoken in this country, while the surrounding smaller countries such as Morocco and Tunisia speak a dialect of Arabic. The Afro-Asiatic language has fifteen main dialects and 300 subdialects.[13] The most spoken language is Arabic; however, the Amazigh (Berber) language is also part of the nation's profile.[14] Most Amazigh people raise crops and livestock. Their artistic creations such as music, wood carving, jewellery, rug weaving, pottery and leather are among the many features that make this region of Africa so enticing.[15] Algerians also host several traditions related to weddings, funerals, childbirths, and food.

As is true of nations all over the world, the concept of religion is a part of the foundation of Algerian fabric. Religion is at the heart of culture and political thought. Unlike the polytheistic cultures of ancient Egypt and Nubia, Algeria embraced a monotheistic belief system. Algerian citizens adhere to a few of the major world religions: Judaism, and Islam, and there is a small population of Christians, however, the dominant religion embraced by the people is Islam.[16] The small Christian population in Algeria believes that Jesus Christ of Nazareth is the crucified and resurrected son of God. This belief also goes together with the belief in a triune God: God the Father, God the Son, and God the Holy Spirit. This population follows the beliefs and traditions described in the *Bible*, believed to be the word of God.

Islam has a long history and is believed to be an Abrahamic religion, along with Judaism. It was founded in Arabia during the seventh century AD by the prophet Muhammad. The word Islam means 'surrender' and coincides with the belief that it is essential for one to surrender to the god, Allah.[17] Islam, Judaism, and Christianity are imperative to include in the study of the ancient queens since religion has held the founding principles of humanity tracing back to the belief in humanity's origins. Just as polytheism was integrated into every piece of ancient Egyptian and Nubian culture, the major religious shift to monotheism was integrated into the cultural, social, and political climate of Algeria. Islam spread rapidly throughout the Middle East, China, the Indian subcontinent, Africa, Southeast Asia, and Europe.[18] Islam is the primary religion in Algeria, and the sacred text embraced by the people is the *Qur'an* (also spelled *Koran*). The Qur'an, which consists of 114 chapters, is believed to be the verbatim speech that God delivered through the vessel of the archangel Gabriel to Muhammad.[19] The *Hadith* is regarded as the sayings and traditions of Muhammad.[20] The Islamic doctrine establishes the laws of thinking. The *Qur'an* dictates the fundamental principles of living. The Sunnah institutes the traditions, Ijma is the consensus, and the Ijtihad is individual thought.[21]

One of the most important concepts in Islamic practice is the Five Pillars. The Pillars consist of the Shahadah (profession of faith), prayer, the Zakat (purification), fasting, and the Hajj (pilgrimage to Mecca).[22] The Shahada is the proclamation of faith and commitment for Muslims. To become a true Muslim, the proclamation that there is only one god, Allah, and recognition that Muhammad is the messenger and prophet of god must be recited three times in the company of witnesses.[23] The Salah is the ritual of Islamic prayer, performed in the direction of Mecca five times per day.[24] Fridays are the designated day for congregational prayer. Zagat is an obligatory financial offering.[25] Some of the financial giving helps fund charities that aid environmental disasters and war zones. Sawn is the ritual of fasting, particularly during the religious holiday, Ramadan, which occurs during the ninth month of the Islamic calendar.[26] During this time of fasting, abstaining from food, drink, sex, and smoking must be abstained from sunrise until sunset.[27] This practice allows the exemption of pregnant women, the ill, and children from taking part. Hajj is the journey Muslims embark on to the city of Mecca at least once in one's lifetime. One must be in the right spiritual mindset before travelling, following the example of the prophet, Muhammad. The Ka'bah sanctuary is a sacred and holy place for Muslims, believed to be built by Abraham.[28]

Differences in Islamic theology arose after Muhammad's death. Branches of Islam were formed such as Sunnis, Quraysh, Kharijites, and Mu'tazilah. The Sunnis are traditionalists, making up the majority of Muslims.[29] Quraysh is the ruling tribe of Mecca.[30] The Kharijites' name is derived from the Arabic word *Kharaju* which means to 'withdraw'.[31] This group believes that unconfessed sin causes one to no longer be Muslim. Proclamation to Allah is not believed to be enough but must accompany righteous deeds. The Mu'tazilah means 'those who stand apart'.[32] While Islam is the dominant religion in Algeria, the queen of this chapter is of the Jewish faith.

Judaism is a monotheistic religion that goes back to the ancient Hebrews. One of the primary beliefs is in a transcendent God who revealed himself to Abraham, Moses, and prophets.[33] This belief system describes the unique relationship between God and his people, and God's sovereignty over all mankind. Abrahamic religion is believed to stem from his son, Isaac, and Islam through Abraham's other son, Ishmael (born of Hagar).[34] Abraham's descendants were enslaved by the Egyptians for hundreds of years until their divine deliverance through Moses. The sacred text of Judaism is the *Torah* which includes the first five books of the Christian Bible: Genesis, Exodus, Leviticus, Numbers, and Deuteronomy, also called the Pentateuch.[35] It is believed to be the word of God, given to Moses at Mount Sinai, also including a genealogical record.[36] In addition to the *Torah*, the *Talmud* is the collection of Jewish laws and customs and is understood to be more of an oral historical account.[37] One of the most recognized accounts in history of divine intervention is the story of the Jewish liberation in the book of Exodus when Moses performs the works of God to the hard-hearted Egyptian Pharoah, Rameses II, whose defiance against the Hebrew God brought about the ten plagues of Egypt. It is this ancient religion that has persevered throughout the course of human history that was embraced by Queen Dahia al Kahina.

Dahia (also spelled Dihya) al Kahina (the word Kahina historically means 'prophetess' or 'witch') is among the more obscure queens in African history, with the exception of her military conquests.[38] Most of her upbringing is unknown besides that she was raised in the Aures Mountains in Algeria and was presumably the daughter or niece of the Berber king, Mathia ben Tifan, however, some scholars place her as the daughter of Aksel, a freedom fighter for the Amazigh people, also known as 'the free people'.[39] If she was the daughter of Aksel, then she came into the world of military conflict honestly. Aksel fought against Uqba ibn Nafi in AD 683 and killed him after the defeat of the Islamic army.[40] Dahia fought alongside Aksel in the early 680s and proved her ferocity on the battlefield. Dahia was destined for war.

After his victory, Aksel expanded his territory, however, he was later killed in battle against Hasaan ibn Nu'man. Aksel was succeeded by a woman named Kocelia who was either his wife or another female relative. However, she must not have ruled very long because by 690, Dahia al Kahina assumed command over the Berber army and people. The Imazighen people were matrilineal, meaning that most of the historical lineage is traced via the female bloodline. Interestingly however, despite the genealogical record adhering mostly to the female line, the name of her mother or any other possible dominant womanly influence has remained elusive throughout the course of history. The term 'Berber' is a derivative term of the Greek word for savage and is interpreted as a derogatory term by some.[41] It is not known if she was born into the Jewish faith or if she converted along with her Gerawa tribe. Regardless of the origins of her religious affiliations, she is mostly believed to have been a follower of Judaism. Her origins and religious affiliation are widely contested with some asserting that she was a Christian due to the spread of Christianity during the Roman conquests that led to widespread African and European occupation.[42]

Dahia was not a dainty or fragile woman. She was a woman who, to her enemies, appeared larger than life. She was a ruthless warrior who would not be subdued by her enemies without a ferocious fight and would certainly not be taken alive. She was the liberator of slaves and a champion of her people. There is some debate regarding her physical appearance due to some believing she had some Greek ancestry, however, most accounts, particularly those of the Muslim army she fought against, describe her as beautiful, dark-skinned, tall, and with long dreadlocked hair.[43] She is depicted wearing traditional Numidian royal attire such as a loose-fitting tunic with a sash or belt fastened around her waist and sandals.[44] In addition to her intimidating physical appearance, she is also known for having an unquenchable sexual thirst. But perhaps her thirst for freedom was by far the most unquenchable desire. This woman warrior would draw her sword in battle and lead her people against the Arab invasion of North Africa during the seventh century, vowing to fight without compromise even if it led to her own demise by the sword of her enemies. The relentless wielding of her sword in war and the roar of her battle cry riled her troops up. Dahia knew the uplifting feelings of pride when her people claimed victory in conflict just as she did the sting of overwhelming and devastating defeat. Her defeated enemies believed Dahia's victories were the result of sorcery as if she chanted spells of defeat and concocted a brew of devilish schemes over them.[45] This is where the story of Dahia and her defence against the powerful Arab army takes centre stage in Algerian history. This climatic event in history will not disappoint.

It is paramount to understand the military weaponry and tactics of an army to best comprehend how a battle is fought in a war that has all the passions of world dominance fuelled in part by religious foundations and ethnic creep. It is an aggressive attempt to not only spread religion to the surrounding lands (leading to worldwide conversion) but also a method to increase the population of any specific ethnic demographic in addition to breeding another out. Ancient African battles were brutal due to the type of weaponry and the menacing hands that wielded them. These weapons were designed to distract, pierce, and kill. The khopesh is a sickle-shaped sabre, and while it originated in Egypt, this sword has been adopted throughout Northern Africa.[46] It consists of three parts in one, with a straight edge that acts as the handle with a pronounced curvature in the blade. This sabre was designed to trap an opponent's arm or pull the shield out of the way, which provided an opportunity for the opposite arm to swing death blows with another more powerful weapon.[47] Perhaps one of the most significant items in the Berber artillery is the flyssa, a razor-sharp sword that reaches twelve to thirty-eight inches in length. It was designed to have the capability of slicing through chainmail, causing devastating wounds to the recipient of the blade's rage.[48] The koummya is a dagger used by the Berber and Arabic armies. This curved, double-edged blade often resembles the tusk of a boar, which is useful for intimidation.[49] This blade is not all-bark-no-bite as it can deliver deep, slashing cuts. The shotel is a type of sickle-curved sword. This semicircular, single-edged blade originated in Ethiopia. The blade was often long enough to reach around an opponent, slicing and stabbing through vital organs such as the kidneys and lungs.[50] The most sinister of all of these weapons is the ida. This blade was multifunctional as some used it for agricultural purposes. It was highly useful in cutting down crops that were ready to be harvested. However, it was also a menacing tool in battle. This blade was laced with poisonous herbs, peppers, and deadly insects, causing paralysis to the one struck or sliced with it.[51] Once paralysis set in, which was often swift, the ida swordsman could deliver death to his or her enemies in as many strikes as necessary. As time marched on, the nimcha was introduced to African warfare, however, this sword was not widely used until the sixteenth century.[52] The Muslim army possessed a similar artillery of weaponry consisting of long sabres and daggers for close encounters in hand-to-hand combat.

While effective and efficient weaponry is essential for any gifted soldier to have, the formation and tactics of the military are paramount too. The methods employed during battle are essentially methodical communication within the army. These methods can consist of formations that require a head-on attack, an attack from the rear, or an all-out surprise attack. One of the most effective and devastating military tactics against an adversary in war is the 'Scorched Earth Policy'.[53] This method has been used for thousands of years; however, it has evolved as military intelligence has improved and changed. This war device dates to ancient Egypt and Mesopotamia and was later used by the Roman Empire and even during the American Civil

War when General Sherman marched through Atlanta to the Atlantic Ocean, burning everything in the Union Army's way.[54] During the Second World War, this was used in the form of 'carpet bombing' and was among Hitler's favourite devices of war, even against the German people.[55]

This policy destroys everything the enemy army can use to wage war, including crops, livestock, infrastructure, and buildings that are used as army shelters. It becomes increasingly difficult for the army under attack to retreat or flee. Fields are burned to ashes, effectively starving the people inside their cities, leaving them vulnerable and weakened. The water supply is often cut off, only increasing the devastation felt by the enemy's army and civilians.[56] The Muslim army had an impressive number of cavalry, and the army had thousands of skilled horsemen trained and ready to ride hard into battle.

While this book is not intended to focus on the heated passions of ancient conflict between Muslims and Jews, it is important to acknowledge. Tensions have been present for almost 2,000 years, which have not dulled over time, but rather have increased and become more severe. During the reign of Dahia, the spread of Islam was rampant across Northern Africa, with the army setting its sights on the populated Jewish tribes. Wars are fought for various reasons; with power, glory, heritage, and fortune being among the top pursuits. The protection of people, culture, and faith may be some of the most virtuous causes of conflict. Queen Dahia had pride in her culture, people, territory, and convictions so she was not going to offer all that she had with open palms to the aggressors marching toward her village. Despite the history of her early life being overwhelmingly elusive, her military conquests did not shy away from the centre stage but rather relished in the blinding light of its recognition as a major battle in North African history. Her adversary was not to be dismissed and he gave Dahia the fight of a lifetime. Leading the Muslim army was General Hasaan ibn al Nu'man. Word had reached his ears of the Jewish queen known as 'the priestess' or 'sorceress', and he was eager to face her and the Berber army on the battlefield.[57] This caliphate was a dominant force that established Islamic rule in North Africa, having led several successful campaigns.[58] According to historical records, the size of his army was unprecedented. He had cavalry and hundreds of thousands of infantry. His command of the Muslim army was well known, and among some, respected. During his campaigns, some of his quests for dominance were met with little to no opposition. On the contrary, some nations or tribes were eager to welcome Nu'man.[59] This may not have been an eagerness to embrace Islam as it was that they did not see the necessity of going up against an army that was notorious for being victorious. To go up against an army such as the one led by General Hasaan ibn al Nu'man would most certainly cost resources and many lives.[60] North Africa was the direction Nu'man sent his army, sights set on the Berber tribe, and in an even more pinpointed direction, Queen Dahia. She was not eager to accept defeat before a battle even commenced and declared that she would lead a force to drive the Arab army back. His army was dispatched from Egypt in AD 693 toward modern-day Algeria. The Berber tribe lived in independence and enjoyed autonomy, so this foreign invader was unsurprisingly met with great opposition and resistance. Dahia led her troops to victory over the Islamic army in 698.[61] Nu'man's army retreated and was driven out of Ifriqiya (region of North Africa and Tunisia).[62] This defeat was most likely a blow to the great leader's ego and postponed the plans of spreading Islam throughout North Africa. Despite the Berber army being numerically smaller than the Muslim army, Dahia proved her and her army's capabilities in battle and made the opposing army acutely aware of the measure of her resolve. The defeat left hundreds of Muslim soldiers dead and close to 100 captured.[63] Nu'man's son was among those she captured. Despite her reputation for violence and hot temperedness, she took pity on a young man named Khalid ben Yazid, the son of her enemy, and adopted him as her own.[64] According to historical accounts, she was not cruel to those she captured. Dahia made sure the prisoners of war were well-fed, clothed, and not treated with harsh severity as other enemy forces may have done. She was not going to be an easy force to subdue. Nu'man's army laid back in a position of observance. One of the best things an army can do is to study the enemy. It is a grave mistake to underestimate one's opponent as this mistake is often met with one's doom. The Muslim army waited for the right time to strike.[65] The battle that would decide the fate of Islamic spread in Algeria was just ahead.

After Dahia al Kahina delivered her initial defeat of Hassan ibn al Nu'man and his army, the great Berber queen did not want to leave any opportunity for her enemies to plunder and pillage her lands. She ordered the 'scorched earth policy' to be employed in her own lands believing her land and all of its riches were better off reduced to ashes than in the hands of her enemies.[66] She had fields and precious resources, including the riches dug up from the earth, burned and destroyed.[67] The people of these lands were left devastated since they and their livestock relied on the land to be healthy and plentiful. As a result of this maniacal order from the queen, many fled the tribe. Others sent word to Nu'man, begging him to invade and intervene.[68]

Smelling the stench of their desperate situation, Nu'man realized the opportunity for victory and assembled his army once again in what was sure to be an epic battle. His army had swelled to an impressive number and is believed to have been the largest army he had yet commanded.[69] Twenty-four thousand men stood shoulder to shoulder, ready with swords, spears, axes, and shields. The army marched toward Ifriqiya once again. They met Dahia's army at Gabes.[70] The fighting was an intense engagement, resulting in the capture of Dahia's sons. They were welcomed into the Muslim army and promoted to officers if they converted to Islam. The captured young men were eager to oblige. Scholars believe that one of Dahia's men betrayed her after they were captured, informing the Islamic warlord of her military battle plans and revealing the Berber army's position.[71] Queen Dahia tried to flee to her stronghold, the Aures Mountains, only to be caught up in what became the final military engagement between her army and the Muslim army of Nu'man. This battle took place in Tarfa (although some call it Tabarka), which is a region located between Tunisia and Libya.[72] Nu'man defeated the Berber army in 701. Despite much of Dahia's history being saturated with legend and lore, what is definitive is her relentless spirit and pride. This would not have been an easy victory for the Muslim army. Despite her intense valour, she had no option but to succumb to defeat. The exact manner of her death is still debated. Some scholars believe that she was killed fighting in battle, while others assert that she chose to part from the earth on her own terms.[73] Perhaps in the more entertaining story, it is said that Dahia refused to be taken captive by her enemy, so she threw herself into a deep well, killing herself.[74] This well is now called, 'Kahina's Well.' When Arab soldiers pulled her limp body up from the well, they severed the queen's head, holding it up for both armies to see who had taken the glory from that battlefield.[75] Surrendering troops of the Berber army were granted amnesty if they converted to Islam. It is believed that over 12,000 men were persuaded from their original faiths. This was only the beginning of the Islamic takeover of Africa. To this day, Islam is the dominant faith system in Algeria.

The legends surrounding the demise of Dahia al Kahina are just as fascinating as her life's conquests. Much of her history is wrapped in some sort of lore and legend that can require a bit more digging to decipher the historical truth. As stated before, there is a legend that she threw herself into a well rather than become a captive of her enemy's army. 'Kahina's Well' is located in Bir el-Kahen, Algeria, and is believed to be the location where she committed this act of suicide. This well still serves as a water source for part of the town. Another theory also located at this well is that the Muslim army surrounded her there, apprehended the Berber queen, forcing her to the ground on her knees, arms bound behind her. With a swift swing of a soldier's sword, her head was taken from her body.[76] Her head was then presented to Hasaan ibn Nu'man like a trophy. Others say she poisoned herself before the Arab soldiers could catch up to her location at the well. One more legend states that she died valiantly in battle, cut down by the enemy, and was found lying on the ground still clutching her sword, positioned as if she would never be willing to relinquish her sword to a foreign ruler. Nu'man offered her a chance to surrender along with her army, to which she replied, 'Kings do not flee', or at least that is what the legend says.[77] As a result of that battle, an estimated 30- to 60,000 Algerians were sold into slavery. Those who begged Nu'man to intervene may have not suspected this to be the outcome of his victory. Some of the villagers refused to be taken as slaves so they committed suicide before their would-be captors could fasten their shackles.

The dates of her death are just as hotly debated as the cause. Some scholars believe that she died in 689 during the war with Hasaan ibn Nu'man's army. Others surmise that she died between 701 and 702 at the end of the war, which is where the stories of 'Kahina's Well' are attributed.[78] Considering ancient texts that describe the war between the Berber tribe and the Islamic army, it is more widely accepted that she died at the end of that conflict in 701 or 702

The future of Algeria was certain, at least as far as religious thought was concerned. Islam was the uncontested majority religion of North Africa, which is still true of the region.

Her reputation of being a cruel leader who turned her power and fury against her own people is also a fascinating road to explore and one that has many twists, turns, and unexpected curves. She was convinced that her land and all its precious resources were the primary reason Nu'man's army was in such hot pursuit. She ordered all the gold and silver that could be found to be melted down until the material could no longer be recognized.[79] She ordered prosperous fields and lush gardens of her own and that of all the people to be burned. Crops that would have continued to sustain families and livestock were now nothing but charred fragments blowing away in a fog of billowing, black smoke. People watched their homes and livelihoods disintegrate before their eyes. Disbelief in what their queen had ordered turned to disdain and she lost a great deal of support from her people.

However, once again this is not the only theory that exists. Perhaps it was Hasaan ibn Nu'man who ordered his army to invade her lands under a blanket of darkness, rousing the people with the flickering flame that grew with each passing minute until fields and homes were beyond redemption.[80] Either way, Queen Dahia was held to blame, some asserting that if she had not resisted Nu'man and his army, they would not have been punished with the extreme severity they had endured.

Perhaps one of the most alluring of her legends is that she was believed to be a prophetess or a sorceress. In the present day, it may seem that resorting to her being a sorceress is a bit outlandish or hasty, but to the people of the ancient world, it seemed to be one of the most viable options to explain her actions. According to lore, Dahia prophesized the troop formation of her enemy's army, and even knew the intricate and intimate details of their military tactics and intended movements as they travelled.[81] It is also claimed that she predicted her death down to the date and act. Those who were in her presence and knew of these predictions had only sorcery to point to as a plausible explanation. Her legend is an exaggerated tale, but it has held the interest of scholars and history enthusiasts alike for centuries. Another legend is that she married a man, whose name is unknown, under political pretext, only to brutally murder him on their wedding night.[82] There is nothing concrete to validate this legend. Unfortunately, any record of her predictions or any other claim made about her is either lost or perhaps never existed; being nothing more than a twisted tale that has been altered just a tad as the centuries have passed.

Dahia's memory is not completely shrouded in legend and lore. There is much truth to this uncompromising woman. She did indeed lead her army against strong, Islamic forces, achieving victory as well as defeat. When the battle lines were drawn, she did not cower in the face of her enemies or hide away in a palace but rather planted her feet firmly on the ground and drew her sword. She is a celebrated figure known the world over, and for those who are not acquainted, she is worth knowing. Dahia is praised as a symbol of female power. In 2001, a statue designed by artist Rachid Khimoune was erected in her honour in Parc de Bercy, Paris, as a part of the 'Children of the World' ('Les Enfants du Monde') exhibit that celebrates global miscellany.[83] She is the chosen piece to represent Algeria. A statue was later erected in Baghai, Khenchela Province in Algeria in 2003.[84]

Our compass continues to point in the direction of exciting histories of women who once walked the sands and fields of this earth. Our travels take us to West Africa to the country of Nigeria where one can see the antelope prancing in fields and lions stalking in the tall grasses. This country is a global leader with a booming economy and diverse climate, culture, people, and religious affiliations. Nigeria is home to an estimated 218,000,000 people. The population is split between rural and urban settlements. There are rivers that rush during rainy seasons but halt to rest in times when rain is scarce. Its most western border cosies up to the Gulf of Guinea which leads to the Atlantic Ocean. This is the country that claims the exciting historical narrative of another warrior queen. Welcome to Nigeria in 1533.

Chapter 7

Amina: 'Warrior Queen of Zazzau'

[AH-*MEE*-NAH]

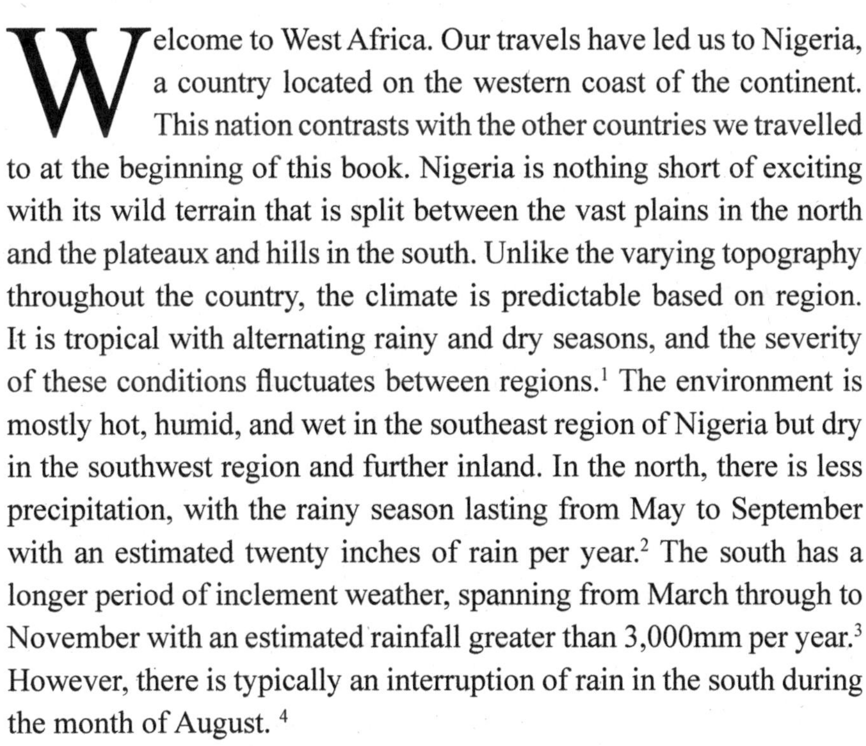

Welcome to West Africa. Our travels have led us to Nigeria, a country located on the western coast of the continent. This nation contrasts with the other countries we travelled to at the beginning of this book. Nigeria is nothing short of exciting with its wild terrain that is split between the vast plains in the north and the plateaux and hills in the south. Unlike the varying topography throughout the country, the climate is predictable based on region. It is tropical with alternating rainy and dry seasons, and the severity of these conditions fluctuates between regions.[1] The environment is mostly hot, humid, and wet in the southeast region of Nigeria but dry in the southwest region and further inland. In the north, there is less precipitation, with the rainy season lasting from May to September with an estimated twenty inches of rain per year.[2] The south has a longer period of inclement weather, spanning from March through to November with an estimated rainfall greater than 3,000mm per year.[3] However, there is typically an interruption of rain in the south during the month of August. [4]

The climate impacts the land and its ability to harvest. Nigerian soil is mostly poor quality in comparison to surrounding countries. During the dry season in the north, the soil has a dense layer of laterite which is rich in iron and aluminium, making it extremely challenging to nurture into producing viable crops.[5] In the savannah, the soil is thick with red laterite, making it much less fertile.[6] There is not as much rainfall or seasonal drying. The forest has the most productive soil and vegetation, making it the best for farming. Nigerian farmers have had to get creative to produce a harvest from their lands. Agricultural techniques such as 'intercropping' (the process of growing two or more crops at the same time in the same field) and 'slash and burn' (cutting down trees and woody plant life, in the dry season, which is then left to dry out).[7]

The Nigerian landscape boasts tall mountains, lakes, and rivers, and its most western border cosies up to the Gulf of Guinea that flows out to the Atlantic Ocean. In the northwestern region are the Sokoto Plains and to the west are the Borno Plains. The Sokoto plains are where some of the richest and most fertile farming soil is located.[8] In the southeast, the most mountainous area borders the Cameroon Highlands.[9] Facing eastward is the Udi-Nsakka plateau whose mountains offer continuous elevation for one hundred miles to the south until it reaches Okigwi.[10] The Gotel Mountains extend to the east all the way to the border of Cameroon. Travelling north you will find the Jos plateau near the centre of Nigeria. This is also where some of the most diverse cultures and languages call their home.[11] It also hosts various ecosystems, including grasslands, forests, and savannahs. One of the most elevated summits is Mount Dimlang in the Shebshi Mountains. Its peak reaches 2,042m (6,699ft).[12] However, this is not quite the highest point in Nigeria. That distinction goes to Chappal Wadi, with a heavenly reach of 2,419m (7,936ft).[13]

As we trek down the mountains, let's take a closer look at the exciting things Nigeria has to offer on the ground level. Several rivers and lakes serve as a source of nourishment and cleansing for the land, animals, and people. The Niger River and Niger Benue are the largest rivers. The Niger River has many wild rapids and waterfalls while the Niger Benue is far more docile, making it more navigable.[14] Other rivers include the Sokoto, Kaduna, and Gongola. All three of these rivers drain into Lake Chad. Coastal areas are drained by short rivers that flow to the Gulf of Guinea. The Niger Delta is a sizeable, low-lying region that drains into the Gulf of Guinea as well.[15] There are freshwater swamps and characteristic landforms such as oxbow lakes, conspicuous levees, and river meander belts.[16] One of the most important wet ecosystems in West Africa is Lake Chad. It used to be one of the largest lakes in the world, but drought and extensive use of the lake have decreased its size quite substantially.[17]

The plant and animal life of Nigeria is an exciting blend of diversity. Nigeria is economically valuable due to the abundant growth of the oil palm. Tropical grasslands grow baobab, tamarind, and the locust bean tree.[18] The baobab tree grows a large green fruit with a slightly prickly shell, known to the natives as a 'super fruit' and is often called the 'tree of life' since the fruit is said to promote good health.[19] The tamarind tree produces a bulb-like acidic fruit that is brown or reddish in colour.[20] The fleshy fruit has a sweet and sour taste. The locust bean tree blooms red, spherical flowers that grow into pods up to 30cm in length. The pod holds a sweet pulp that is used for medicinal and food purposes. The fruit is often used to sweeten soups and other foods, as well as clean teeth due to its compounds that can form a lather.[21] The savannah has more scattered vegetation of short trees and grasses. Near Lake Chad, species of acacia and the doum palm are common. The doum palm (also called the 'gingerbread tree') has a variety of uses going far beyond a food source. The tree's subtly sweet fruit contains antioxidants, and metabolites, and is even believed to promote intestinal health. Its leaves are used to weave baskets.[22]

Many exotic animals occupy the lands, rivers, and seas, each maintaining the vast ecosystem they inhabit. In the savannah, camels, antelope, hyenas, lions, baboons, and giraffe are the most common wildlife found.[23] The rainforest belt is home to red river hogs, elephant, and chimpanzees.[24] Animals such as leopards, gorillas, golden cats, wild pigs, and monkeys are common in both the savannah and rainforest belt.[25] Smaller animals such as squirrels, cane rats, and porcupines are found in abundance and serve the predators as a primary source of food.[26] Several species of birds can be seen flying high across the horizon such as the guinea fowl, quail, kites, grey parrots, and vultures circling on high.[27] The river keeps animals such as crocodiles, hippopotamuses, and a large variety of fishes. The diversity of plant and animal life is among the most exciting things to see in Nigeria, but one may argue that among the beautiful results of its creation, the people and their unique cultures are the most thrilling.

There are over 250 ethnic groups in Nigeria, however, there are three that are considered the primary groups. The Hausa-Fulani, Yoruba, and Igbo. The Hausa people are mostly cattle farmers and silversmiths.[28] Many grow cotton which is spun into cloth by the women of the villages. The Yoruba men are also farmers who grow yams, maize (corn), peas, plantains, peanuts, millet (grain), and beans.[29] The women spin cotton, weave baskets, and die cloth into vibrant colours. The men are skilled blacksmiths, leathermakers, wood carvers, and glass makers. Like the previous two groups, the Igbo people are crop and cattle farmers. Men are responsible for growing yams, while the women tend to other crops such as beans, pumpkins, okra, melons, taro (a root vegetable like a potato but with the sweetness of a parsnip), and cassava (a root vegetable that also resembles a potato).[30] The main exports of the Igbo people are palm oil and palm kernels.[31] Trading of local craftsmanship and goods is important to these three tribes. Nigerian women were well known for having skills in trade and were considered crucial to the success of long-distance and local exchange of goods. Religion is varied between the groups, but most of the people are Sunni Muslim. The other practised religions are Christianity, and indigenous beliefs, including ancestral worship and divination.[32] The cattle were sometimes used for spiritual sacrifices.

The kingdom discussed in this chapter adhered to the Islamic religion. It is this kingdom that debuts another woman who is proudly known as a warrior and champion of her people.

The kingdom of Zazzau, or as it is presently called, Zaria, is one of the oldest kingdoms in Nigeria. It is located on the Kubanni River, which served as an abundant water source for the people and animal life that lived there. Another prominent water source is the Kaduna River, a tributary of the mighty Niger River.[33] Zazzau was a primary emirate, which is a territory ruled by an emir (a title used for high officials or rulers in Muslim culture).[34] This territory was abundant in cotton (particularly in the savannah), tobacco, ginger, sugar cane, shea nuts, peanuts, and soybeans.[35] This made the region a desirable trading partner with the surrounding cities of Kano and Katsina. Salt was one of the prime items of trade and was often exchanged for slaves, cloth, grain, and even fine leather.[36] Most of the Zarian citizens were farmers who raised cattle, goats, and guinea fowl for meat. Other crops that were not used much for trade were millet and sorghum, but they served as staple foods in the Nigerian diet.

The Zarian people were artistic and lived their lives loud through the expressive uses of vibrant colours that they incorporated into their pottery and weaved goods. Cotton grew in abundance and was used for weaving cloth into clothing and blankets. The cotton was dyed with bright colours and patterns. These same vibrant hues were used in pottery painting, which was among the items sold or traded to foreign travelling merchants.[37] Zarian women were skilled weavers, making many baskets using the method of 'raffia weaving' since it is made of a natural fibre from the palmyra palm that is durable, excellent at holding dye colours, and pliable.[38] Adding to the aesthetics of their crafts, Zarian women embellished their artistries with beautiful ribbons made with the palmyra palm leaves.

Since Zaria was a desirable trading post, the surrounding cities became trade rivals in constant competition to get the first pick of the goods from the Zarian lands and people. Most notably, the cities of Kano and Katsina were the fiercest competitors. The kingdom of Kano is a traditional emirate in Northern Nigeria and was founded as one of the 'Seven True Hausa States' (Biram, Rano, Kano, Gobir, Katsina, Daura and Zazzau).[39] These regions are known for being part of the major Islamic district. Up until the fourteenth century, these regions were not a part of any authority, making them vulnerable to foreign domination. Eventually, these kingdoms were conquered, including Zazzau, and were ruled by the Kororofa (also known as Kwararafa).

The city of Nupe was a land of fishermen and merchants, called the 'river people'.[40] Their communities could consist of just a few families or several thousand people. They were ruled by a chief whose primary responsibilities were settling disputes amongst his people and effectively managing the land's resources. The people of Nupe were excellent glass bead makers that were designed for jewellery. They also made fine leather with intricate designs, brass trays, and woven mats. The men were mostly blacksmiths, brass smiths, and tailors. The women were excellent trade brokers.

The Jukun people lived on the upper Benue River. They are descendants of the Kororofa, which is one of the most powerful Sudanic kingdoms.[41] Their communities consisted of many groups that were smaller in size. Most families were polygamous, meaning the men had more than one wife. Most had several. The ruins of this land and its people have yet to be more thoroughly discovered and interpreted due to limited archaeological efforts.

Men's and women's roles were what some may call traditional, but with a twist. For the most part, men dominated the political sphere, occupying leadership roles, however, women were not absent from political platforms. The family was a central focus of the community and women were given an immense amount of responsibility over the rearing of their children, which included training them to be a contributing member of the workforce. This child-rearing extended far beyond domestic responsibilities. In Nigerian culture, age is not just a number. The elderly were highly revered, including women. Elderly women had a voice in politics as well due to the belief that they held a significant level of wisdom.[42] It was also believed that women had the power to summon spirits and sway them to act in their favour. In addition to these beliefs, Nigerians hold the Hausa proverbs as a moral code by which to live, to maintain the utmost happiness and prosperity in life. They possess a poetic structure and serve as a guide to history and a moral compass for virtue. These proverbs, also known as 'Karin Magana' are not necessarily considered a religious text, however, they are highly regarded and considered a primary ingredient to fulfilment and purpose and have been practised since the middle ages.[43] There are several proverbs still studied today, however there are two referenced in this chapter that are at the heart of human decency, happiness, and contentedness. A primary belief is that the events of life do not occur by coincidence but are rather a part of an orchestrated plan that was meant to be. No one is designed to walk this earth alone, not only for the sake of community but also because strength lies in numbers. The proverbs also express the importance of avoiding idleness. Hard work is an essential aspect of life and procrastination is viewed as futile. Among the many Hausa proverbs is a key lesson that echoes throughout humanity. 'A shining face comes with a full belly.'[44] This proverb is not one-dimensional. It means that contentment is the key to happiness. If one's basic needs are met and one is free to bless others with the overflow, emotional contentment should be a natural human response. While the Nigerian queen discussed in this chapter may or may not have embodied many of these proverbs, there is perhaps one that is at the heart of all the others. '*Mutum ba shi shigga mahauta shiji'n tsoro'n jinni*' (a man does not enter a slaughterhouse if he fears blood).[45]

This chapter differs somewhat from the others. While warfare is a primary concept among this collection of queens, this woman truly stands alone. The Zazzau queen in this chapter did not fear blood but rather welcomed the opportunity to shed it whether her enemies' or her own. Even from an early age, she seemed to crave conflict, and her life was filled with several opportunities to fulfil her quest for triumph on and off the battlefield. History is brutal and warfare has been as consistent in settling foreign disputes as the sun rising in the sky each day. Her taste for glory and lust for warfare seem to contrast greatly with any moral code of contentment and peace. However, if war was to be had, then she was going to charge in, giving her most ferocious efforts to win each battle. The kingdom of Zazzau benefited by increasing its lands – a tale as old as time – and protection from potential invaders.

Despite a male-dominated culture, women still held a significant amount of respect. Unlike many other cultures that confined women within domestic fences, there were a few who would not be restrained. Among the women who had the power to wield their influence in word and sword is the warrior queen of Zazzau, Amina.

Amina was born in Zazzau, Nigeria, in 1533 in the Hausa community. Her people called the mountains their home and were led by her father, who is believed to be King Nikatau, and mother, Queen Bakwa Turunku.[46] The ruling family was wealthy and instituted a lucrative trade business, exchanging foreign goods and even slaves for salt, horses, colourful fabric, and kola nuts.[47] The kola nut is a valuable resource and was highly sought after in ancient times due to its believed health benefits. It is high in caffeine, acting as an effective nervous system stimulant, and is alleged to assist in battling fatigue and depression.

From an early age, Amina possessed an interest and skill in the sword. She was caught holding a dagger and studying its craftsmanship when she was only six years old. By her adolescence, Amina had begun her instruction in military tactics and weapons training.

She trained vigorously and learned how to fight in close-quarter hand-to-hand combat, and she was a proficient archer. She was also highly trained in fighting with the cavalry. Amina was the perfect candidate for taking charge of an army, having proven her competency and confidence. When her parents died around the year 1566, her brother Karama became king of the Zazzau people.[48] He appointed her as the leader of his army and she headed several military campaigns that resulted in success for her kingdom, expanding Zazzau's land and increasing its wealth.

Whether it was her beauty or the power she wielded, the men of the region flocked to her. Several suitors brought gifts such as cloth and slaves in exchange for her hand in marriage. Unwilling to forfeit her autonomy, she refused them all, believing that she would be seen as inferior by her people and any potential enemies; she believed that the institution of marriage would quickly diminish any power she had achieved, and her influence would consequently dim. When her brother died, Amina took the throne. This was not a seamless ascent as there had never been a female ruler to lead as the head of the nation autonomously. The political leaders and those within the royal sphere held many lengthy discussions about who could or should become king of Zazzau. However, considering Amina's longstanding reputation of political savviness and undeniable skill and courage on the field of battle, it was clear that she was more than capable and qualified to sit on the throne. She now had authority over the vast army of 20,000 soldiers marching on foot, 1,000 cavalry, and the entire kingdom. She was the first of her people to rule independently. Amina was the woman who was 'as capable as a man'; a phrase that expresses the confidence her people possessed for their new female authority.[49] She is also called 'the pink-heeled warrior' which describes the strength and courageous spirit of women.[50] Just like her sword in battle, her courage and tenacity were unsheathed.

Armies that attempted to conquer Zazzau must have approached the battles against her army with a great deal of apprehension, for she was no ordinary woman. Like so many influential women of the ancient past, war victories and the personalities that led them through their campaigns often become subjects of embellished legends that precede them long before arrows are drawn, and swords glint in the sun light. For Amina, her reputation as a great warlord reached the battlefield before she did. As legend tells it, even her horse, named 'Demon' was said to be feared due to stories that steam came out of its nostrils and evaporated into the air.[51] Amina led her people to victory, reclaiming lands that had been previously conquered by foreign enemies.

According to legend, Amina captured one man from each region she conquered to spend one night with her. The man was her personal sex slave, but upon the rise of the morning, Amina would have the man dragged from her quarters and beheaded.[52] It is unknown if the man chosen for sexual satisfaction with the queen knew that his end would be met so soon after he beheld the queen of Zazzau. She did not do the beheading herself but appointed one of her soldiers to do the work for her. Despite her many one-night stands with countless men, she never gave birth to any children. It is unknown if she could not bear children or if she sabotaged any pregnancies herself. Either way, Amina had no desire to birth and raise children.

During her reign as queen, she led a thirty-four-year military campaign, conquering the surrounding regions. She expanded her kingdom's territory and increased wealth. To show her dominance in each military victory, Amina ordered massive walls to be built around each region. These are called 'Ganuwar Amina' meaning 'Amina's Walls'.[53] The immense walls she had built were comparable to how she viewed her victories: solid, immovable, and inevitable. But even the greatest of warriors must meet their end. The death of Amina is inconclusive. Some scholars assert that she died in battle in 1610. This is not an outlandish theory as there have been several leaders to wet the sands with their own blood until their life was vanquished. Some believe that Amina was killed on the battlefield after being shot with a poisoned arrow. Others are not so certain that she met her end on the battlefield. Some believe that the queen of Zazzau simply disappeared as if she walked off and vanished beneath the blanket of dusk. After her death (or disappearance), women saw their autonomy and authority dwindle and revert to the male-dominated cultural norms that existed before her rule. Unfortunately, the efforts she put forth to pave the way for future female successors to rule independently were unsuccessful. Since we are robbed of a definitive conclusion about this queen, we must instead feast on the information available regarding her military exploits. We must understand the 'why' of her war.

Ancient civilizations like the one in Zazzau did not exist in isolation. It was surrounded by several other regions that were in hot pursuit of expansion, wealth, and power. Sometimes, all a kingdom wanted was the continuation of protection from potential invaders who would plunder treasures, resources, people, and culture, and ultimately leave the kingdom in ruins. No empire strives to be a charred smudge on the pages of history. During the reign of Amina, Zazzau had a long-standing track record of being one of the wealthiest kingdoms, full of hard-working people and resources that could fetch a fine price at trade dealings. Her brother is not known as a great leader, he was believed to be weak since it was his sister, Amina, who served him as his royal advisor and military leader. The kingdom was thriving because of Amina. However, she was not content to remain simply in a supportive role. Her inner strength and uncompromising will could not be settled into any form of submissiveness. She grew up with a front-row seat to the political arena, surrounded by military influences. As a woman, she still received training in all responsibilities that are traditionally domestic, such as weaving, cooking, cleaning, and the proper rearing of children. It was most likely presumed that she would assume a maternal role and fill the palace with children, however, Amina would not so much as glance at any other path than the one that led to the battlefield and ultimately to glory for her and her kingdom. From a very early age, Amina was present for countless discussions, plans, preparations, and arguments revolving around the expansion of Zazzau's territory. During the reign of her brother, she maintained royal court status. She also had ideas for her country that most probably would not have been understood unless she claimed victory on the battlefield and showed her dominance to all those who rested their eyes upon her.

Upon the death of her brother, she did not waste any time putting her nose to the grindstone. She grabbed her responsibilities by the reigns and snapped her submissives into action. Amina assembled thousands of Zazzau's trained military men, clothed in thick chainmail, and armed with swords, axes, spears, bows, and arrows, and led them forward in several successful military campaigns against Kwararafa and Nupe.[54] She commanded some of the best archers who could loose their arrows with perfect timing and distance. What is even more fascinating is the respect and confidence the Zazzau military had for Amina. She marched her army to locations that would give her the greatest advantage during active engagement with the enemy such as very narrow valleys and steep hillsides. Her cavalry would mow down the enemy with Amina in the front riling up her soldiers with a fierce battle cry and her raised sword shining brilliantly in the sun before it was dimmed with the scarlet blood of her enemies. Amina was victorious on the battlefield, and now finally she could display the vision she kept in her mind for the world to see. She expanded Zazzau's territory and wealth. She successfully established trade routes throughout North Africa, inaugurated statehood in Zazzau, and built massive walls that stretched for up to ten miles.[55] She employed thousands of workers to perform public work such as building roads and public buildings. Amina was not interested singularly in land expansion and wealth. She had a deep desire for her people to develop a style that was culturally unique and relevant, and she gave her people the freedom to do just that. Amina supported her people to create music, literature, and art that was culturally significant to the

Zazzau people, believing it would strengthen their identity. Amina was a lover of rich literature, poetry, and storytelling. She encouraged her people to tell stories and legends, believing in the value of words and the lasting impact their tales would have. When all the monuments were reduced to dust, their stories would remain.

One of the greatest legacies a nation, family, or person can have, are the legends that are faithfully passed down to the generations. She wanted those who succeeded her to know of the victories of her and the Zazzau people and show the world that a kingdom can thrive under the supremacy of a woman. The 'whys' of her wars were not shrouded by complicated tales but were rather point-blank. Despite the legends that have endured over the last many centuries, she is perhaps one of the most transparent of ancient African queens regarding her motives for the conquests she led. She remains one of Nigeria's most recognized leaders. Her sister, Zaria (whom the region is now named after) led as Zazzau's queen after the death of Amina for a short time. The kingdom then reverted to the patriarchal ruling system.

After the reign of Amina, Zazzau went through a series of changes. After the successful conquests that led to victory in Kano, Katsina, Jukun, and Nupe, Zazzau eventually fell under the control of Kwararafa (a Jukun kingdom).[56] Zazzau became a tribute state of the Bornu Kingdom. The region's good fortune declined; however, it has remained one of Nigeria's traditional emirate regions.[57]

Zaria has maintained its good standing as a profitable nation of trade. Its main exports include cocoa beans and tobacco. Nigeria is one of the primary merchants of petroleum gas, natural gases, and cotton, which is perhaps one of its most valuable items.[58] Nigeria's main trading partners include India, Spain, France, and the Netherlands.[59] Its main imports are mineral fuels, oil, machinery, electric equipment, and cars.[60] However, Nigeria imports far more goods than it exports. Nigeria has gone through growing pains just like every other country that has floated upon the seas of this earth. Its history is a colourful and sorted tale that has contributed not only to African history but to world history as well. Queen Amina and her ferocious reign on the battlefield and upon her Zarian throne contributed to the rich past of Nigeria. She is a revered part of history and has become a figure of pride for women of African descent, believing that she helped pave the way for women to pursue roles that require more leadership abilities, resilience to opposition, and tenacity of spirit. Qualities such as this, when displayed in productive ways, have the capability to spread like wildfire, not in a destructive manner but one that is inspiring to those who have unbridled strengths and are not afraid to showcase them to the world. That is perhaps the most prominent feature in Amina's legacy.

Queen Amina of Zazzau is the last of the most obscure queens discussed in this book. Many of the monuments that could give historians and archaeologists better insight and understanding into the life and reign of Amina remain obscure due to being lost with time. Certain locations throughout Africa are either forbidden to dig (and some are severely limited even with permission to investigate) or the locations are not entirely known. So much of ancient history is yet to be excavated, but once these monuments and artifacts are brought back up to where the surface meets the sun, we will have an abundance of information to learn from. The wealth of knowledge is immeasurable.

Let's board our boat and sail where our compass points us to next; to a land further south that sits along the coast of the great Atlantic Ocean. The great mountains of Nigeria slowly fade away in the distance until all we see and hear is the churning sea. If we were to board a boat to sail through the South Atlantic seas, we would experience a phenomenon known as the 'Coriolis Effect' which is when the water in the Southern Atlantic flows counterclockwise, contrasting to the North Atlantic which flows clockwise. This is yet another example of the earth's infinite splendour. Finally, we reach the foamy surface of another African nation and our next remarkable female.

Chapter 8

Njinga: 'The Infernal Queen'

[N-JING-GAH]

Welcome to Angola, a place where the palm trees sway with the breath of tropical breezes. Angola is located on the southwest coast of Africa, hugging the southern Atlantic Ocean. This country is a gem, materialistically and historically speaking. Angola is known for its precious gems, metals, and even petroleum. Materials such as copper, gold, uranium, and manganese are mined in abundant quantities.[1] The northeast rivers sparkle with diamonds like the glinting of the beaming sun in the afternoon. Alluvial diamonds are found in river gravel, clay, and sand.[2]

Precious gems and materials are not the only dazzling thing to be seen in Angola. Like other African countries, many wild animals roam in savannahs, forests, and rivers. Hyenas, leopards, lions, hippopotamuses, giraffes, zebras, buffalo, monkeys, antelopes, wildebeests, and crocodiles bask in their natural habitats.[3] Many exotic birds soar high in the sky, their colourful feathers casting a rainbow of shadows along the ground when the sun shines onto their outstretched wings. During the time of Njinga, the land was mostly made up of dense rainforests, however, due to agricultural efforts, the terrain has shifted in the landscape's makeup.[4] The land is now predominantly a savannah.

As abundant as its wildlife, so are its people diverse. The culture is vibrant with expressive art forms that saturate their music, dance, and expression. Jewellery is made from carved wood, seashells, and clay, even the human body is decorated into an artistic masterpiece.[5] Music is a massive part of the culture as well. Dances are choreographed to pair with musical instruments such as the *ngoma* (bongo drum), *mpwita* (another drum), *mpungu* (trumpet), and *hungu* (a musical bow).[6]

Many Angolans in ancient times were farmers. Corn, cotton, millet, sorghum, and sisal (a fibre extracted from the sisal leaf) are the primary crops harvested from the cultivated soil.[7] Farmers also raised livestock such as pigs, chickens, and goats. Fishing was and still is a primary method of putting food on the table. The rivers are well-stocked with catfish, sardines, tuna, and mackerel.[8] The ocean provides the ingredients for a great meal, such as crabs and lobsters. Unlike the African countries discussed in previous chapters, the dominant religion of Angola is Catholicism.[9] This is a glaring contrast to the belief system of the earlier queens and has much to do with foreign influence. Portuguese conquistadors, merchants, and settlers arrived in Angola around 1575 and established the first European colony in Luanda, the capital of Angola.[10] The dynamic of Angolan culture was permanently altered. Many goods were transported to Angola including silks, knives, cotton, mirrors, and jewellery beads.[11] These goods were exchanged for flesh, in one of the most abominable institutions invented by humanity, the slave trade. People of the Kongo kingdom assisted the Portuguese by capturing their people and selling them to be transported to foreign cane fields as sugar had become a commodity in high demand, particularly in Europe.[12] Eventually, the Portuguese began employing efforts of their own to capture vulnerable and unsuspecting Angolans. Not only was labour needed in the sugar fields, but the Portuguese had an unquenchable lust for gold. Countless slaves were sold for thousands of glinting pieces of gold. Disagreements between the Kongo kingdom and Portuguese involvement in the capture and selling of slaves sprouted quickly and the Portuguese had to devise an alternative plan to continue their involvement in the slave trade, which was proving to be quite profitable.[13] The Portuguese turned their sights to the kingdom of Ndongo as a new partner in the slave trade. Slave traders were not the only ones to set their sights on the nation of Angola.

Along with the arrival of Portuguese conquistadors (conquerors) were the Jesuits, a male missionary group that dedicated themselves to charity and converting as many Africans to Catholicism as possible.[14] The missionaries spent many months trying to get the Angolan people to learn the Portuguese language, which assisted in their evangelical efforts. The more the African people adapted to the foreign language of the Portuguese, the conversion to Catholicism would increase.[15] Unlike Jesuit missionaries, the conquistadors were not as patient with conversion efforts. Invaders wearing masks of righteousness rode through the Mbundu villages demanding the enlightenment of Angolans (meaning to adhere to their religious beliefs) either by force or apprehensive cooperation.[16] They wielded several menacing weapons such as crossbows, lances, swords, and armed cavalry. Perhaps one of the most terrifying weapons unleashed on the Angolan people was specific breeds of dogs. The Irish Wolfhound, Deerhound, and Mastiff (all of them are large dog breeds) were bred and trained to hunt and capture human beings, specifically Africans.[17] Sometimes, these dogs were employed to deliver a slow and excruciating method of execution.[18] The conquistadors raided villages and captured livestock and people. Those who did not submit to this foreign ruler were murdered and had their noses cut off. The noses were collected as a method to score the death count.[19] The violence was justified as a religious purification from their pagan ways. Those that were successfully captured were taken to the Brazilian cane fields. The slave trade grew to horrifying heights of popularity with the discovery of America. A treacherous triangle was drawn on the map of world history and some became acquainted with this passage that seemed to have no more of an end than that of a circle.[20] The Ngola people found themselves in a nightmare from which there was no waking. Death was the most merciful outcome in comparison to the shackled journey so many found themselves on.

The Atlantic Slave Trade is the largest forced migration effort in history. From the sixteenth to nineteenth centuries, slave ships crammed with close to 12,000,000 captured human beings crossed the Atlantic Ocean by way of what is known as the 'Middle Passage'.[21] An additional 2,000,000 slaves died before they made it to their destined ports. The institution of slavery existed in Africa long before the Atlantic Slave Trade, however, the dynamic was not as extreme. Slaves were of course labourers, and some were convicted criminals. The flesh for gold and goods became far more lucrative and many wanted a share in the profit. Slavers were made up of both men and women.[22] Those who dared walk alone or leave their children unattended became prime targets to be captured.

People captured for transport across the Atlantic Ocean were separated by gender and age. Men were shackled together in pairs and crammed into small compartments on a lower deck of the ship.[23] These compartments were stacked on top of each other, leaving no room for the slightest movement or shifting. The women were not shackled but were confined on another deck of the ship.[24] Children were kept in a compartment away from the adult African slaves and could roam a bit more freely.[25] The women were raped on a regular basis by the ship's crew, and many of them were impregnated by their captors.[26] This was a result of constant forced sexual intercourse to feed their inhumane lust for dominance and power. The other outcome was that any baby born to their African mother would be considered property of the traders.

The conditions on the ships were deplorable. The heat of hundreds of bodies shackled together mixed with little to no ventilation made

Above: Jar sealing impressed with Queen Neithhotep's name. Early Dynastic Period. 3100 BC. (The Metropolitan Museum. New York)

Right: Neith Statuett. (The Metropolitan Museum. New York)

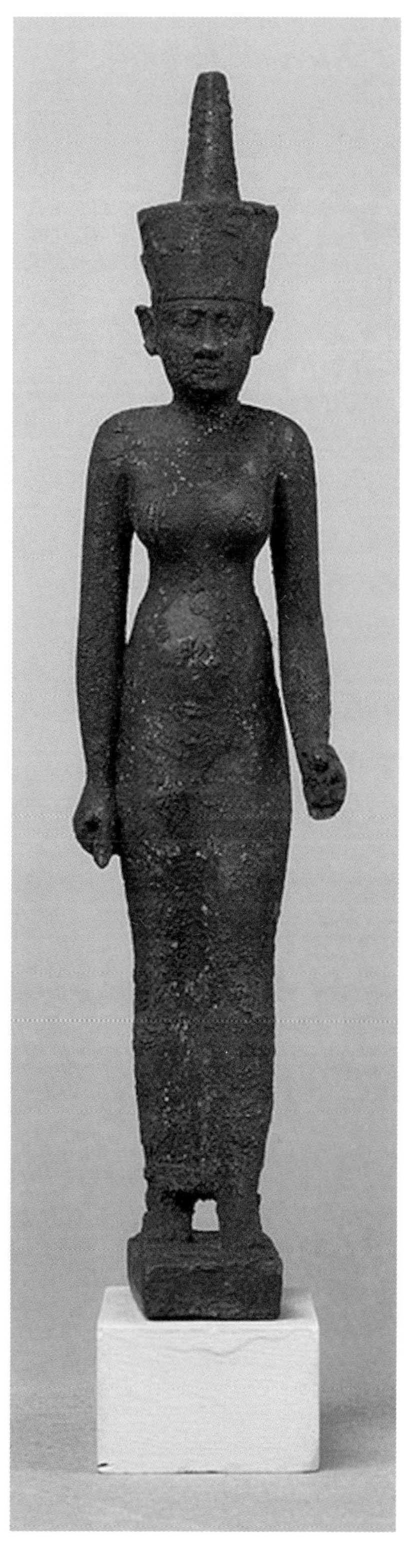

Above left: Narmer Palette, 31st century BC. (Anonymous)

Above right: Aegis of Isis, 924–600 BC. (The Metropolitan Museum. New York)

Left: Seated Statue of Hatshepsut, 1479–1458 BC. Eighteenth Dynasty. (The Metropolitan Museum. New York)

Right: Nefertiti's bust.
(Giovanni from Firenze, Italy. 17 April 2008)

Below: Akhenaten, Nefertiti and Their Children.
(Gerbil. 1 October 2006)

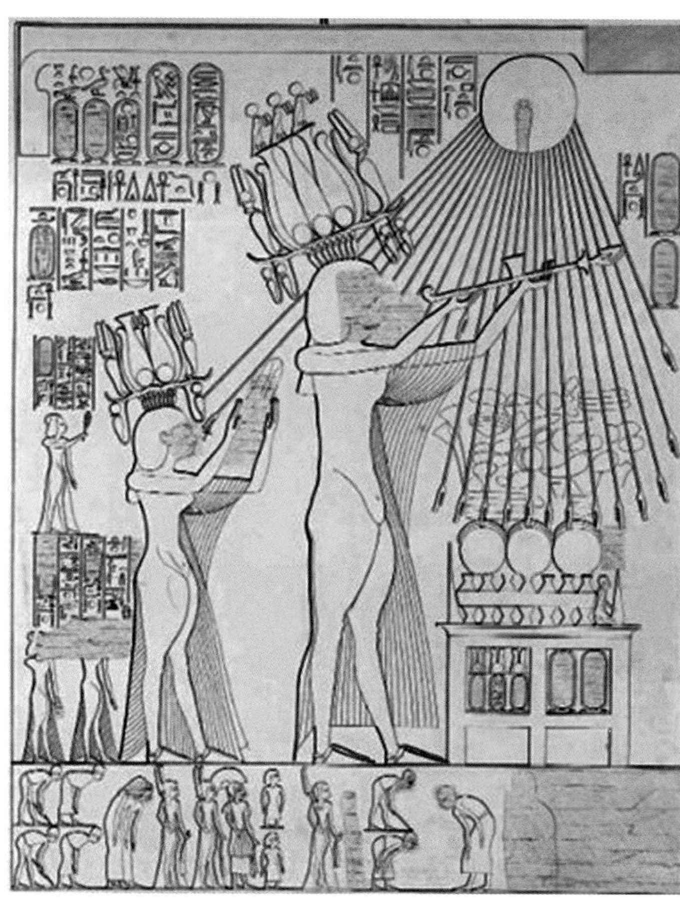

Left: Panehsy Tomb-Akhenaten-Nefertiti-Atef. (Lepsius. 1848)

Below: Ruins of Mahram Bilqis. (Bernard Gagnon. 18 August 1986)

Bronze Head of Caesar Augustus. (Carole Raddato. 12 July 2014)

Dahia al-Kahina. (Numide05. 25 April 2010)

Left: Queen Njinga by Achille Deveria (1800–1857).

Below: Njinga Sitting on Slave. (Author: Njinga, Reine d'Angola. A Relação de Antonio Cavazzi de Montecuccolo. 5 June 2018)

Ranavalona I. (Philippe-Auguste Ramanankirahina (1860–1915) 1905)

Les Martyrs d'Ampamarinana. (G. Mondain. 8 October 2014)

for hellish surroundings.[27] There were no areas to dispose of human waste, so slaves were forced to defecate where they lay. They vomited from the stench, only exacerbating their already horrible situation. The only meal provided was rice and beans. Slaves that refused to eat had their mouths pried open with a device called the '*speculum oris*'. This contraption was effective at making sure a slave consumed their food. Two scissor-like rods were on one end and a thumb screw was fastened on one side that was turned, prising open the mouths and jaws of the slaves, allowing the food to be forced down their throats.[28] Slaves who were deemed disobedient were severely punished by flogging. This punishment was performed in the presence of other slaves to dissuade them from following in disobedience. The flogging was torturous as flesh was ripped open with relentless rage until the hands holding the whips became tired. Many slaves attempted to commit suicide by trying to jump off the ship. Death by drowning seemed like a much more humane option than anything that they were living through or what awaited them when the ship reached its port. To prevent slaves from taking their own lives, suicide nets were set up.[29] Any slave caught trying to escape the ship was severely punished. Those that succeeded in jumping off the ship were caught in the nets (which prevented drowning) and lifeboats were lowered to bring them back aboard.

Disease spread like wildfire aboard slave ships, claiming millions of lives in horrifying conditions. The overcrowded, filthy quarters became breeding grounds for deadly illnesses, with smallpox, influenza, malaria, measles, scurvy, and dysentery among the most common killers. Smallpox ravaged the body, covering it in painful, pus-filled sores that left survivors permanently scarred. Influenza brought fever, relentless coughing, and crippling fatigue, offering little respite in the suffocating, disease-ridden air below deck. Malaria, carried by mosquitoes, drained the body of its strength, leading to convulsions, jaundice, and bloody urine. Measles, highly contagious in such close quarters, caused agonizing fevers, blinding red rashes, and, in many cases, left its victims permanently blind. Scurvy, brought on by severe malnutrition, caused teeth to rot, gums to bleed, and limbs to swell as the body broke down from within. Yet the most feared of all was dysentery – a brutal, relentless illness that tore through the intestines, leaving its victims doubled over in excruciating pain, their bodies wasting away from bloody diarrhoea and dehydration. With no medical care and little access to clean water, those who fell ill were often left to die, their suffering ignored, their bodies discarded like refuse. Disease was not just an affliction aboard these ships – it was a death sentence, tightening its grip on the enslaved with every passing day.[30]

The conditions of these slave ships were a frightening reality. Diseases that could only have manifested in the darkest of nightmares clawed their way out of hell and sank their fangs into humanity. It is difficult to fathom humans forcing other humans into a life of slavery, let alone the settings we know existed on these slave ships. As stated before, slavery is among the worst institutions to arise from human invention and is a true crime against humanity. There were about 35,000 slave ships that transported 12,000,000 Africans across the Atlantic before the trade had run its course and was eventually deemed illegal, and was eventually banned in America by the Act Prohibiting the Importation of Slaves, in 1808.[31] Angola was very involved in this trade, especially with the arrival of Portuguese conquistadors. This is where the story of our next queen begins. Little did the Mbundu people know that their defender would be a woman who was not expected to live beyond her first few feeble breaths.

In 1569 a Mbundu baby girl named Njinga was born (also known as Nzinga). Her grand entrance into this world was difficult since her tiny neck was bound by the umbilical cord like the winding root of a tree.[32] She was named after the Kimbunu tree root, 'Kujinga' meaning twist or wrap.[33] The village oracles predicted that she would not survive, however, they did not consider the fighting spirit that was already at work within the child. Njinga survived her traumatic birth and continued to strengthen each day. She was the granddaughter of the Mbundu ruler Kasenda and daughter of Mbande a Ngola (reigned 1592–1617) and his favourite concubine, Kengela ka Nkombe.[34] He was the reigning king over the village of the Mbundu people. Their village worshipped nature and gave homage to their ancestors. Ngangas (spiritual leaders) communicated with deceased ancestors, performed healing rituals for the sick and wounded, worshipped to bring rain, and took part in human sacrifice, including children.[35]

Like many other cultures throughout Africa, Mbande a Ngola had a chief wife with whom he had one son (his eldest child) and many concubines. He had four more children with his favourite concubine, Ngola Mbande, Njinga, Kambu, and Funji.[36] Throughout her youth and even adulthood, Njinga and Ngola Mbande had a long-standing sibling rivalry. Her father's rule was marked by tireless conflict and struggle. Conflict with the Portuguese was constant, especially when the Portuguese joined forces with the Imbangala in 1607. The Imbangala were extremely violent, and war-like, and participated often in human sacrifice and cannibalism.[37] They had a reputation for being ruthless and dedicated to violence and ravaging the villages they conquered. Their ruthlessness was not only carried out against outsiders. Their own camps were marked with the bloodshed of each other. Women who were with child had to give birth to their babies outside of the camp. If they were born inside, the babies were slaughtered in front of their weeping mothers. This tribe was dominantly made up of mercenary soldiers who enjoyed the taste of human flesh and blood, however, women were not normally the victims of their cannibalistic customs. One method the Imbangala used to grow their forces was to kidnap young boys from the surrounding villages and recruit them into their army. The Imbangala exacerbated the slave trade's efforts by aiding the Portuguese in capturing many from the Mbande villages throughout Angola. In desperation, King Mbande a Ngola attempted to employ diplomacy with the Portuguese by submitting to becoming baptized and allowing Jesuits access to his lands. As a result of this agreement, many Angolans were converted to Christianity.[38]

From an early age, Njinga showed an intense passion for fighting. She learned to fight, was taught military tactics and agility, and was introduced to the Mbundu arsenal. Her father not only supported her natural affinity for warfare, but fostered her abilities, allowing her to practice wielding swords, daggers, and axes.[39] She received training in combat and cavalry fighting. Her father also allowed her to build her political knowledge by having her sit in during political discussions among the court and his advisers. She was intelligent and soaked up all that she heard like a sponge. Njinga had a strong knack for negotiation. She grew to be persuasive and had the ability to think quickly but strategically. Her observations in the political sphere with her father gave her an arsenal of skills that she would later employ when her people and kingdom needed them the most.

She had two sisters and a brother, and it is unknown if they possessed the same passion for fighting. She was raised in the royal kingdom and was gifted concubines and enjoyed their company as often as she pleased. She was impregnated by one of them and gave birth to a son who would have been a potential heir to the throne.[40] In the Mbundu culture, rights to the throne were based on birth order. Her father was betrayed by a member within his trusted sphere of men, ambushed, and murdered.[41] Njinga's brother saw this as a ripe opportunity to ensure he was the uncontested ruler of the Mbundu people. Based on Mbundu's heirship rules, Mbande a Ngola's oldest son would have taken the throne. However, his mother (who was also the chief wife of Mbande a Ngola) was accused of adultery and imprisoned.[42] This tarnished her son's image and called into question his legitimacy. Ngola Mbande murdered his half-brother, his stepmother, and her siblings as well, severing any opposition to his ascent to the throne.[43] He was declared the new ruler of Ngola, and he threatened the life of anyone who dared protest his right to rule. He surrendered his own son to the Imbangala to receive military training and perhaps turn his enemy into his military ally. He made drastic efforts to ensure that his sisters would never rule the kingdom nor have a viable heir that could challenge his ascent to kingship. He murdered Njinga's infant son and had all three of his sisters sterilized.[44] He had oils and herbs boiled to hellish temperatures and poured onto each sister, burning through their tender flesh, and killing any chance of bearing children.[45]

After her sterilization, Njinga moved away from the kingdom, along with her male and female concubines to Matamba. It was at this point that Njinga decided that she would sleep with whoever she wanted and have her sexual needs fulfilled as many times as she yearned for it.[46] She had no desire to be domesticated or told what she could and could not do. Whatever tenderness she may have had toward the world was burned, and cruelty and thirst for bloodshed grew solid roots in the ashes. The woman that was born of her tragedies was uncompromising, immovable as iron, and at times, vicious and cruel. She had the capability of luring the innocent into the clutches of death, laying words like bear traps and her smile like a snare.

During her exile in Matamba, Njinga nurtured her inner strength that would manifest itself outwardly on the battlefield and in the political courts of her rivals. During this time, she refused to adhere herself to a chief husband, maintaining her autonomy. Thanks to her upbringing and exposure to the political meetings her father brought her to during her youth, she was able to demonstrate her capability in negotiations and conversations regarding peace and war. She demonstrated her abilities along with her sense of pride in herself and her country during a visit to Luanda to meet the Portuguese governor. She arrived dressed in traditional Ndongo attire of quality cloth of vibrant colours and patterns. Feathers were weaved in her hair and crown. Her wrists and ankles were wrapped in bracelets and anklets, all adorned with priceless gems. She refused to dress in traditional Portuguese attire.[47] Her meeting with the governor became known the world over. To show their dominance and assign Njinga to the status they believed she held, the Portuguese had a carpet laid on the floor instead of a chair. Realizing the lowered status they had given her she made the quick decision to correct their assumption of her political status. With a snap of her fingers, one of her female slaves kneeled on the floor and assumed the position of a chair. Njinga sat on her slave for hours while political discussions were being had.[48]

She was the leading negotiator and representative for the king, her brother. She negotiated the desire for a military alliance, peace, and the return of any runaway slaves.[49] The Portuguese governor countered with the demand for an annual tribute of Mbundu slaves. She assertively rejected this demand, believing that a tribute such as that was only fitting for a conquered king, and her brother and their kingdom were still free. This bold assertion had far more to do with her preserving the kingdom and her intention of ruling it, than securing her brother's royal legacy. To sweeten the pot, she agreed to be baptized in the Catholic faith and assumed a new Christian name, Ana de Sousa, of which the Portuguese governor was pleased.[50] Her brother, Mbande, was satisfied and named his sister Njinga as royal regent of his kingdom. It was at this point that Njinga began to seriously undermine her brother's authority. She whispered to those in the political and military sphere that Mbande was an incompetent ruler who would certainly cause the kingdom to plummet. She accused him of not being a real man or leader to his face, suggesting that it would be more useful for him to surrender his seat on the throne and live as a recluse on a farm.[51] Sensing his support waning from his subjects and advisors, and now his own sister and regent, Mbande plunged into a deep depression. In 1624 he was found dead by poisoning. It is unknown if his poisoning was self-inflicted or if he was secretly murdered.[52] Most scholars believe the king carried out his own demise.

The king was dead, eliminating a major obstacle to Njinga and the empire she intended to create. She was not only regent over Mbande's kingdom, but she was also regent over his young son.[53] Her next task was the elimination of the boy. Mbande's son was with the Imbangala tribe, learning from the tribe's chief, Kasa (also known as Kasanje). To maintain her role as regent over the boy, she needed to get married. Considering Njinga and Kasa had somewhat of a romantic history, she declared her love for him, suggesting a marital union. She gave him many gifts that would have been enticing to the leader of a tribe that took such pleasure in plundering any village they set foot into. Despite the Imbangala's former cooperation with the Portuguese, the Death tribe was willing to offer their services to the highest bidder. Kasa obliged her suggestion of marriage.[54]

The day of their planned nuptials arrived, and Njinga had excited her nephew by telling him he was going to be a part of the ceremony. However, before the ceremony began, she grabbed the boy who was only about seven years old, and swiftly snuffed the life out of him. Her guests were armed, and a panic ensued upon seeing the horror of a boy murdered in front of their eyes. A bloody fight followed, wedding guests were running away in every direction, unsure if they or their loved ones were intended targets.[55] During the chaos, Njinga dragged her nephew and threw him into the Kwanza River, laughing in celebration. She declared that the murder of her infant son at the hands of her brother was finally avenged. Any contest to her ascent to the throne was removed. The wedding was off, and she did not need a chief husband to achieve what she sought, at least at that time.

Njinga did not waste a moment. She formed allies with eastern sobas (three kingdoms in present-day Sudan). The kingdoms were located in Nubia, Makuria, and Alodia. In 1628 she reoccupied the Kindonga Islands. She successfully blocked roads used for government slave markets.[56] Njinga's power was growing, and her enemies knew it. Sensing the rising threat, Captain Paio de Arau'jo de Azevedo decided that war with Njinga and her army was inevitable and necessary. His army marched out of Luanda and pursued her army's position in the Kindonga Islands. Not yet ready for war, Njinga abandoned her base and retreated to Matamba. However, Azevedo's army eventually caught up with her and cornered her army at the base of a cliff.[57] Faithful to the fearless leader, her soldiers created a wall around her, giving her enough time to find a vine and climb down the steep cliffs of the mountain until her feet reached the safety of the ground below. The fight on the cliff commenced, ultimately favouring the Portuguese army. Azevedo captured Njinga's sisters, Kambu and Funji. He stripped them of their clothing and brought them back to Luanda completely exposed and publicly humiliated.[58] After the attack, Njinga did not have much of an army or enough people to rebuild her kingdom. This is when she sought an alliance with the Imbangalas.

Chief Kasa agreed to protect Njinga and join her in battle under one condition, she had to marry him. She did not want the union, but she needed protection from her enemies, and she needed a strong army for the future attacks that were sure to come. In silent desperation, Njinga submitted to Kasa's terms. She followed the example of Tempo a Ndumbo who was a former Imbagalan queen. Tempo established tenets and sacraments for female leaders in the Imbangala to participate in. Among these creeds were infanticide, ritual human sacrifice, and cannibalism.[59] For her initiation, Njinga participated in the *cuia* (drinking of human blood).[60]

Before battle, warriors would anoint themselves in 'holy oil' which is the greasy oils derived from the human body after it has been crushed and pounded between a mortar and pestle. The oils are spread all over the body of the warrior.[61] As a part of her final initiation into the Imbangala army, Njinga participated in a ritual known as *maji ma samba* which is where the woman sacrifices the life of her own baby.[62] Since she did not have a baby of her own to sacrifice, Njinga took the baby of one of her slaves. She sacrificed the infant, crushing its body in the pestle until it produced the desired oily substance. She smeared the innocent blood all over her face and body without reservation or remorse. She was officially baptized into the Imbangala tribe.

Now that she had a formal alliance forged in blood, the time for war planning was underway. In 1631 Njinga and her army of bloodthirsty soldiers and mercenaries invaded Matamba. The invasion was successful. She captured many Mbundu soldiers, some of whom were made into slaves, while others became meals for the ferocious army. Whether it was out of admiration or fear of Njinga (I'm inclined to the latter), many Mbundu soldiers abandoned their army and took up arms with her. It was better to be enlisted in her army than be captured and most likely eaten. She successfully blended the Mbundu culture with the Imbangala, which was no small feat.[63] Njinga had recruited soldiers who had once stood as her enemies. Now it was time to hit the Portuguese where it would hurt most, their economy. She ordered Portuguese trade routes to be blocked. She showed off her alliance with the Imbangala tribe, whom the Portuguese rulers outwardly feared due to the tribe's reputation for brutality and plundering. By 1633 she successfully choked her enemy's economy by cutting off the roads used for slave markets, the Portuguese colony's primary source of financial stability and social control. In 1641 a new threat could be seen in the distance as ships bearing a flag with a foreign design waved in the wind and the seas pushed the vessels onto the shores of Angola. The Dutch had arrived.

It is wise to never underestimate those you do not know. Njinga understood this concept well and played her cards carefully until she could determine if these newcomers would become friends or foes. For the time being, Njinga played along, supplying the Dutch with slaves until she secured an alliance with them, which included the addition of over 2,000 Dutch and Brazilian soldiers. Njinga had an impressive force that she fully intended to use to unleash hell on the Portuguese. In yet another successful raid, Njinga's army pursued the Portuguese, capturing many and intending them for slavery. However, before she could secure them for trade, the Imbangalas beheaded them. With each victory, Njinga increased her wealth. She built impressive *kilombos* (communities or camps) that could house the many she took as captives as well as the 80,000 soldiers she led under her command. Her army was well-supplied with ammunition and food, which was an advantage that the Portuguese army lacked in comparison.

Njinga was not tired of war by any means, but she wanted to ensure that the timing was going to work in her favour. Consulting her oracles, she requested a sign to decide the right time to strike the Portuguese army once again. The oracles pitted a white rooster against a black one. The two birds embraced their own battle with the white rooster resulting in the victory. Njinga took this as an undisputable sign that it was time for another raid. Her raid was successful initially; however, the Portuguese later attacked her guard and a portion of her army, slaughtering most of them. The Portuguese left a couple alive to bring her the message that many of hers lay dead on the ground. Enraged by the news, Njinga beheaded the messengers that had been left alive. Never one to accept any measure of defeat, she once again prepared for battle.

While she prepared, the Portuguese army cut off her supply of ammunition and reinforcements from the Dutch.[64] They intended to attack her army in the Dembos region in Ndongo. She received word of the enemy's movements and attempted to slow their progress by setting a blaze to their path, however, it was not nearly as successful as she had hoped. The Portuguese may have expected some sort of interception of their plans; however, it did not slow them down. They marched through the scorched path and advanced. The Portuguese army attacked Njinga's army and succeeded, causing many of her soldiers to flee the battlefield. She left behind precious gems, weapons, silks, and even her sister, Kambu.[65]

Her palace was raided by the Portuguese army and Kambu was raped. Kambu embodied a proud spirit, much like her sister Njinga. Kambu refused to let the assault tarnish how she presented herself outwardly. Whatever pain, anger, or shame she may have felt internally, she never allowed her chin to drop. She stood before the Portuguese general dressed in splendour, for which she gained a measure of respect from her captors. Her sister, Funji was not as fortunate. She was still a captive at Massangano, a Portuguese stronghold. Her captors were unaware that she was acting as a military spy for her sister, Njinga, passing along many letters and notes exposing the Portuguese army's plans and movements. Her reports were discovered hidden beneath a Catholic altar. Upon the discovery of her efforts against the Portuguese, Funji was bound and dragged to the Kwanza River. She was thrust under while the river's currents rushed over her face until she drowned. The murder of Njinga's sister fuelled yet another motive for the continued war with the Portuguese army. She prepared her counterattack for 1647.

To make this attack successful, Njinga needed the military and political cooperation of the Dutch. The two forces agreed to the terms that neither would negotiate with the Portuguese. Believing that a strong agreement was secured with the Dutch, Njinga led her army in an attack on 27 October 1647. The ground shook as 10,000 Dembos, 4,000 Imbangala, and 300 Dutch marched behind her.[66] Her army killed over 3,000 Portuguese soldiers and burned countless villages to the ground. The surviving Portuguese soldiers fled for the Massangano Fort. Even with her enemy in ashes, Njinga did not believe her victory was complete without the rescue of her sister, Kambu.

The Massangano Fort was well-fortified and resourced, so Njinga had to wait and devise plans of how to breach its walls. During this time, the Portuguese army and support had swelled. Behind the back of the great warrior queen, the chief of the West India Company severed the agreement with Njinga by signing a treaty with the Portuguese.[67] Without the support of the Dutch, Njinga feared she could not win her conquests against her enemies, but she was not going to let her adversaries know that. For another eight long years, battle raged. She launched another attack against an enemy Imbangala tribe that had forged an alliance with the Portuguese. Her reputation as the 'Infernal Queen', had preceded her and the enemy tribe's chief, Kalandula was fearful of her.[68] Unwilling to endure a massacre of his people at the hands of this warrior queen, Kalandula sent a messenger to Njinga armed with his pledge of allegiance. However, his soldiers were not as devoted. Attempting to flee her army, over 400 of them were apprehended by her soldiers and sold at the slave market. She had Chief Kalandula beheaded.[69]

Warfare remained a constant theme throughout Njinga's rule, however, she eventually retired her sword and axe from the battlefield and wielded her skills in diplomacy instead. She worked for peace with the Portuguese for many years, however, they refused the primary demand, which was her 'claim to their colony'.[70] To help foreign relations, Njinga released the captured priests (some entirely and others who were allowed to reside in her courts and live relatively free lives). She treated Jesuit missionaries well and even kept an altar to Christ in her *kilombo*. Njinga also gave up the practice of cannibalism.

Njinga's willingness to propose peaceful measures with former enemies did not eliminate her willingness for violence if needed. She still had not rescued Kambu. Despite her natural mindset for battle, Njinga first tried a peaceful tactic to rescue her sister, and it succeeded. She gifted the Portuguese ten slaves in exchange for Kambu, along with the agreement that she would be recognized as the ngola of Matamba and she would accept the Portuguese as rulers of Angola.[71] She also instituted religious tolerance by allowing the Portuguese freedom to practise their religion in her lands without interference. The release of Kambu was a huge first step to peace, and a formal treaty followed. The Lucala River was established as the boundary between Angola and Matamba[72] Njinga also agreed to end practices such as infanticide and cannibalism.[73] This treaty helped end the three decades of war. Njinga spent her remaining years devoted to ensuring Matamba's economic and political stability. She never forgot her glories and defeats on the battlefield, and often regaled those in her personal sphere of her days of leading thousands into violence and bloodshed. She was never ashamed of any of it. Near the end of her life, she decided to adhere closer to Catholic beliefs and lifestyle rather than mysticism. She gave up her concubines, several spouses, and many lovers. She officially referred to herself as a 'Catholic King', not a queen.[74] Her funeral was a blend of Mbundu and Catholic traditions, void of human sacrifice.

Njinga's moral compass probably contrasts with many. She not only stood firm in the face of war and violence toward the innocent, but she relished the experience of it all. In addition to her success on the battlefield, she blended cultures that would have remained adversaries. She promoted women in positions of power. Not only did she prove her ability to rule on the battlefield (and inspire scores of women to join her) she was an example of a woman's capability to rule autonomously, negotiate foreign alliances, stabilize a nation's economy, and collaborate to reach national and foreign peace. Perhaps one of her most vibrant achievements is the religious tolerance and cooperation that still endures in Angola today. The export of slaves was banned in Angola in 1836 and officially abolished in the Portuguese Empire in 1875.[75]

Our compass points to the east as we trek through forests, sands, and across rivers. We are about to embark on a journey of our own and cross a sliver of ocean to the island of Madagascar.

Chapter 9

Ranavalona I: The 'Mad Queen of Madagascar' [RA-NA-VA-LOW-NA]

We have arrived at our final land destination and era of history in this book. Madagascar is the fourth largest island in the world and is separated from the African continent by the Mozambique Channel.[1] This island hosts yet another intriguing culture and history. It is made up of five primary topographical regions; the central highlands, east coast, west coast, southwest, and Tsaratanana Massif.[2] Mount Maromokotro is the highest elevation reaching 2,876 metres.[3] There are many rivers and lakes that contribute to the agricultural health of the island as well. The major primary rivers include Mangoro, Maningory, Mananara, Ivondro, and Mananjary. They drain the flood plains, allowing for significantly higher agricultural success.

The primary climate is tropical; however, the climate varies by region. Winds from the Indian Ocean contribute to the climate differences. The western coast is more arid while the inland is primarily temperate. The eastern coast has the most rainfall of all other regions and bears the brunt of wicked thunderstorms. Madagascar is also subjected to cyclones from the Indian Ocean.

There are many natural resources and other treasures found on this island. Mining is a widely worked trade among the people. Materials such as coal, salt, mica, tar sands, graphite, chromate, and bauxite are pulled from the mines and exported globally.[4] Semi-precious stones such as amethyst, garnet, jasper, gold, tourmaline, beryl, quartzite, and sapphires are among the most common and popular among locals and visitors to the island.[5] Mining these precious stones and resources is one of Madagascar's most lucrative trades, producing much of its annual revenue and keeping the economy stable.

Farming is also a common trade among the people, both livestock and crops. Cattle, pigs, chickens, geese, ducks, and turkeys are raised mostly on the plateau regions.[6] Some of the livestock, primarily cattle, are still used today for ceremonial sacrifice. Farms growing crops such as rice (wet, dry, and irrigated), potatoes, yams, bananas, and corn are grown and used as a staple in the peoples' diet.[7] Sugarcane is also grown in the northwest plantations. Fruits such as oranges, apples, plums, avocados, grapefruits, grapes, pineapples, guavas, passion fruit, and papaya grow in lush abundance.[8] In addition to these staple foods, crops such as tobacco, coffee, cacao, vanilla, cotton, pepper, peanuts, and lima beans are grown and exported.[9] Even marine wildlife serves as an abundant source of food and trade export such as shellfish and crustaceans. The large export of shrimp that is fished off Madagascar's coast is among the most lucrative goods in international trade.[10]

The nation is made up of several ethnic groups, the most common being the Malagasy people (which then breaks up into about twenty additional ethnic groups). The people predominantly follow the Christian faith, including Catholic and Protestant beliefs as the next leading religious groups. There is a small percentage of practising Sunni Muslims and ancestral worship.[11] The high percentage of practicing Christians in Madagascar is credited to

European colonization, like that of Angola. Christianity was not always openly accepted. Fiercely resisting European colonization and influence, Christians were subjected to brutality, starvation, and slaughter during the reign of our final queen.

Details of Ranavalona I's origins are limited, however, the events leading to her rise to power are documented. Ranavalona (birth name Ramavo) was born in 1778 in Madagascar. Some scholars believe that she came from humble origins, being born to a prince's cousin while others assert that she is the daughter of Prince Andriantsalamanjaka.[12] Regardless of her origins, when she was very young, her father, prince or peasant, thwarted an assassination attempt on the ruler of Madagascar, King Andrianampoinimerina, by the king's uncle, Andrianjafy. King Andrianampoinimerina was so grateful that his life was saved, that he promised Andriantsalamanjaka that his daughter, Princess Ramavo would be given to his son and heir, Radama, in matrimony.[13] Despite Ramavo being Radama's first wife, she was far from his favourite. She had to compete for his affection and favour along with his other eleven wives. If Ramavo was going to secure her place in the Madagascar royalty, she needed to devise a strategy since she had not secured a royal heir with King Radama.

King Radama's reign was a prosperous time for Madagascar. He signed a commercial treaty with the British Empire in 1820 which secured military equipment and training for his army.[14] In addition to expanding the Merina kingdom, he collaborated with the London Missionary Society. This society opened schools, improved literacy among the population, and converted many Malagasy people to Christianity. Madagascar's involvement in the slave trade was brought to an end. Radama did not always maintain the popular vote among his people due to his progressive ideas that contrasted with traditional values that were still upheld and revered among many of his people. An example of this is the order he gave his soldiers to keep their hair short. This may seem like a simple and reasonable demand, however, for the Malagasy people, it was an insult to tradition and a robbery of sacred rituals. Traditional women were accustomed to braiding the long hair of their men before war and this new demand eliminated their involvement in such a sacred practice.[15] Radama did not take to the criticism well. When the traditionalist women revolted against his nontraditional decrees, he had them brutally killed and their remains fed to wild dogs.[16] It's no surprise that King Radama's death is somewhat suspicious. One theory is that Ramova poisoned her husband, while another suggests that the king was enduring debilitating cirrhosis and syphilis. It is believed that the king, not being able to withstand his suffering any longer, slit his own throat in 1828 at age thirty-six.[17] Another possibility is that he drank himself to death.

The king was dead but that did not mean that Ramova had an easy path to ascension. King Radama's nephew, Prince Rakatobe was next in line for the throne. However, if Ramova had a child, he or she would be the rightful heir to become the royal sovereign. Rakatobe did not want his right to rule to slip through his fingers, so it's possible that murder awaited Ramova. However, Ramova employed strategy to where it would benefit her most. She rallied support through her public declaration to re-establish ancestral customs. Many of her supporters were members of the aristocracy. She seized control of the palace and declared herself the uncontested Queen of Madagascar on 1 August 1828. She made sure all loose ends were tied. Prince Rakatobe had a spear plunged into his throat and his mother was starved to death.[18] Any contest to the throne was eliminated. Queen Ranavolona I began what would later be known as a reign of terror, as she would be known as Ranavalona, the 'Mad Queen of Madagascar.'

During her coronation, Queen Ranavalona was a striking vision of royal splendour, dressed in a magnificent French-made gown as she was paraded through the villages. Parisian fashion dominated the elite wardrobes of Europe, Africa, and the Americas, and Ranavalona's attire reflected this influence. Her gown featured a fitted bodice with a modest neckline and a voluminous dome-shaped skirt that swept the floor, creating the illusion of gliding as she moved. The sleeves, in keeping with contemporary trends, were wide and structured, with delicate embellishments at the cuffs. The soft salmon-pink hue of her dress may have appeared to shift in different lighting, a popular effect achieved through 'shot silk' weaving techniques. A long, elegant cape cascaded from her shoulders, further enhancing her regal presence. Her hair was styled in tight ringlets that framed her face, and atop her head sat a crown that matched the soft pink of her gown, completing the image of royal authority.

Despite this display of European-inspired grandeur, Ranavalona later cast aside her ceremonial finery in favour of a more personal and symbolic act of sovereignty. In a dramatic rejection of foreign traditions and an assertion of her own power, she performed a private initiation, having the blood of a freshly slaughtered bull smeared across her body. This ritual, deeply rooted in Malagasy custom, underscored her defiance of European influence and reinforced her position as an independent and formidable ruler.[19]

The queen's first order of business was to do away with European customs and religious practices that had been adopted under the previous reign. She severed ties with the British and re-established the traditional religious practices and customs, attempting to do away with Christian manners of worship. In November 1831, Ranavalona banned sacraments and Christian baptism. Any Malagasy people who had not been baptized into the Christian faith were forbidden to do so. Communion was considered a crime and any boys attending the London Missionary Society schools were unenrolled in the education system and placed in the army.[20]

She interrupted the importation of supplies, as well as blocking Madagascar's main exports, cattle and rice. This did not sit well with many in her lands, leading to the revolt of the Sakalava people.

On 26 February 1835, the queen announced that Christians, particularly missionaries could stay in her lands if they did not participate in their worship practices such as baptism and if they had any useful knowledge or skill that could be applied to the benefit of her kingdom and people. Her tolerance was short-lived, and soon afterward she issued another decree. Queen Ranavalona began to spiral into hatred against the Christian inhabitants in her lands. On 1 March 1835, she demanded every Christian to denounce their faith. Any who opposed this decree would be punished to the highest degree and it wasn't long before she acted on her harsh threats. A Christian preacher named Rainitsandavana refused to turn away from his faith and several of his followers refused as well. Not only did he openly disobey her command, but he also had the audacity to compare her status (in the sense of humanity) to being equal to a slave. In a rage at his disobedience and insults about her status, she ordered her soldiers to lower the preacher and all his followers' heads into a pit; boiling water was poured over them until they died.[21] Their death was excruciating and slow. Her soldiers and trusted advisors fed her the narrative that Christians were disobedient and hostile to the ancient Malagasy religion and expected many more Christians to refuse her attempts to rid Madagascar of their biblical message. The queen was not done with her murderous conquests yet and vowed that death awaited all Christians.

Ranavalona was influenced heavily by her prime minister and lover (as he was rumoured to be) Andriamihaja. He is also rumoured to be the father of the queen's son, Rokoto. The prime minister was a big supporter of King Radama's policies and cooperation with British influence in the Malagasy kingdom. Despite his close relations with the queen and powerful influence, he had enemies who wielded just as powerful influence over the queen. Perhaps his biggest adversaries and competition for the queen's confidence were three brothers of the Andafiavaratra family. It is rumoured that two of the brothers were lovers of the queen as well.[22] Whether it was jealousy in sharing the queen's affection or unresolved malice in the political realm, Prime Minister Andriamihaja was accused of betraying the queen with another woman. This was a serious accusation, and the queen did not tarry on putting her lover on trial, the Tangena Trial to be exact. However, Andriamihaja knew that this would be met with almost certain death . He opted to have his throat pierced by a spear instead and he was granted his request.[23]

The Tangena Trial was a favoured method of torture used by the queen. Those on trial were forced to eat the Tangena nut which contains a poison that induces profuse vomiting. Once the nut was ingested, the presumed guilty had to eat three pieces of raw chicken skin. If all three pieces were vomited, one was considered innocent. If one died from the poison, guilt was assumed, and that just punishment had been carried out. However, if one survived and did not vomit the chicken skins, they were also assumed guilty of the charges, and executed.[24] The Tangena Trial is credited to have taken 100,000 Malagasy lives. Another form of torture and punishment the queen subjected her people to was 'progressive amputation'.[25] This means that a small part of the body was cut off first, followed by larger chunks until most or all of it was removed. This procedure was done without the benefit of anesthetics. Not all her punishments resulted in certain death. Those that were poor and could not afford to pay their taxes were subjected to Fanampoana, which forced people into unpaid labour such as becoming soldiers or waste collectors.[26]

Deciding she had demonstrated enough tolerance with the Christians in her kingdom, she demonstrated her disdain for all the Malagasy people to see. In 1836, she ordered her soldiers to capture fourteen Malagasy Christian leaders who had openly refused to give up their religion or stop their worship practices. Unfortunately, among those captured for this display was a woman named Ranivo, whom Queen Ranavalona had once considered her kinswoman.[27] Ranivo was previously active in the ancient religious worship traditions but had since embraced Christianity and was captured along with the Christian missionaries. They were bound by ropes and dangled high above rocky ravines long enough for them to see the sharp rocks that awaited below. Ranavalona was deeply distressed when her friend Ranivo was among those to be executed so she gave orders for her to witness the execution rather than endure it, hoping that she would become fearful of her impending death and turn from her newfound faith.[28] The soldiers seized her from the group and brought her to the edge of the steep cliff where she received only a stinging slap across the face. She faced her Christian brothers, watching while their ropes were cut, plummeting them to the rocks below where their flesh was ripped open, and bones crushed. As for Ranivo, the queen sent her away to the far countryside, hiding her away from punishment from any of her cruel decrees. Ranivo married a Christian man, raised children, and lived many years in her hidden solitude.[29] This was not the last time that the people saw premature mortality at the queen's whims. The story of the four condemned nobles instilled fear in those who witnessed their execution.

The four nobles were condemned for embracing European Christianity and among them was the wife of a noble who was with child and very close to delivering her baby. While waiting for their sentence to be carried out, the small group began singing Christian hymns, which infuriated the queen and her soldiers. Ranavalona ordered them to be gagged so that their praises would be muffled to a dull hum until their tongues got in the way and silenced their worship.[30] A huge brush fire and wooden stakes were lit, and the soldiers grabbed the queen's captives, dragging them toward the fire. Before the condemned could be thrown into the fire, a torrential rainfall soaked the land and extinguished the fire, temporarily halting the execution. Paying no heed to the abrupt storm, the soldiers worked to rekindle the fire since the queen was not going to let a little rain thwart her demands. The soldiers began lighting the wood again, which was of course taking a long time, and more dry brush was needed. According to historical records, as the soldiers worked to relight the flames, a massive triple rainbow burst across the sky like a canopy over the execution site.[31] Many who had gathered to witness the executions were filled with fear, believing they were in the presence of a divine, supernatural power. They fled the site as fast as their feet could carry them. Staying obedient to their queen and duty, the soldiers (regardless of any fear they may have had) threw the victims into the raging fires. While the pregnant woman was enduring excruciating pain, the physical shock caused her body to go into swift labour, and she delivered her baby while her flesh was burning. The baby was thrown into the fires as well, only living long enough to give the world its short-lived cries.[32] After such a sight, those who stayed to watch this event may have wished they had fled with the others. This execution succeeded in the greater purpose that Ranavalona had all along. It wasn't just about delivering punishment; it was about deterring others from abandoning their ancient faith.

In 1845 Ranavolona led her people on a wild buffalo hunt. This order came from the queen during a time when her rule seemed to give way to darkness and further morbid punishments. She ordered her slaves and servants to dig roads for her chariots and accompanying aristocratic members to travel and hunt the elusive buffalo herds.[33] Those bound in servitude were not supplied with enough food to sustain them through the long sixteen-week hunt. When the large entourage passed through villages, many carried off what resources they could find, hoping it would sustain them for a while longer. However, starvation and diseases such as malaria spread through the large group like wildfire, claiming the lives of over 10,000 men, women, and children.[34] According to the record, no buffalo were shot during this hunt.[35] Ranavalona had a strategy to ensure a replenished body count of servants. On 13 May 1845, she passed a new law ordering all foreigners to perform free labour and other forms of public work.[36]

As the years continued, the queen's relationship with France and England deteriorated. Her husband Radama had cooperated with the foreign European powers, but Ranavalona resisted any alliance that existed between her kingdom, France and England. The two

European powers refused to allow Madagascar's queen to sever ties so easily. This deeply offended the French King Charles X. He sent fleets of ships to the island and launched an attack in 1839. The attack was unsuccessful since the Malagasy people fought back. Despite the decreasing popularity Ranavalona had with her own people, they held fast to national pride, refusing to be conquered by a foreign ruler.[37] Her resistance was temporary though. If Ranavalona was going to modernize her island, she needed to do more than cooperate. She needed French and English support and influence. Under the flag of truce, she sent delegates to Paris and London, hoping to reform Madagascar and open trade relations with her enticing offer of rice and cattle. The Malagasy delegates were unsuccessful in their mission. France and England did not accept the queen's proposals and in 1845, the two European nations invaded the island again.

Madagascar was consistently pursued by France and England from 1817, each wanting to dominate foreign influence throughout the island. Despite King Radama's previous cooperation with the Europeans, the Hovas tribe (who also happened to be the dominant tribe in Madagascar at that time) were unhappy with the presence of any foreign influence. Madagascar's relationship with France and England deteriorated substantially, especially with Queen Ranavalona's labour declaration in May 1845. Any who refused to abide were forced to vacate the island within eleven days. British subjects living on the island wrote grievances home describing the queen's constricting decrees, making it almost impossible for them to remain on the island and maintain whatever freedom they felt entitled to as British subjects who had purchased lands under Radama's reign.[38] Captain Kelly of the British naval fleet boarded his ship, the HMS *Conway*, and sailed for the shores of Madagascar to investigate the current political and social climate that had caused such a stir between the locals and the foreign inhabitants.[39]

A primary piece of Captain Kelly's investigation was the ensured protection of land that was purchased from King Radama during his reign as well as the safety of British merchants who were residing within the Hovan government. Kelly instigated discussions with the government in Madagascar, however, he was met with fierce opposition. The British were given one year to relinquish their purchased lands and vacate the island. This angered Captain Kelly, and he swiftly wrote correspondence to French officials to discuss the queen's breach of their foreign contract. Kelly met with two French naval captains and the trio formed an alliance with war laid as its foundation. The French ships *Berceau* and *Zelee* were launched toward Madagascar with Captain Kelly's ship HMS *Conway* positioned on their right for the upcoming assault.[40] This conflict, also known as The Storming of Madagascar 1845 is believed to be Britain's shortest battle in its history.[41] The British and French underestimated the quality of the Tamatave Fort. The escarp (the inner slope of the wall surrounding the defensive wall of the city) was at least nine feet thick of solid stone.[42] The foundation was at least two feet deep, and the interior wall was three feet thick.[43] *Conway's* log details the strength of this fort and the need for a more strategic tactic for breaching the well-fortified walls of Tamatave.[44] In the end, the British and French suffered defeat and it is recorded that twenty-one lost their lives and fifty-three were left wounded to varying degrees. This attack deeply wounded the already deteriorating relationship between the French, British, and Malagasy people, which endured for many years. Ranavalona was not going to let this attack go unpunished and she was determined to make a public spectacle of her attackers, especially since this was not the first time that foreign nations had tried to break the walls and spirits of the queen and her people.

Just like the previous attack, the Malagasy people prevailed. As a deterrent for future attacks, she mounted the skulls of the dead on pikes and lined them along the beach.[45] Ranavalona decided that since amicable relations with France and England were an impossibility (at least during her reign), she resolved to promote independence in her nation by setting up factories to manufacture their own goods such as ink, porcelain, guns, ammunition, silks, and bricks.[46] These factories created over 20,000 jobs for the Malagasy people. She employed thousands of workers to build her luxurious palace which was filled with Napoleonic art.

By 1853, hostilities between Ranavolna and the English and French had dissipated enough for the nations to resume trade, but the Europeans' trust in the Malagasy queen was apprehensive and limited. However, relations with her son, Rakoto Radama were far more estranged. Rakoto Radama resisted many of his mother's policies and abhorred her brutal punishments against her own people as well as foreign inhabitants on the island. He conspired with the English and French to overthrow Ranavalona and place himself on the throne. On 28 June 1855, Rakoto Radama signed an agreement with Joseph Francois Lambert to overthrow the queen.[47] Lambert secured support in Europe for this quest in exchange for access to valuable minerals dug up from the earth and the forests in Madagascar. All Rakoto Radama required was ten per cent of the profits.[48] The alliance was sealed, supported, and progressing according to plan. However, the conspirators made the mistake of including the wrong individuals in their plans such as the queen's advisor and presumed lover, who informed Ranavalona of her son's intentions. She was greatly disturbed by him making secret alliances with her foreign enemies and plans to remove her from the throne. The conspirators were captured by her spies and forced to march through the thick swamps where they died of heat exhaustion and malaria.[49] Only her son and Joseph Francois Lambert were kept alive.

Ranavalona I enjoyed a long life, much to the dismay of her enemies and the people whom she kept suppressed under her strict policies. The queen finally entered into an eternal sleep on 16 August 1861. Her death was not accomplished on the battlefield nor of plague or other illness like some of the other queens in this book. She died amid a midnight slumber, peacefully relinquishing her grip on the world she tried to control. Many came to the queen's funeral to bid farewell. During the ceremony, a barrel of gunpowder accidentally detonated, killing several mourners in attendance.[50] Her son Rokoto Radama II succeeded her to the throne.

Unlike his mother, Radama II sought to re-establish relations with European powers by overturning Ranavalona's policies and allowing foreign influence to spread into Madagascar once again. However, his reign was short-lived. There were many among the Malagasy people who abhorred European colonization and were furious with Radama's declaration of alliance. While few contest the length of his reign, most scholars believe he was overthrown by a Marina oligarchy and assassinated. Madagascar needed a new ruler to assume the throne and lead the nation into a long overdue period of political and social stability.

The string of royal leadership would eventually bring Madagascar to a kneeling stance before foreign invaders, however, the women who succeeded Ranavalona I were nothing short of extraordinary in the face of opposition and strife. Since the 'Mad Queen of Madagascar' only had one heir (who had been assassinated), authority was passed to her Prime Minister, Rainivoninahitriniony. He was a cunning man with a knack for ensuring his enduring political voice and influence. He silenced Malagasy worship and ancestral beliefs as well as mandated that education be enforced for everyone, however, this mostly applied to males. European ministries were given provinces throughout Madagascar as well. He had support from his foreign alliances, only needing to ensure his royal right to rule. One method of securing his uncontested leadership was by marrying Rasoherina.[51] The union was more of a political alliance than a union of love.

Queen Rasoherina was born to royalty to Prince Andriantsalamandriana and Princess Rafaramanjaka and was the niece of Ranavalona I. She was the divorcée of a well-known statesman, Raharolahy.[52] The pair divorced the same year she married Radama II. She was aware of the passionate feelings regarding her husband's political positions though she may not have known about the planned coup (a violent seizure of power). This violent uprising is believed to have been organized by two brothers, Rainivoninahitriniony and Rainilaiarivony. They successfully had the reigning king killed; however, regicide made them very unpopular among some of the Malagasy people.[53]

The Prime Minister had a hot temper that was exacerbated by his excessive drinking. There were times in which he would exercise his frustrations by subjecting his wife, the queen, to physical abuse and even threatened to end her life with a knife on several occasions. Refusing to give in to her husband's intimidation, repeated abuse and uncontrolled alcohol consumption, she deposed him and declared his brother, Rainilaiarivony Prime Minister.[54] A major point in her reign was when she signed a treaty with the United States and began conversations for a treaty with France, however, the treaty was not signed until after she died in 1868.

After the demise of Queen Rasoherina, Madagascar went through another royal transition, and the next ruling monarch was the cousin of the 'Mad Queen', Ranavalona II. Despite her blood ties to the formerly feared ruler, Ranavalona II possessed an entirely different spirit and method of governing her people. She still embodied the inner strength of the women who ruled before her, but she also expressed a love for her people and developed policies that would benefit the whole of her island, especially women.[55] Just like the previous queen, she married Prime Minister Rainilaiarivony. She welcomed missionaries and allowed them to practice their Christianity openly and instituted religious freedom. During her reign she participated in secret prayer and worship meetings.[56] Now, she and her people could pray and worship without the severe persecution that many had feared previously. She encouraged her people to adhere to the moral code promoted in Christianity including abolishing polygamy and prohibiting the trade of slaves and alcohol.[57] In addition to her progressive orders, she declared that education be extended as a right and duty for all children up to age fourteen, including girls.[58]

She ordered the destruction of idols and talismans in 1869 and was baptized into the Christian faith on 29 February 1869.[59] She was also a generous financial giver, taking part in a yearly Christmas tithe in which the funds would be used for missionary work and the people they would encounter.[60] Madagascar was in sufficient financial standing to enable a law that allowed the use of brick and stone in construction, whereas before, perishable materials were used. Several churches were erected, some of which were dedicated to the martyrs whose lives were taken under Ranavalona I's reign. These churches include Ambohipotsy (Rasalama martyr), Faravohitra (martyrs burned by fire), and Ampamarinana (martyrs thrown off the cliffs). Ranavalona II died on 13 July 1883.[61]

Upon the death of the second Ranavalona, Madagascar crowned its last queen Ranavalona III. Queen Ranavalona III was born Princess Razafindrahety in 1861. She received educational instruction from the London Missionary Society and was raised Protestant. She was married to a nobleman named Ratrimo, however, he suddenly died under what is believed to be suspicious circumstances in 1883, two months before Ranavalona II passed.[62] Since the political system was established with the signing of power being given to the Prime Minister with the passing of Radama II via Rasoherita's signature, Rainilaiarivony once again gained supreme power when he married Ranavalona III.[63] Her reign was tumultuous since she and her Prime Minister husband could not encourage France to cooperate to at least an amicable level. In a massive invasion, France conquered Madagascar in 1896. She and the royal family were exiled to Algiers, the primary seaport in Algeria.[64] After conquering the island, the French maintained slavery, closed some of the schools, and forced the Malagasy people to learn and speak French. During this invasion, thousands of Malagasy people were murdered. Ranavalona III eventually travelled to France and was quite taken by the extravagant beauty of Parisian finery, fashion, and elegance of the women.[65] The 'Last Queen of Madagascar' died in 1917.

Madagascar remained a French colony until 1960 when the country regained its independence.

Ranavalona I's legacy differs depending on who one asks. She is notoriously known for her brutal tactics and punishments, persecution of Christians, and the 'Great Buffalo Hunt' that led to thousands of people needlessly dying while the hunted buffalo remained elusive, thriving under the sun and sleeping soundly under a blanket of stars, untouched by gunfire. Her violence became widely feared and increased during a time when many believed she was spiralling into a mental decline. However, some argue that her violence was not the all-encompassing theme of her reign as queen. Many assert that Ranavalona I was a trailblazer in ensuring freedom and autonomy from European influence. She fought hard against the English and French from colonizing and dominating the political, economic, and social climate of Madagascar. For those who detested the 'Mad Queen's' policies, it certainly served as an example for those succeeding her, the kind of ruler they did not want to embody. Despite her distaste for foreign influence, she made sure she dressed the part of a respected royal, clothing herself in extravagant Parisian fashion and embellished with her Malagasy crown. Whether she was right, wrong, cruel, strategic, or any other characteristic in between, Queen Ranavalona I forged her name into the books of African and world history.

Conclusion

Through the journeys in this book, we have traversed deserts and mountains, waded through rivers, and stood in the heart of bustling cities, all in pursuit of understanding the remarkable women who shaped history. These queens, consorts, and warriors were more than figures of power; they were architects of their own legacies, navigating the complex intersections of leadership, culture, religion, and geopolitics. Their stories reveal the depth of their influence – not only in the moments they reigned but in the echoes of their rule that still resonate today. The past is not a simple narrative of victories and defeats; it is a tapestry of human ambition, resilience, and sacrifice.

History is not meant to comfort us. It demands reflection, often stirring emotions of pride and sorrow, admiration and grief. It leaves scars – some physical, like Amanirenas' blinded eye or the burn marks on Njinga's belly, and others cultural, wounds that have taken centuries to begin to heal. But scars are not just reminders of pain; they are testaments to endurance. These women bore their scars with unwavering resolve, refusing to surrender to circumstance or victimhood.

Neithhotep commanded expeditions that expanded Egypt's wealth when women were expected to remain behind palace walls.

Hatshepsut redefined kingship, daring to rule as a man and securing the future of her dynasty. Nefertiti, nearly erased from history, endures as a symbol of influence and power, her image so coveted that even Adolf Hitler refused to part with it. Makeda, in her quest for wisdom, carried a faith back to Ethiopia that would shape its religious identity for millennia.

Other queens stood at the frontlines, wielding swords and strategy against empires that sought to consume them. Amanirenas, her body still healing, lifted her shield and rode into battle against Rome. Dahia stood firm in her faith, choosing death over surrender. Amina, mounted on her warhorse Demon, fought fiercely to defend her homeland. Njinga, from the moment she entered the world in crisis, refused to accept submission, spilling blood when necessary and fighting relentlessly to save her sisters. Ranavalona I defied colonial rule, paying any price to preserve Madagascar's sovereignty.

These women were warriors, visionaries, and rulers, each unique in her approach yet united in their refusal to be forgotten. Their legacies endure, not just in the histories of their nations, but in the indelible mark they have left on the world. They remind us that power is not granted – it is taken, fought for, and fiercely defended.

Notes

Chapter 1

1. Oakes, Lorna, and Lucia Gahlin. 2022. *The Illustrated Encyclopaedia of Ancient Egypt: An Illustrated Reference to the Myths, Religions, Pyramids and Temples of the Land of the Pharaohs*. Edited by Helena Sudell. Cambridgeshire: Anness Publishing Limited. Page 14.
2. Oakes, Lorna, and Lucia Gahlin. 2022. *The Illustrated Encyclopaedia of Ancient Egypt: An Illustrated Reference to the Myths, Religions, Pyramids and Temples of the Land of the Pharaohs*. Edited by Helena Sudell. Cambridgeshire: Anness Publishing Limited. Page 15.
3. Oakes, Lorna, and Lucia Gahlin. 2022. *The Illustrated Encyclopaedia of Ancient Egypt: An Illustrated Reference to the Myths, Religions, Pyramids and Temples of the Land of the Pharaohs*. Edited by Helena Sudell. Cambridgeshire: Anness Publishing Limited. Pages 44-45, 422.
4. Britannica, T. Editors of Encyclopaedia. 'Crowns of Egypt.' Encyclopaedia Britannica, 31 October, 2008. www.britannica.com/topic/crowns-of-Egypt.
5. Oakes, Lorna, and Lucia Gahlin. 2022. *The Illustrated Encyclopaedia of Ancient Egypt: An Illustrated Reference to*

the Myths, Religions, Pyramids and Temples of the Land of the Pharaohs. Edited by Helena Sudell. Cambridgeshire: Anness Publishing Limited. Page 314.

6. Mark, Joshua. 2016. 'Neith.' WorldHistory.org. September 14, 2016. www.worldhistory.org/Neith/.
7. Britannica, T. Editors of Encyclopaedia. 'Crowns of Egypt.' Encyclopaedia Britannica, October 31, 2008. www.britannica.com/topic/crowns-of-Egypt.
8. Mark, Joshua J. 2016. 'Ancient Egyptian Religion.' World History Encyclopaedia. January 20, 2016. www.worldhistory.org/Egyptian_Religion/.
9. Oakes, Lorna, and Lucia Gahlin. 2022. *The Illustrated Encyclopaedia of Ancient Egypt: An Illustrated Reference to the Myths, Religions, Pyramids and Temples of the Land of the Pharaohs*. Edited by Helena Sudell. Cambridgeshire: Anness Publishing Limited. Pages 412.
10. Mark, Joshua. 2016. 'Osiris.' World History Encyclopaedia. March 6, 2016. www.worldhistory.org/osiris/.
11. Mark, Joshua. 2016. 'Osiris.' World History Encyclopaedia. March 6, 2016. www.worldhistory.org/osiris/.
12. Oakes, Lorna, and Lucia Gahlin. 2022. *The Illustrated Encyclopaedia of Ancient Egypt: An Illustrated Reference to the Myths, Religions, Pyramids and Temples of the Land of the Pharaohs*. Edited by Helena Sudell. Cambridgeshire: Anness Publishing Limited. Pages 310-311.
13. Mark, Joshua. 2016. 'Osiris.' World History Encyclopaedia. March 6, 2016. www.worldhistory.org/osiris/.
14. Mark, Joshua. 2016. 'Osiris.' World History Encyclopaedia. March 6, 2016. www.worldhistory.org/osiris/.
15. Oakes, Lorna, and Lucia Gahlin. 2022. *The Illustrated Encyclopaedia of Ancient Egypt: An Illustrated Reference to the Myths, Religions, Pyramids and Temples of the Land of the Pharaohs*. Edited by Helena Sudell. Cambridgeshire: Anness Publishing Limited.

16. Klimczak, Natalia. 2017. 'Searching for the Lost Footsteps of the Scorpion Kings.' Ancient-Origins.net. Ancient Origins. February 23, 2017. www.ancient-origins.net/history-famous-people/searching-lost-footsteps-scorpion-kings-007598.
17. Klimczak, Natalia. 2017. 'Searching for the Lost Footsteps of the Scorpion Kings.' Ancient-Origins.net. Ancient Origins. February 23, 2017. www.ancient-origins.net/history-famous-people/searching-lost-footsteps-scorpion-kings-007598.
18. Klimczak, Natalia. 2017. 'Searching for the Lost Footsteps of the Scorpion Kings.' Ancient-Origins.net. Ancient Origins. February 23, 2017. www.ancient-origins.net/history-famous-people/searching-lost-footsteps-scorpion-kings-007598.
19. Mark, Joshua. 2016. 'Narmer.' World History Encyclopaedia. February 1, 2016. www.worldhistory.org/Narmer/.
20. Oakes, Lorna, and Lucia Gahlin. 2022. *The Illustrated Encyclopaedia of Ancient Egypt: An Illustrated Reference to the Myths, Religions, Pyramids and Temples of the Land of the Pharaohs*. Edited by Helena Sudell. Cambridgeshire: Anness Publishing Limited.
21. Oakes, Lorna, and Lucia Gahlin. 2022. *The Illustrated Encyclopaedia of Ancient Egypt: An Illustrated Reference to the Myths, Religions, Pyramids and Temples of the Land of the Pharaohs*. Edited by Helena Sudell. Cambridgeshire: Anness Publishing Limited.
22. World History Edu. 2021. 'Neith – Origins, Family, Meaning, Symbols & Powers.' World History Edu. March 25, 2021. www.worldhistoryedu.com/neith-origins-family-meaning-symbols-powers/.
23. Oakes, Lorna, and Lucia Gahlin. 2022. *The Illustrated Encyclopaedia of Ancient Egypt: An Illustrated Reference to the Myths, Religions, Pyramids and Temples of the Land of the Pharaohs*. Edited by Helena Sudell. Cambridgeshire: Anness Publishing Limited.

24. Britannica, T. Editors of Encyclopaedia. 'Menes.' Encyclopaedia Britannica, December 17, 2020. www.britannica.com/biography/Menes.
25. Mark, Joshua. 2017. 'Great Female Rulers of Ancient Egypt 2017.' World History Encyclopaedia. March 29, 2017. www.worldhistory.org/article/1040/great-female-rulers-of-ancient-egypt/.
26. Hill, J. 2018. 'Neithhotep.' Ancient Egypt Online: Ancient Egyptian History and Art. 2018. www.ancientegyptonline.co.uk/neithhotep/.
27. World History Edu. 2022. 'Neithhotep: History, Facts, & Achievements.' World History Edu. April 15, 2022. www.worldhistoryedu.com/neithhotep-history-facts-achievements/.
28. World History Edu. 2022. 'Neithhotep: History, Facts, & Achievements.' World History Edu. April 15, 2022. www.worldhistoryedu.com/neithhotep-history-facts-achievements/.
29. World History Edu. 2022. 'Neithhotep: History, Facts, & Achievements.' World History Edu. April 15, 2022. www.worldhistoryedu.com/neithhotep-history-facts-achievements/.
30. World History Edu. 2022. 'Neithhotep: History, Facts, & Achievements.' World History Edu. April 15, 2022. www.worldhistoryedu.com/neithhotep-history-facts-achievements/.
31. Hill, J. 2018. 'Neithhotep.' Ancient Egypt Online: Ancient Egyptian History and Art. 2018. www.ancientegyptonline.co.uk/neithhotep/.
32. World History Edu. 2022. 'Neithhotep: History, Facts, & Achievements.' World History Edu. April 15, 2022. www.worldhistoryedu.com/neithhotep-history-facts-achievements/.
33. Moll, Michele. 2011. 'Burial Practices at Naqada.' Archaeology of Ancient Egypt. July 14, 2011. www.anthropology.msu.edu/egyptian-archaeology/2011/07/14/burial-practices-at-naqada/.
34. Cox, Jessica. 2012. 'Trade and Power: The Role of Naqada as a Trading Centre in Predynastic Egypt.' *Egyptology in Australia and New Zealand 2009: Proceedings of the Conference Held*

in Melbourne, September 4th-6th, January. www.academia.edu/2980599/Trade_and_Power_The_Role_of_Naqada_as_a_Trading_Centre_in_Predynastic_Egypt.

35. Oakes, Lorna, and Lucia Gahlin. 2022. *The Illustrated Encyclopaedia of Ancient Egypt: An Illustrated Reference to the Myths, Religions, Pyramids and Temples of the Land of the Pharaohs*. Edited by Helena Sudell. Cambridgeshire: Anness Publishing Limited.
36. Oakes, Lorna, and Lucia Gahlin. 2022. *The Illustrated Encyclopaedia of Ancient Egypt: An Illustrated Reference to the Myths, Religions, Pyramids and Temples of the Land of the Pharaohs*. Edited by Helena Sudell. Cambridgeshire: Anness Publishing Limited.
37. Oakes, Lorna, and Lucia Gahlin. 2022. *The Illustrated Encyclopaedia of Ancient Egypt: An Illustrated Reference to the Myths, Religions, Pyramids and Temples of the Land of the Pharaohs*. Edited by Helena Sudell. Cambridgeshire: Anness Publishing Limited.
38. Oakes, Lorna, and Lucia Gahlin. 2022. *The Illustrated Encyclopaedia of Ancient Egypt: An Illustrated Reference to the Myths, Religions, Pyramids and Temples of the Land of the Pharaohs*. Edited by Helena Sudell. Cambridgeshire: Anness Publishing Limited. Page 36.
39. Oakes, Lorna, and Lucia Gahlin. 2022. *The Illustrated Encyclopaedia of Ancient Egypt: An Illustrated Reference to the Myths, Religions, Pyramids and Temples of the Land of the Pharaohs*. Edited by Helena Sudell. Cambridgeshire: Anness Publishing Limited.
40. Oakes, Lorna, and Lucia Gahlin. 2022. *The Illustrated Encyclopaedia of Ancient Egypt: An Illustrated Reference to the Myths, Religions, Pyramids and Temples of the Land of the Pharaohs*. Edited by Helena Sudell. Cambridgeshire: Anness Publishing Limited.

41. Hill, J. 2018. 'Neithhotep.' Ancient Egypt Online: Ancient Egyptian History and Art. 2018. www.ancientegyptonline.co.uk/neithhotep/
42. Mark, Joshua. 2016. 'Narmer.' World History Encyclopaedia. February 1, 2016. www.worldhistory.org/Narmer/.

Chapter 2

1. Oakes, Lorna, and Lucia Gahlin. 2022. *The Illustrated Encyclopaedia of Ancient Egypt: An Illustrated Reference to the Myths, Religions, Pyramids and Temples of the Land of the Pharaohs*. Edited by Helena Sudell. Cambridgeshire: Anness Publishing Limited. Page 152.
2. World History Edu. 2020. 'Khonsu: Ancient Egyptian God of the Moon and Time.' World History Edu. October 21, 2020. www.worldhistoryedu.com/khonsu-ancient-egyptian-god-of-the-moon-and-time/.
3. World History Edu. 2020. 'Khonsu: Ancient Egyptian God of the Moon and Time.' World History Edu. October 21, 2020. www.worldhistoryedu.com/khonsu-ancient-egyptian-god-of-the-moon-and-time/.
4. World History Edu. 2020. 'Khonsu: Ancient Egyptian God of the Moon and Time.' World History Edu. October 21, 2020. www.worldhistoryedu.com/khonsu-ancient-egyptian-god-of-the-moon-and-time/.
5. Cassar, Claudine. 2023. 'The Nightly Journey of Khonsu - the Ancient Egyptian God of the Moon.' Anthropology Review. September 4, 2023. www.anthropologyreview.org/history/ancient-egypt/egyptian-god-of-the-moon/.
6. Oakes, Lorna, and Lucia Gahlin. 2022. *The Illustrated Encyclopaedia of Ancient Egypt: An Illustrated Reference to the Myths, Religions, Pyramids and Temples of the Land of the*

Pharaohs. Edited by Helena Sudell. Cambridgeshire: Anness Publishing Limited. Page 154.

7. Oakes, Lorna, and Lucia Gahlin. 2022. *The Illustrated Encyclopaedia of Ancient Egypt: An Illustrated Reference to the Myths, Religions, Pyramids and Temples of the Land of the Pharaohs*. Edited by Helena Sudell. Cambridgeshire: Anness Publishing Limited. Page 154.
8. Oakes, Lorna, and Lucia Gahlin. 2022. *The Illustrated Encyclopaedia of Ancient Egypt: An Illustrated Reference to the Myths, Religions, Pyramids and Temples of the Land of the Pharaohs*. Edited by Helena Sudell. Cambridgeshire: Anness Publishing Limited. Page 154.
9. Drower, M. Stefana and Dorman, Peter F. 'Karnak.' Encyclopaedia Britannica, October 2, 2023. www.britannica.com/place/Karnak.
10. Oakes, Lorna, and Lucia Gahlin. 2022. *The Illustrated Encyclopaedia of Ancient Egypt: An Illustrated Reference to the Myths, Religions, Pyramids and Temples of the Land of the Pharaohs*. Edited by Helena Sudell. Cambridgeshire: Anness Publishing Limited. Pages 154-155.
11. Drower, M. Stefana and Dorman, Peter F. 'Karnak.' Encyclopaedia Britannica, October 2, 2023. www.britannica.com/place/Karnak.
12. Mark, Joshua J. 2016. Review of *Karnak*. World History Encyclopaedia. September 16, 2016. www.worldhistory.org/Karnak/.
13. Drower, M. Stefana and Dorman, Peter F. 'Karnak.' Encyclopaedia Britannica, October 2, 2023. www.britannica.com/place/Karnak.
14. Britannica, T. Editors of Encyclopaedia. 'Ahmose I.' Encyclopaedia Britannica, November 8, 2017. www.britannica.com/biography/Ahmose-I.
15. Britannica, T. Editors of Encyclopaedia. 'Ahmose I.' Encyclopaedia Britannica, November 8, 2017. www.britannica.com/biography/Ahmose-I.

16. Britannica, T. Editors of Encyclopaedia. 'Ahmose I.' Encyclopaedia Britannica, November 8, 2017. www.britannica.com/biography/Ahmose-I.
17. World History Edu. 2021. 'Ahmose I: History, Accomplishments and Facts.' World History Edu. October 13, 2021. www.worldhistoryedu.com/ahmose-i-history-accomplishments-and-facts/.
18. Britannica, T. Editors of Encyclopaedia. 'Amenhotep I.' Encyclopaedia Britannica, February 12, 2024. www.britannica.com/biography/Amenhotep-I.
19. World History Edu. 2021. 'Ahmose I: History, Accomplishments and Facts.' World History Edu. October 13, 2021. www.worldhistoryedu.com/ahmose-i-history-accomplishments-and-facts/.
20. Britannica, T. Editors of Encyclopaedia. 'Thutmose I.' Encyclopaedia Britannica, April 3, 2014. www.britannica.com/biography/Thutmose-I.
21. Britannica, T. Editors of Encyclopaedia. 'Thutmose I.' Encyclopaedia Britannica, April 3, 2014. www.britannica.com/biography/Thutmose-I.
22. Cooney, Kara. 2015. *Woman Who Would Be King: Hatshepsut's Rise to Power in Ancient Egypt.* New York: Broadway Books. Page 33.
23. Cooney, Kara. 2015. *Woman Who Would Be King: Hatshepsut's Rise to Power in Ancient Egypt.* New York: Broadway Books. Page 33-34.
24. Cooney, Kara. 2015. *Woman Who Would Be King: Hatshepsut's Rise to Power in Ancient Egypt.* New York: Broadway Books. Pages 22, 24.
25. Oakes, Lorna, and Lucia Gahlin. 2022. *The Illustrated Encyclopaedia of Ancient Egypt: An Illustrated Reference to the Myths, Religions, Pyramids and Temples of the Land of the*

Pharaohs. Edited by Helena Sudell. Cambridgeshire: Anness Publishing Limited. Pages 346-347.

26. Oakes, Lorna, and Lucia Gahlin. 2022. *The Illustrated Encyclopaedia of Ancient Egypt: An Illustrated Reference to the Myths, Religions, Pyramids and Temples of the Land of the Pharaohs*. Edited by Helena Sudell. Cambridgeshire: Anness Publishing Limited. Pages 346-347.
27. Oakes, Lorna, and Lucia Gahlin. 2022. *The Illustrated Encyclopaedia of Ancient Egypt: An Illustrated Reference to the Myths, Religions, Pyramids and Temples of the Land of the Pharaohs*. Edited by Helena Sudell. Cambridgeshire: Anness Publishing Limited. Pages 346-347.
28. Oakes, Lorna, and Lucia Gahlin. 2022. *The Illustrated Encyclopaedia of Ancient Egypt: An Illustrated Reference to the Myths, Religions, Pyramids and Temples of the Land of the Pharaohs*. Edited by Helena Sudell. Cambridgeshire: Anness Publishing Limited. Page 347.
29. Oakes, Lorna, and Lucia Gahlin. 2022. *The Illustrated Encyclopaedia of Ancient Egypt: An Illustrated Reference to the Myths, Religions, Pyramids and Temples of the Land of the Pharaohs*. Edited by Helena Sudell. Cambridgeshire: Anness Publishing Limited. Page 347.
30. Oakes, Lorna, and Lucia Gahlin. 2022. *The Illustrated Encyclopaedia of Ancient Egypt: An Illustrated Reference to the Myths, Religions, Pyramids and Temples of the Land of the Pharaohs*. Edited by Helena Sudell. Cambridgeshire: Anness Publishing Limited. Page 269.
31. Cooney, Kara. 2015. *Woman Who Would Be King: Hatshepsut's Rise to Power in Ancient Egypt.* New York: Broadway Books. Page 36.
32. Oakes, Lorna, and Lucia Gahlin. 2022. *The Illustrated Encyclopaedia of Ancient Egypt: An Illustrated Reference to the Myths, Religions, Pyramids and Temples of the Land of the*

Pharaohs. Edited by Helena Sudell. Cambridgeshire: Anness Publishing Limited. Page 366.

33. Oakes, Lorna, and Lucia Gahlin. 2022. *The Illustrated Encyclopaedia of Ancient Egypt: An Illustrated Reference to the Myths, Religions, Pyramids and Temples of the Land of the Pharaohs*. Edited by Helena Sudell. Cambridgeshire: Anness Publishing Limited. Page 366.
34. Oakes, Lorna, and Lucia Gahlin. 2022. *The Illustrated Encyclopaedia of Ancient Egypt: An Illustrated Reference to the Myths, Religions, Pyramids and Temples of the Land of the Pharaohs*. Edited by Helena Sudell. Cambridgeshire: Anness Publishing Limited. Page 367.
35. Cooney, Kara. 2015. *Woman Who Would Be King: Hatshepsut's Rise to Power in Ancient Egypt.* New York: Broadway Books. Page 38, 39.
36. Cooney, Kara. 2015. *Woman Who Would Be King: Hatshepsut's Rise to Power in Ancient Egypt.* New York: Broadway Books. Page 40.
37. Cooney, Kara, and National Geographic Society (U.S. 2018. *When Women Ruled the World: Six Queens of Egypt*. Washington, D.C.: National Geographic. Page 105.
38. Cooney, Kara, and National Geographic Society (U.S. 2018. *When Women Ruled the World: Six Queens of Egypt*. Washington, D.C.: National Geographic. Page 52.
39. Cooney, Kara. 2015. *Woman Who Would Be King: Hatshepsut's Rise to Power in Ancient Egypt.* New York: Broadway Books. Page 53.
40. Cooney, Kara. 2015. *Woman Who Would Be King: Hatshepsut's Rise to Power in Ancient Egypt.* New York: Broadway Books. Page 53.
41. Cooney, Kara. 2015. *Woman Who Would Be King: Hatshepsut's Rise to Power in Ancient Egypt.* New York: Broadway Books. Page 55.

42. Cooney, Kara. 2015. *Woman Who Would Be King: Hatshepsut's Rise to Power in Ancient Egypt.* New York: Broadway Books. Page 55.
43. Cooney, Kara. 2015. *Woman Who Would Be King: Hatshepsut's Rise to Power in Ancient Egypt.* New York: Broadway Books. Page 54.
44. Cooney, Kara. 2015. *Woman Who Would Be King: Hatshepsut's Rise to Power in Ancient Egypt.* New York: Broadway Books. Page 56.
45. Cooney, Kara. 2015. *Woman Who Would Be King: Hatshepsut's Rise to Power in Ancient Egypt.* New York: Broadway Books. Page 61.
46. Cooney, Kara. 2015. *Woman Who Would Be King: Hatshepsut's Rise to Power in Ancient Egypt.* New York: Broadway Books. Page 68.
47. Cooney, Kara. 2015. *Woman Who Would Be King: Hatshepsut's Rise to Power in Ancient Egypt.* New York: Broadway Books. Page 70.
48. Cooney, Kara. 2015. *Woman Who Would Be King: Hatshepsut's Rise to Power in Ancient Egypt.* New York: Broadway Books. Page 62.
49. Schwarz-Bart, Simone, André Schwarz-Bart, Rose-Myriam Réjouis, Val Vinokur, Stephanie Daval, and Stephanie K Turner. 2001. *In Praise of Black Women.* Madison, Wi: The University of Wisconsin Press. Page 44.
50. Cooney, Kara, and National Geographic Society (U.S. 2018. *When Women Ruled the World: Six Queens of Egypt*. Washington, D.C.: National Geographic. Page 107.
51. Cooney, Kara, and National Geographic Society (U.S. 2018. *When Women Ruled the World: Six Queens of Egypt*. Washington, D.C.: National Geographic. Page 107.
52. Cooney, Kara, and National Geographic Society (U.S. 2018. *When Women Ruled the World: Six Queens of Egypt*. Washington, D.C.: National Geographic. Page 126.
53. Cooney, Kara, and National Geographic Society (U.S. 2018. *When Women Ruled the World: Six Queens of Egypt*. Washington, D.C.: National Geographic. Page 127-128.

54. Oakes, Lorna, and Lucia Gahlin. 2022. *The Illustrated Encyclopaedia of Ancient Egypt: An Illustrated Reference to the Myths, Religions, Pyramids and Temples of the Land of the Pharaohs*. Edited by Helena Sudell. Cambridgeshire: Anness Publishing Limited. Page 364.
55. Oakes, Lorna, and Lucia Gahlin. 2022. *The Illustrated Encyclopaedia of Ancient Egypt: An Illustrated Reference to the Myths, Religions, Pyramids and Temples of the Land of the Pharaohs*. Edited by Helena Sudell. Cambridgeshire: Anness Publishing Limited. Pages 190-191.
56. Schwarz-Bart, Simone, André Schwarz-Bart, Rose-Myriam Réjouis, Val Vinokur, Stephanie Daval, and Stephanie K Turner. 2001. *In Praise of Black Women*. Madison, Wi: The University of Wisconsin Press. Page 48.
57. Cartwright, Mark. 2019. 'Cosmetics in the Ancient World.' World History Encyclopaedia. September 6, 2019. www.worldhistory.org/article/1441/cosmetics-in-the-ancient-world/.
58. Oakes, Lorna, and Lucia Gahlin. 2022. *The Illustrated Encyclopaedia of Ancient Egypt: An Illustrated Reference to the Myths, Religions, Pyramids and Temples of the Land of the Pharaohs*. Edited by Helena Sudell. Cambridgeshire: Anness Publishing Limited. Pages 154-155.
59. Mark, Joshua. 2017. 'Thutmose III.' World History Encyclopaedia. July 20, 2017. www.worldhistory.org/Thutmose_III/.
60. Drower, M. Stefana and Dorman, Peter F. 'Thutmose III.' Encyclopaedia Britannica, January 30, 2024. www.britannica.com/biography/Thutmose-III.
61. Mark, Joshua. 2017. 'Thutmose III.' World History Encyclopaedia. July 20, 2017. www.worldhistory.org/Thutmose_III/.
62. Mark, Joshua. 2017. 'Thutmose III.' World History Encyclopaedia. July 20, 2017. www.worldhistory.org/Thutmose_III/.
63. Oakes, Lorna, and Lucia Gahlin. 2022. *The Illustrated Encyclopaedia of Ancient Egypt: An Illustrated Reference to*

the Myths, Religions, Pyramids and Temples of the Land of the Pharaohs. Edited by Helena Sudell. Cambridgeshire: Anness Publishing Limited. Page 92.

64. Cooney, Kara, and National Geographic Society (U.S. 2018. *When Women Ruled the World: Six Queens of Egypt*. Washington, D.C.: National Geographic. Page 151.
65. Britannica, T. Editors of Encyclopaedia. 'Heb-Sed.' Encyclopaedia Britannica, June 1, 2016. www.britannica.com/topic/Heb-Sed.
66. Oakes, Lorna, and Lucia Gahlin. 2022. *The Illustrated Encyclopaedia of Ancient Egypt: An Illustrated Reference to the Myths, Religions, Pyramids and Temples of the Land of the Pharaohs*. Edited by Helena Sudell. Cambridgeshire: Anness Publishing Limited. Page 348.
67. Wilford, John Noble. 2007. 'Tooth May Have Solved Mummy Mystery.' *The New York Times*, June 27, 2007, sec. World. www.nytimes.com/2007/06/27/world/middleeast/27mummy.html
68. Wilford, John Noble. 2007. 'Tooth May Have Solved Mummy Mystery.' *The New York Times*, June 27, 2007, sec. World. www.nytimes.com/2007/06/27/world/middleeast/27mummy.html
69. 'Study Finds Skin Cream Caused Egyptian Queen's Death.' 2011. Biblical Archaeology Society. August 22, 2011. www.biblicalarchaeology.org/daily/news/study-finds-skin-cream-caused-egyptian-queens-death/.
70. Oakes, Lorna, and Lucia Gahlin. 2022. *The Illustrated Encyclopaedia of Ancient Egypt: An Illustrated Reference to the Myths, Religions, Pyramids and Temples of the Land of the Pharaohs*. Edited by Helena Sudell. Cambridgeshire: Anness Publishing Limited. Page 165.
71. Oakes, Lorna, and Lucia Gahlin. 2022. *The Illustrated Encyclopaedia of Ancient Egypt: An Illustrated Reference to the Myths, Religions, Pyramids and Temples of the Land of the*

Pharaohs. Edited by Helena Sudell. Cambridgeshire: Anness Publishing Limited. Pages 396-399.

72. Oakes, Lorna, and Lucia Gahlin. 2022. *The Illustrated Encyclopaedia of Ancient Egypt: An Illustrated Reference to the Myths, Religions, Pyramids and Temples of the Land of the Pharaohs*. Edited by Helena Sudell. Cambridgeshire: Anness Publishing Limited. Page 190-191.
73. Oakes, Lorna, and Lucia Gahlin. 2022. *The Illustrated Encyclopaedia of Ancient Egypt: An Illustrated Reference to the Myths, Religions, Pyramids and Temples of the Land of the Pharaohs*. Edited by Helena Sudell. Cambridgeshire: Anness Publishing Limited. Page 107.
74. HISTORY.COM EDITORS. 2009. 'Hatshepsut.' HISTORY. December 16, 2009. www.history.com/topics/ancient-egypt/hatshepsut.
75. Oakes, Lorna, and Lucia Gahlin. 2022. *The Illustrated Encyclopaedia of Ancient Egypt: An Illustrated Reference to the Myths, Religions, Pyramids and Temples of the Land of the Pharaohs*. Edited by Helena Sudell. Cambridgeshire: Anness Publishing Limited. Page 106.
76. Cooney, Kara. 2015. *Woman Who Would Be King: Hatshepsut's Rise to Power in Ancient Egypt.* New York: Broadway Books. Page 88.
77. Cooney, Kara. 2015. *Woman Who Would Be King: Hatshepsut's Rise to Power in Ancient Egypt.* New York: Broadway Books. Pages 66-67, 90.
78. Schwarz-Bart, Simone, André Schwarz-Bart, Rose-Myriam Réjouis, Val Vinokur, Stephanie Daval, and Stephanie K Turner. 2001. *In Praise of Black Women*. Madison, Wi: The University of Wisconsin Press. Page 50.
79. Schwarz-Bart, Simone, André Schwarz-Bart, Rose-Myriam Réjouis, Val Vinokur, Stephanie Daval, and Stephanie K Turner.

2001. *In Praise of Black Women*. Madison, Wi: The University of Wisconsin Press. Page 50.

80. Schwarz-Bart, Simone, André Schwarz-Bart, Rose-Myriam Réjouis, Val Vinokur, Stephanie Daval, and Stephanie K Turner. 2001. *In Praise of Black Women*. Madison, Wi: The University of Wisconsin Press. Page 50.

Chapter 3

1. Oakes, Lorna, and Lucia Gahlin. 2022. *The Illustrated Encyclopaedia of Ancient Egypt: An Illustrated Reference to the Myths, Religions, Pyramids and Temples of the Land of the Pharaohs*. Edited by Helena Sudell. Cambridgeshire: Anness Publishing Limited. Page 377.
2. Editors at Britannica. 'Ancient Egypt - Thutmose IV.' 2019. In *Encyclopaedia Britannica*. www.britannica.com/place/ancient-Egypt/Thutmose-IV.
3. Editors at Britannica. 'Ancient Egypt - Thutmose IV.' 2019. In *Encyclopaedia Britannica*. www.britannica.com/place/ancient-Egypt/Thutmose-IV.
4. Smith, Cathy Anne. n.d. 'Mutemwiya and the Divine Birth of Amenhotep III | World History.' www.worldhistory.us/ancient-history/ancient-egypt/mutemwiya-and-the-divine-birth-of-amenhotep-iii.php.
5. Tyldesley, Joyce A. 2005. *Nefertiti: Egypt's Sun Queen*. London; New York: Penguin. Page 46.
6. Tyldesley, Joyce A. 2005. *Nefertiti: Egypt's Sun Queen*. London; New York: Penguin. Page 46.
7. Schwarz-Bart, Simone, André Schwarz-Bart, and Unesco. 2001. *In Praise of Black Women*. Madison: The University of Wisconsin Press; Houston, Tex. Page 56

8. NatGeoUK. 2021. 'These Pharaohs' Private Letters Expose How Politics Worked 3,300 Years Ago.' National Geographic. January 8, 2021. www.nationalgeographic.co.uk/history-and-civilisation/2021/01/.
9. Knott, Elizabeth. 2019. 'The Amarna Letters.' Metmuseum.org. 2019. www.metmuseum.org/toah/hd/amlet/hd_amlet.htm.
10. 'Amenhotep III and Tiye Colossal Statue.' Egymonuments.gov.eg. www.egymonuments.gov.eg/en/collections/amenhotep-iii-and-tiye-colossal-statue-6/.
11. Cooney, Kara, and National Geographic Society (U.S. 2018. *When Women Ruled the World: Six Queens of Egypt*. Washington, D.C.: National Geographic. Page 176.
12. Cooney, Kara, and National Geographic Society (U.S. 2018. *When Women Ruled the World: Six Queens of Egypt*. Washington, D.C.: National Geographic. Page 176.
13. Dorman, P. F. 'Akhenaten.' Encyclopaedia Britannica, February 9, 2024. www.britannica.com/biography/Akhenaten.
14. Tyldesley, Joyce A. 2005. *Nefertiti: Egypt's Sun Queen*. London; New York: Penguin. Pages 94-95.
15. Tyldesley, J. 'Nefertiti.' Encyclopaedia Britannica, February 25, 2024. www.britannica.com/biography/Nefertiti.
16. DHWTY. 2016. 'Mythical Benben Stone: The Landing Site of Egyptian God Atum.' Ancient-Origins.net. Ancient Origins. August 25, 2016. www.ancient-origins.net/artifacts-other-artifacts/mythical-benben-stone-landing-site-egyptian-god-atum-006513.
17. Dodson, Aidan. 2020. *Nefertiti, Queen and Pharaoh of Egypt*. American University in Cairo Press. Page 10.
18. Communications, Office of Public Affairs &. n.d. 'Pharaoh's Unusual Feminine Appearance Suggests Two Gene Defects.' Medicine.yale.edu. www.medicine.yale.edu/news-article/pharaohs-unusual-feminine-appearance-suggests-two-gene-defects/.

19. Spence, Kate. 2011. 'BBC - History - Ancient History in Depth: Akhenaten and the Amarna Period.' Bbc.co.uk. 2011. www.bbc.co.uk/history/ancient/egyptians/akhenaten_01.shtml.
20. Britannica, T. Editors of Encyclopaedia. 'Amarna style.' Encyclopaedia Britannica, June 28, 2013. www.britannica.com/art/Amarna-style.
21. Dodson, Aidan. 2020. *Nefertiti, Queen and Pharaoh of Egypt*. American University in Cairo Press. Page 24.
22. Oakes, Lorna, and Lucia Gahlin. 2022. *The Illustrated Encyclopaedia of Ancient Egypt: An Illustrated Reference to the Myths, Religions, Pyramids and Temples of the Land of the Pharaohs*. Edited by Helena Sudell. Cambridgeshire: Anness Publishing Limited. Page 156-157.
23. Oakes, Lorna, and Lucia Gahlin. 2022. *The Illustrated Encyclopaedia of Ancient Egypt: An Illustrated Reference to the Myths, Religions, Pyramids and Temples of the Land of the Pharaohs*. Edited by Helena Sudell. Cambridgeshire: Anness Publishing Limited. Page 157.
24. Oakes, Lorna, and Lucia Gahlin. 2022. *The Illustrated Encyclopaedia of Ancient Egypt: An Illustrated Reference to the Myths, Religions, Pyramids and Temples of the Land of the Pharaohs*. Edited by Helena Sudell. Cambridgeshire: Anness Publishing Limited. Page 157.
25. Dodson, Aidan. 2020. *Nefertiti, Queen and Pharaoh of Egypt*. American University in Cairo Press. Page 44.
26. Mark, Joshua. 2017. 'Amarna Period of Egypt.' World History Encyclopaedia. August 3, 2017. www.worldhistory.org/Amarna_Period_of_Egypt/.
27. Dorman, Peter. 'Akhenaten - Religion of the Aton.' Encyclopaedia Britannica. www.britannica.com/biography/Akhenaten/Religion-of-the-Aton.

28. Stevens, Anna. Review of *Akhenaten, Nefertiti & Aten: From Many Gods to One*. American Research Center in Egypt. University of Cambridge & Monash University. www.arce.org/resource/akhenaten-nefertiti-aten-many-gods-one.
29. Oakes, Lorna, and Lucia Gahlin. 2022. *The Illustrated Encyclopaedia of Ancient Egypt: An Illustrated Reference to the Myths, Religions, Pyramids and Temples of the Land of the Pharaohs*. Edited by Helena Sudell. Cambridgeshire: Anness Publishing Limited. Page 157.
30. Tyldesley, Joyce A. 2005. *Nefertiti: Egypt's Sun Queen*. London; New York: Penguin. Page 76.
31. Oakes, Lorna, and Lucia Gahlin. 2022. *The Illustrated Encyclopaedia of Ancient Egypt: An Illustrated Reference to the Myths, Religions, Pyramids and Temples of the Land of the Pharaohs*. Edited by Helena Sudell. Cambridgeshire: Anness Publishing Limited. Page 301.
32. Smith, Cathy Anne. 2019. 'Akhenaten and Nefertiti's Children | World History.' September 20, 2019. www.worldhistory.us/ancient-history/ancient-egypt/akhenaten-and-nefertitis-children.php.
33. Cooney, Kara, and National Geographic Society (U.S. 2018. *When Women Ruled the World : Six Queens of Egypt*. Washington, D.C.: National Geographic. Pages 184-185.
34. Smith, Cathy Anne. 2019. 'Akhenaten and Nefertiti's Children | World History.' September 20, 2019. www.worldhistory.us/ancient-history/ancient-egypt/akhenaten-and-nefertitis-children.php.
35. Smith, Cathy Anne. 2019. 'Akhenaten and Nefertiti's Children | World History.' September 20, 2019. www.worldhistory.us/ancient-history/ancient-egypt/akhenaten-and-nefertitis-children.php.
36. Cooney, Kara, and National Geographic Society (U.S. 2018. *When Women Ruled the World: Six Queens of Egypt*. Washington, D.C.: National Geographic. Page 189.

37. Cooney, Kara, and National Geographic Society (U.S. 2018. *When Women Ruled the World: Six Queens of Egypt*. Washington, D.C.: National Geographic. Page 190.
38. Cooney, Kara, and National Geographic Society (U.S. 2018. *When Women Ruled the World: Six Queens of Egypt*. Washington, D.C.: National Geographic. Page 195.
39. Tyldesley, Joyce A. 2005. *Nefertiti: Egypt's Sun Queen*. London; New York: Penguin. Page 176.
40. Tyldesley, Joyce A. 2005. *Nefertiti: Egypt's Sun Queen*. London; New York: Penguin. Page 153.
41. Cooney, Kara, and National Geographic Society (U.S. 2018. *When Women Ruled the World: Six Queens of Egypt*. Washington, D.C.: National Geographic. Page 195.
42. Cooney, Kara, and National Geographic Society (U.S. 2018. *When Women Ruled the World: Six Queens of Egypt*. Washington, D.C.: National Geographic. Page 196.
43. Cooney, Kara, and National Geographic Society (U.S. 2018. *When Women Ruled the World: Six Queens of Egypt*. Washington, D.C.: National Geographic. Page 196.
44. Cooney, Kara, and National Geographic Society (U.S. 2018. *When Women Ruled the World: Six Queens of Egypt*. Washington, D.C.: National Geographic. Page 198.
45. Cooney, Kara, and National Geographic Society (U.S. 2018. *When Women Ruled the World: Six Queens of Egypt*. Washington, D.C.: National Geographic. Page 197.
46. Cooney, Kara, and National Geographic Society (U.S. 2018. *When Women Ruled the World: Six Queens of Egypt*. Washington, D.C.: National Geographic. Page 197.
47. Tyldesley, J. 'Nefertiti.' Encyclopaedia Britannica, February 25, 2024. www.britannica.com/biography/Nefertiti.
48. Brown, Nicholas. Review of *The KV55 Coffin*. American Research Centre in Egypt. Department of Near Eastern

Languages and Cultures, University of California, Los Angeles. The KV55 Coffin.

49. 'Ray Johnson on the Forensic Reconstruction of the "Younger Lady"| Institute for the Study of Ancient Cultures.' 2018. Isac. uchicago.edu. www.isac.uchicago.edu/article/ray-johnson-forensic-reconstruciton-younger-lady.
50. Mark, Joshua J. 2011. Review of *Tiye*. World History Encyclopaedia. July 18, 2011. www.worldhistory.org/tiye/.
51. 'Ray Johnson on the Forensic Reconstruction of the "Younger Lady" | Institute for the Study of Ancient Cultures.' 2018. Isac. uchicago.edu. www.isac.uchicago.edu/article/ray-johnson-forensic-reconstruciton-younger-lady.
52. 'Ray Johnson on the Forensic Reconstruction of the "Younger Lady"| Institute for the Study of Ancient Cultures.' 2018. Isac. uchicago.edu. www.isac.uchicago.edu/article/ray-johnson-forensic-reconstruciton-younger-lady.
53. Tyldesley, J. 'Nefertiti.' Encyclopaedia Britannica, February 25, 2024. www.britannica.com/biography/Nefertiti.
54. Tyldesley, Joyce A. 2005. *Nefertiti: Egypt's Sun Queen*. London; New York: Penguin. Page 195.
55. Editors, History com. 2019. 'Nefertiti.' HISTORY. June 7, 2019. www.history.com/topics/ancient-egypt/nefertiti.
56. Dodson, Aidan. 2020. *Nefertiti, Queen and Pharaoh of Egypt*. American University in Cairo Press. Page 124.
57. Editors, History com. 2019. 'Nefertiti.' HISTORY. June 7, 2019. www.history.com/topics/ancient-egypt/nefertiti.
58. Editors, History com. 2019. 'Nefertiti.' HISTORY. June 7, 2019. www.history.com/topics/ancient-egypt/nefertiti.
59. Dodson, Aidan. 2020. *Nefertiti, Queen and Pharaoh of Egypt*. American University in Cairo Press. Page 125.
60. Dodson, Aidan. 2020. *Nefertiti, Queen and Pharaoh of Egypt*. American University in Cairo Press. Page 127.

Chapter 4

1. Britannica, T. Editors of Encyclopaedia. 'Blue Nile River.' Encyclopaedia Britannica, March 9, 2024. www.britannica.com/place/Blue-Nile-River.
2. 'Blue Nile - New World Encyclopaedia.' www.newworldencyclopedia.org. www.newworldencyclopedia.org/entry/Blue_Nile.
3. Crummey, D. Edward, Marcus, Harold G. and Mehretu, Assefa. 'Ethiopia.' Encyclopaedia Britannica, March 9, 2024. www.britannica.com/place/Ethiopia.
4. Crummey, D. Edward, Marcus, . Harold G. and Mehretu, Assefa. 'Ethiopia.' Encyclopaedia Britannica, March 9, 2024. www.britannica.com/place/Ethiopia.
5. AnnaEverywhere. 2020. 'Ethiopian Food Guide: Best Ethiopian Dishes to Try.' Anna Everywhere. July 6, 2020. www.annaeverywhere.com/ethiopian-food-guide
6. Britannica, T. Editors of Encyclopaedia. 'Queen of Sheba.' Encyclopaedia Britannica, March 6, 2024. www.britannica.com/biography/Queen-of-Sheba.
7. Serjeant, R. Bertram, Ghul, Mahmud Ali, Ochsenwald, William L. and Beeston, Alfred Felix L. 'History of Arabia.' Encyclopaedia Britannica, April 30, 2020. www.britannica.com/topic/history-of-Arabia-31558.
8. Cartwright, Mark. 2019. 'Trade in the Ancient World.' World History Encyclopaedia. February 22, 2019. www.worldhistory.org/collection/39/trade-in-the-ancient-world/.
9. Ryckmans, J. 'Arabian religion.' Encyclopaedia Britannica, January 19, 2024. www.britannica.com/topic/Arabian-religion.
10. Britannica, T. Editors of Encyclopaedia. 'Queen of Sheba.' Encyclopaedia Britannica, March 6, 2024. www.britannica.com/biography/Queen-of-Sheba.

11. Mark, Joshua J. 2018. Review of *Kingdom of Saba*. World History Encyclopaedia. March 2, 2018. www.worldhistory.org/Kingdom_of_Saba/.
12. Mark, Joshua J. 2018. Review of *Kingdom of Saba*. World History Encyclopaedia. March 2, 2018. www.worldhistory.org/Kingdom_of_Saba/.
13. Mark, Joshua J. 2018. Review of *Kingdom of Saba*. World History Encyclopaedia. March 2, 2018. www.worldhistory.org/Kingdom_of_Saba/.
14. Britannica, T. Editors of Encyclopaedia. 'Maʾrib.' Encyclopaedia Britannica, September 13, 2023. www.britannica.com/place/Marib.
15. Mark, Joshua J. 2018. Review of *Kingdom of Saba*. World History Encyclopaedia. March 2, 2018. www.worldhistory.org/Kingdom_of_Saba/.
16. 'Temple of Awwam - AtlasIslamica.' 2021. May 24, 2021. www.atlasislamica.com/temple-of-awwam/.
17. Britannica, T. Editors of Encyclopaedia. 'Ea.' Encyclopaedia Britannica, March 1, 2024. www.britannica.com/topic/Ea.
18. *Life Application Study Bible*. 2019. 3rd ed. Vol. NIV. Carol Stream, Illinois: Tyndale House and Zondervan. (Orig. pub. 1988.). Pages 509-510.
19. Knox, John. 2017. 'Solomon.' World History Encyclopaedia. January 25, 2017. www.worldhistory.org/solomon/.
20. Knox, John. 2017. 'Solomon.' World History Encyclopaedia. January 25, 2017. www.worldhistory.org/solomon/.
21. *Life Application Study Bible*. 2019. 3rd ed. Vol. NIV. Carol Stream, Illinois: Tyndale House and Zondervan. (Orig. pub. 1988.). Page 511-512.
22. Mark, Joshua J. 2018. Review of *Queen of Sheba*. World History Encyclopaedia. March 26, 2018. www.worldhistory.org/Queen_of_Sheba/.

23. Wallis, A. 2020. *The Kebra Nagast*. Page 16.
24. Schwarz-Bart, Simone, André Schwarz-Bart, and Unesco. 2001. *In Praise of Black Women*. Madison: The University of Wisconsin Press; Houston, Tex. Page 78.
25. 2020. Metmuseum.org. 2020. www.metmuseum.org/art/collection/search/465954.
26. Schwarz-Bart, Simone, André Schwarz-Bart, and Unesco. 2001. *In Praise of Black Women*. Madison: The University of Wisconsin Press; Houston, Tex. Page 78.
27. Schwarz-Bart, Simone, André Schwarz-Bart, and Unesco. 2001. *In Praise of Black Women*. Madison: The University of Wisconsin Press; Houston, Tex. Page 79.
28. Wallis, A. 2020. *The Kebra Nagast*. Page 17.
29. Schwarz-Bart, Simone, André Schwarz-Bart, and Unesco. 2001. *In Praise of Black Women*. Madison: The University of Wisconsin Press; Houston, Tex. Page 80.
30. Wallis, A. 2020. *The Kebra Nagast*. Page 26.
31. 'History Channel Documentary - Ancient History - the Queen of Sheba.' 2017. www.youtube.com. Accessed March 10, 2024. www.youtube.com/watch?v=F9zW85DgfW4.
32. Schwarz-Bart, Simone, André Schwarz-Bart, and Unesco. 2001. *In Praise of Black Women*. Madison: The University of Wisconsin Press; Houston, Tex. Page 80.
33. Wallis, A. 2020. *The Kebra Nagast*. Page xliii.
34. Wallis, A. 2020. *The Kebra Nagast*. Page xlix.
35. Wallis, A. 2020. *The Kebra Nagast*. Page xli.
36. Wallis, A. 2020. *The Kebra Nagast*. Page xli-xlii.
37. Wallis, A. 2020. *The Kebra Nagast*. Page xlii.
38. Wallis, A. 2020. *The Kebra Nagast*. Page xlii.
39. Wallis, A. 2020. *The Kebra Nagast*. Page xlii.
40. Wallis, A. 2020. *The Kebra Nagast*. Page xlii-xliii.
41. Wallis, A. 2020. *The Kebra Nagast*. Page xliii.

42. Magazine, Smithsonian, and Max Kutner. October 20, 2018 'Unearthing America's Lawrence of Arabia, Wendell Phillips.' Smithsonian Magazine. www.smithsonianmag.com/smithsonian-institution/unearthing-americas-lawrence-arabia-wendell-phillips-180953059/.
43. Jerusalem, The Hebrew University of. n.d. 'Popular Archaeology - a Sabaean Inscription on a Large Clay Jar Deciphered and Discovered Less than 300 Meters from the Site of the Jerusalem Temple.' Popular Archaeology. www.popular-archaeology.com/article/a-sabaean-inscription-on-a-large-clay-jar-deciphered-and-discovered-less-than-300-meters-from-the-site-of-the-jerusalem-temple/.
44. 'History Channel Documentary - Ancient History - the Queen of Sheba.' 2017. www.youtube.com. Accessed March 10, 2024. www.youtube.com/watch?v=F9zW85DgfW4.
45. 'History Channel Documentary - Ancient History - the Queen of Sheba.' 2017. www.youtube.com. Accessed March 10, 2024. www.youtube.com/watch?v=F9zW85DgfW4.

Chapter 5

1. 'The History of Ancient Nubia | Institute for the Study of Ancient Cultures.' Isac.uchicago.edu. www.isac.uchicago.edu/museum-exhibits/history-ancient-nubiaOLD.
2. 'The History of Ancient Nubia | Institute for the Study of Ancient Cultures.' Isac.uchicago.edu. www.isac.uchicago.edu/museum-exhibits/history-ancient-nubiaOLD.
3. Mark, Joshua J. 2018. 'The Kingdom of Kush.' World History Encyclopaedia. February 26, 2018. www.worldhistory.org/Kush/.
4. Mark, Joshua J. 2018. 'The Kingdom of Kush.' World History Encyclopaedia. February 26, 2018. www.worldhistory.org/Kush/.

5. The British Museum, 'Ancient Nubia and the Kingdom of Kush, an introduction,' in *Smarthistory,* March 9, 2021, www.smarthistory.org/ancient-nubia-kingdom-kush-intro/.
6. The British Museum. 'Ancient Nubia and the Kingdom of Kush, an Introduction (Article).' Khan Academy. www.khanacademy.org/humanities/ancient-art-civilizations.
7. The British Museum, 'Ancient Nubia and the Kingdom of Kush, an introduction,' in *Smarthistory,* March 9, 2021, www.smarthistory.org/ancient-nubia-kingdom-kush-intro/.
8. The British Museum, 'Ancient Nubia and the Kingdom of Kush, an introduction,' in *Smarthistory,* March 9, 2021, www.smarthistory.org/ancient-nubia-kingdom-kush-intro/.
9. Cavazzi, Franco. 2021. 'Roman Military Tactics.' The Roman Empire. December 18, 2021. www.roman-empire.net/army/tactics/.
10. Hanson, Marilee. 2022. 'Roman Weapons - English History.' English History. June 13, 2022. www.englishhistory.net/romans/roman-weapons/.
11. Hanson, Marilee. 2022. 'Roman Weapons - English History.' English History. June 13, 2022. www.englishhistory.net/romans/roman-weapons/.
12. Cavazzi, Franco. 2021. 'Roman Military Tactics.' The Roman Empire. December 18, 2021. www.oman-empire.net/army/tactics/.
13. 'Nubian Archers | Institute for the Study of Ancient Cultures.' Isac.uchicago.edu. www.isac.uchicago.edu/museum-exhibits/nubia/nubian-archers.
14. Magak, Adhiambo Edith. 'The One-Eyed African Queen Who Defeated the Roman Empire.' www.narratively.com/p/the-one-eyed-african-queen-who-defeated-the-roman-empire.
15. The British Museum. 'Ancient Nubia and the Kingdom of Kush, an Introduction (Article).' Khan Academy. Accessed March 13, 2024. www.khanacademy.org/humanities/ancient-art-civilizations/egypt-art/x7e914f5b:kingdom-of-kush/a/ancient-nubia-and-the-kingdom-of-kush.

16. Britannica, T. Editors of Encyclopaedia. 'Piye.' Encyclopaedia Britannica, January 30, 2015. www.britannica.com/biography/Piye.
17. Mora, Kai. 2022. 'The Nubian Queen Who Fought Back Caesar's Army.' HISTORY. March 23, 2022. www.history.com/news/nubian-queen-amanirenas-roman-army.
18. Magak, Adhiambo Edith. 'The One-Eyed African Queen Who Defeated the Roman Empire.' www.narratively.com/p/the-one-eyed-african-queen-who-defeated-the-roman-empire.
19. Magak, Adhiambo Edith. 'The One-Eyed African Queen Who Defeated the Roman Empire.' www.narratively.com/p/the-one-eyed-african-queen-who-defeated-the-roman-empire.
20. Mora, Kai. 2022. 'The Nubian Queen Who Fought Back Caesar's Army.' HISTORY. March 23, 2022. www.history.com/news/nubian-queen-amanirenas-roman-army.
21. Magak, Adhiambo Edith. 'The One-Eyed African Queen Who Defeated the Roman Empire.' www.narratively.com/p/the-one-eyed-african-queen-who-defeated-the-roman-empire.
22. King, Arienne. 'Dodekaschoinos.' October 5, 2017. World History Encyclopaedia. www.worldhistory.org/Dodekaschoinos/.
23. Britannica, T. Editors of Encyclopaedia. 'Gaius Cornelius Gallus.' Encyclopaedia Britannica, March 5, 2024. www.britannica.com/biography/Gaius-Cornelius-Gallus.
24. Magak, Adhiambo Edith. 'The One-Eyed African Queen Who Defeated the Roman Empire.' www.narratively.com/p/the-one-eyed-african-queen-who-defeated-the-roman-empire.
25. Magak, Adhiambo Edith. 'The One-Eyed African Queen Who Defeated the Roman Empire.' www.narratively.com/p/the-one-eyed-african-queen-who-defeated-the-roman-empire.
26. Magak, Adhiambo Edith. 'The One-Eyed African Queen Who Defeated the Roman Empire.' www.narratively.com/p/the-one-eyed-african-queen-who-defeated-the-roman-empire.
27. 'Kom El-Dekka.' www.touregypt.net. Accessed March 13, 2024. www.touregypt.net/alkom.htm.

28. Mora, Kai. 2022. 'The Nubian Queen Who Fought Back Caesar's Army.' HISTORY. March 23, 2022. www.history.com/news/nubian-queen-amanirenas-roman-army.
29. Magak, Adhiambo Edith. 'The One-Eyed African Queen Who Defeated the Roman Empire.' www.narratively.com/p/the-one-eyed-african-queen-who-defeated-the-roman-empire.
30. Magak, Adhiambo Edith. 'The One-Eyed African Queen Who Defeated the Roman Empire.' www.narratively.com/p/the-one-eyed-african-queen-who-defeated-the-roman-empire.
31. Magak, Adhiambo Edith. 'The One-Eyed African Queen Who Defeated the Roman Empire.' www.narratively.com/p/the-one-eyed-african-queen-who-defeated-the-roman-empire.
32. Mora, Kai. 2022. 'The Nubian Queen Who Fought Back Caesar's Army.' HISTORY. March 23, 2022. www.history.com/news/nubian-queen-amanirenas-roman-army.
33. Magak, Adhiambo Edith. 'The One-Eyed African Queen Who Defeated the Roman Empire.' www.narratively.com/p/the-one-eyed-african-queen-who-defeated-the-roman-empire.
34. White, Shelby, and Leon Levy. 2018. 'Amun Sanctuary – Jebel Barkal (Sudan).' Harvard.edu. Program for Archaeological Publications. 2018. www.whitelevy.fas.harvard.edu/amun-sanctuary-%E2%80%93-jebel-barkal-sudan.
35. 'The Lion Temple.' Musawwarat. Accessed March 13, 2024. www.musawwarat.com/about-musawwarat/the-lion-temple/.
36. Mora, Kai. 2022. 'The Nubian Queen Who Fought Back Caesar's Army.' HISTORY. March 23, 2022. www.history.com/news/nubian-queen-amanirenas-roman-army.
37. Mora, Kai. 2022. 'The Nubian Queen Who Fought Back Caesar's Army.' HISTORY. March 23, 2022. www.history.com/news/nubian-queen-amanirenas-roman-army.
38. Mora, Kai. 2022. 'The Nubian Queen Who Fought Back Caesar's Army.' HISTORY. March 23, 2022. www.history.com/news/nubian-queen-amanirenas-roman-army.

39. Mora, Kai. 2022. 'The Nubian Queen Who Fought Back Caesar's Army.' HISTORY. March 23, 2022. www.history.com/news/nubian-queen-amanirenas-roman-army.
40. Koekoe, Jade. March 23, 2017. 'Object in Focus: The Meroe Head of Augustus – World History et Cetera. www.etc.worldhistory.org/photos/meroe-head-augustus/.
41. 'Stela | British Museum.' The British Museum. www.britishmuseum.org/collection/object/Y_EA1650.
42. Editors, History com. 2009. 'Nero.' HISTORY. November 9, 2009. www.history.com/topics/ancient-rome/nero.
43. Britannica, T. Editors of Encyclopaedia. 'Visigoth.' Encyclopaedia Britannica, February 20, 2024. www.britannica.com/topic/Visigoth.
44. Britannica, T. Editors of Encyclopaedia. 'Alaric.' Encyclopaedia Britannica, February 9, 2024. www.britannica.com/biography/Alaric.
45. Mark, Joshua. 2019. 'Western Roman Empire.' World History Encyclopaedia. September 27, 2019. www.worldhistory.org/Western_Roman_Empire/.
46. Mora, Kai. 2022. 'The Nubian Queen Who Fought Back Caesar's Army.' HISTORY. March 23, 2022. www.history.com/news/nubian-queen-amanirenas-roman-army.
47. Lasserre, F. 'Strabo.' Encyclopaedia Britannica, February 8, 2019. www.britannica.com/biography/Strabo.
48. Mora, Kai. 2022. 'The Nubian Queen Who Fought Back Caesar's Army.' HISTORY. March 23, 2022. www.history.com/news/nubian-queen-amanirenas-roman-army.
49. Mora, Kai. 2022. 'The Nubian Queen Who Fought Back Caesar's Army.' HISTORY. March 23, 2022. www.history.com/news/nubian-queen-amanirenas-roman-army.
50. Mora, Kai. 2022. 'The Nubian Queen Who Fought Back Caesar's Army.' HISTORY. March 23, 2022. www.history.com/news/nubian-queen-amanirenas-roman-army.

Chapter 6

1. Zaimeche, S., Sutton, Keith, Brown, L. Carl and Chanderli, Abdel Kader. 'Algeria.' Encyclopaedia Britannica, March 13, 2024. www.britannica.com/place/Algeria.
2. Zaimeche, S., Sutton, Keith, Brown, L. Carl and Chanderli, Abdel Kader. 'Algeria.' Encyclopaedia Britannica, March 13, 2024. www.britannica.com/place/Algeria.
3. Zaimeche, S., Sutton, Keith, Brown, L. Carl and Chanderli, Abdel Kader. 'Algeria.' Encyclopaedia Britannica, March 13, 2024. www.britannica.com/place/Algeria.
4. Zaimeche, S., Sutton, Keith, Brown, L. Carl and Chanderli, Abdel Kader. 'Algeria.' Encyclopaedia Britannica, March 13, 2024. www.britannica.com/place/Algeria.
5. Zaimeche, S., Sutton, Keith, Brown, L. Carl and Chanderli, Abdel Kader. 'Algeria.' Encyclopaedia Britannica, March 13, 2024. www.britannica.com/place/Algeria.
6. Zaimeche, S., Sutton, Keith, Brown, L. Carl and Chanderli, Abdel Kader. 'Algeria.' Encyclopaedia Britannica, March 13, 2024. www.britannica.com/place/Algeria.
7. Zaimeche, S., Sutton, Keith, Brown, L. Carl and Chanderli, Abdel Kader. 'Algeria.' Encyclopaedia Britannica, March 13, 2024. www.britannica.com/place/Algeria.
8. Zaimeche, S., Sutton, Keith, Brown, L. Carl and Chanderli, Abdel Kader. 'Algeria.' Encyclopaedia Britannica, March 13, 2024. www.britannica.com/place/Algeria.
9. Zaimeche, S., Sutton, Keith, Brown, L. Carl and Chanderli, Abdel Kader. 'Algeria.' Encyclopaedia Britannica, March 13, 2024. www.britannica.com/place/Algeria.
10. Zaimeche, S., Sutton, Keith, Brown, L. Carl and Chanderli, Abdel Kader. 'Algeria.' Encyclopaedia Britannica, March 13, 2024. www.britannica.com/place/Algeria.

11. Zaimeche, S., Sutton, Keith, Brown, L. Carl and Chanderli, Abdel Kader. 'Algeria.' Encyclopaedia Britannica, March 13, 2024. www.britannica.com/place/Algeria.
12. Zaimeche, S., Sutton, Keith, Brown, L. Carl and Chanderli, Abdel Kader. 'Algeria.' Encyclopaedia Britannica, March 13, 2024. www.britannica.com/place/Algeria.
13. Zaimeche, S., Sutton, Keith, Brown, L. Carl and Chanderli, Abdel Kader. 'Algeria.' Encyclopaedia Britannica, March 13, 2024. www.britannica.com/place/Algeria.
14. Room, and Hamilton Lugar. n.d. 'National African Language Resource Centre (NALRC).' www.nalrc.indiana.edu/doc/brochures/tamazight.pdf.
15. Zaimeche, S., Sutton, Keith, Brown, L. Carl and Chanderli, Abdel Kader. 'Algeria.' Encyclopaedia Britannica, March 13, 2024. www.britannica.com/place/Algeria.
16. Zaimeche, S., Sutton, Keith, Brown, L. Carl and Chanderli, Abdel Kader. 'Algeria.' Encyclopaedia Britannica, March 13, 2024. www.britannica.com/place/Algeria.
17. Schimmel, A., Mahdi, Muhsin S., and Rahman, Fazlur. 'Islam.' Encyclopaedia Britannica, March 15, 2024. www.britannica.com/topic/Islam.
18. Schimmel, A., Mahdi, Muhsin S., and Rahman, Fazlur. 'Islam.' Encyclopaedia Britannica, March 15, 2024. www.britannica.com/topic/Islam.
19. Schimmel, A., Mahdi, Muhsin S., and Rahman, Fazlur. 'Islam.' Encyclopaedia Britannica, March 15, 2024. www.britannica.com/topic/Islam.
20. Schimmel, A., Mahdi, Muhsin S., and Rahman, Fazlur. 'Islam.' Encyclopaedia Britannica, March 15, 2024. www.britannica.com/topic/Islam.
21. Schimmel, A., Mahdi, Muhsin S., and Rahman, Fazlur. 'Islam.' Encyclopaedia Britannica, March 15, 2024. www.britannica.com/topic/Islam.

22. Schimmel, A., Mahdi, Muhsin S., and Rahman, Fazlur. 'Islam.' Encyclopaedia Britannica, March 15, 2024. www.britannica.com/topic/Islam.
23. Schimmel, A., Mahdi, Muhsin S., and Rahman, Fazlur. 'Islam.' Encyclopaedia Britannica, March 15, 2024. www.britannica.com/topic/Islam.
24. Schimmel, A., Mahdi, Muhsin S., and Rahman, Fazlur. 'Islam.' Encyclopaedia Britannica, March 15, 2024. www.britannica.com/topic/Islam.
25. Schimmel, A., Mahdi, Muhsin S., and Rahman, Fazlur. 'Islam.' Encyclopaedia Britannica, March 15, 2024. www.britannica.com/topic/Islam.
26. Schimmel, A., Mahdi, Muhsin S., and Rahman, Fazlur. 'Islam.' Encyclopaedia Britannica, March 15, 2024. www.britannica.com/topic/Islam.
27. Schimmel, A., Mahdi, Muhsin S., and Rahman, Fazlur. 'Islam.' Encyclopaedia Britannica, March 15, 2024. www.britannica.com/topic/Islam.
28. Schimmel, A., Mahdi, Muhsin S., and Rahman, Fazlur. 'Islam.' Encyclopaedia Britannica, March 15, 2024. www.britannica.com/topic/Islam.
29. Schimmel, A., Mahdi, Muhsin S., and Rahman, Fazlur. 'Islam.' Encyclopaedia Britannica, March 15, 2024. www.britannica.com/topic/Islam.
30. Schimmel, A., Mahdi, Muhsin S., and Rahman, Fazlur. 'Islam.' Encyclopaedia Britannica, March 15, 2024. www.britannica.com/topic/Islam.
31. Schimmel, A., Mahdi, Muhsin S., and Rahman, Fazlur. 'Islam.' Encyclopaedia Britannica, March 15, 2024. www.britannica.com/topic/Islam.
32. Schimmel, A., Mahdi, Muhsin S., and Rahman, Fazlur. 'Islam.' Encyclopaedia Britannica, March 15, 2024. www.britannica.com/topic/Islam.

33. Salo Wittmayer Baron, and Haim Zalman Dimitrovsky. 2018. 'Judaism | History, Beliefs, & Facts.' In *Encyclopedialike Britannica*. www.britannica.com/topic/Judaism.
34. History.com Editors. 2021. 'Israel.' HISTORY. May 11, 2021. www.history.com/topics/middle-east/history-of-israel.
35. Britannica, T. Editors of Encyclopaedia. 'Torah.' Encyclopaedia Britannica, March 15, 2024. www.britannica.com/topic/Torah.
36. Britannica, T. Editors of Encyclopaedia. 'Torah.' Encyclopaedia Britannica, March 15, 2024. www.britannica.com/topic/Torah.
37. Dimitrovsky, H. Zalman and Silberman, Lou Hackett. 'Talmud and Midrash.' Encyclopaedia Britannica, March 10, 2024. www.britannica.com/topic/Talmud.
38. Mark, Joshua J. 2018. Review of *Kahina*. World History Encyclopaedia. March 16, 2018. www.worldhistory.org/Kahina/.
39. Mark, Joshua J. 2018. Review of *Kahina*. World History Encyclopaedia. March 16, 2018. www.worldhistory.org/Kahina/.
40. Mark, Joshua J. 2018. Review of *Kahina*. World History Encyclopaedia. March 16, 2018. www.worldhistory.org/Kahina/.
41. Room, and Hamilton Lugar. 'National African Language Resource Centre (NALRC).' www.nalrc.indiana.edu/doc/brochures/tamazight.pdf.
42. Team, Editorial. 2018. 'Dihya, Queen of the Berbers | African History | ThinkAfrica.' Think Africa. November 14, 2018. www.thinkafrica.net/dihya-kahina/.
43. Mark, Joshua J. 2018. Review of *Kahina*. World History Encyclopaedia. March 16, 2018. www.worldhistory.org/Kahina/.
44. Mark, Joshua J. 2018. Review of *Kahina*. World History Encyclopaedia. March 16, 2018. www.worldhistory.org/Kahina/.
45. Mark, Joshua J. 2018. Review of *Kahina*. World History Encyclopaedia. March 16, 2018. www.worldhistory.org/Kahina/.
46. Flame (Leah), Working the. 2022. '14 Types of African Swords [Ancient to Modern].' Working the Flame. August 14, 2022. www.workingtheflame.com/african-swords/.

47. Flame (Leah), Working the. 2022. '14 Types of African Swords [Ancient to Modern].' Working the Flame. August 14, 2022. www.workingtheflame.com/african-swords/.
48. Flame (Leah), Working the. 2022. '14 Types of African Swords [Ancient to Modern].' Working the Flame. August 14, 2022. www.workingtheflame.com/african-swords/.
49. Flame (Leah), Working the. 2022. '14 Types of African Swords [Ancient to Modern].' Working the Flame. August 14, 2022. www.workingtheflame.com/african-swords/.
50. Flame (Leah), Working the. 2022. '14 Types of African Swords [Ancient to Modern].' Working the Flame. August 14, 2022. www.workingtheflame.com/african-swords/.
51. Flame (Leah), Working the. 2022. '14 Types of African Swords [Ancient to Modern].' Working the Flame. August 14, 2022. www.workingtheflame.com/african-swords/.
52. Flame (Leah), Working the. 2022. '14 Types of African Swords [Ancient to Modern].' Working the Flame. August 14, 2022. www.workingtheflame.com/african-swords/.
53. Vaughan, D. 'scorched-earth policy.' Encyclopaedia Britannica, March 8, 2024. www.britannica.com/topic/scorched-earth-policy.
54. Vaughan, D. 'scorched-earth policy.' Encyclopaedia Britannica, March 8, 2024. www.britannica.com/topic/scorched-earth-policy.
55. Vaughan, D. 'scorched-earth policy.' Encyclopaedia Britannica, March 8, 2024. www.britannica.com/topic/scorched-earth-policy.
56. Vaughan, D. 'scorched-earth policy.' Encyclopaedia Britannica, March 8, 2024. www.britannica.com/topic/scorched-earth-policy.
57. Mark, Joshua J. 2018. Review of *Kahina*. World History Encyclopaedia. March 16, 2018. www.worldhistory.org/Kahina/.
58. Afsaruddin, A. 'Caliphate.' Encyclopaedia Britannica, February 25, 2024. www.britannica.com/place/Caliphate.
59. Team, Editorial. 2018. 'Dihya, Queen of the Berbers | African History | ThinkAfrica.' Think Africa. November 14, 2018. www.thinkafrica.net/dihya-kahina/.

60. Mark, Joshua J. 2018. Review of *Kahina*. World History Encyclopaedia. March 16, 2018. www.worldhistory.org/Kahina/.
61. Mark, Joshua J. 2018. Review of *Kahina*. World History Encyclopaedia. March 16, 2018. www.worldhistory.org/Kahina/.
62. Britannica, T. Editors of Encyclopaedia. 'Aghlabid dynasty.' Encyclopaedia Britannica, October 17, 2017. www.britannica.com/topic/Aghlabid-dynasty.
63. Medievalists.net. 2019. 'The Berber Queen Who Defied the Caliphate: Al-Kahina and the Islamic Conquest of North Africa.' Medievalists.net. December 3, 2019. www.medievalists.net/2019/12/berber-queen-al-kahina/.
64. Medievalists.net. 2019. 'The Berber Queen Who Defied the Caliphate: Al-Kahina and the Islamic Conquest of North Africa.' Medievalists.net. December 3, 2019. www.medievalists.net/2019/12/berber-queen-al-kahina/.
65. Medievalists.net. 2019. 'The Berber Queen Who Defied the Caliphate: Al-Kahina and the Islamic Conquest of North Africa.' Medievalists.net. December 3, 2019. www.medievalists.net/2019/12/berber-queen-al-kahina/.
66. Mark, Joshua J. 2018. Review of *Kahina*. World History Encyclopaedia. March 16, 2018. www.worldhistory.org/Kahina/.
67. Mark, Joshua J. 2018. Review of *Kahina*. World History Encyclopaedia. March 16, 2018. www.worldhistory.org/Kahina/.
68. 'Queen Kahina's Well, Bir El-Kahen, Algeria | Archive | Diarna.org.' Archive.diarna.org. Accessed March 17, 2024. www.archive.diarna.org/site/detail/public/280/.
69. Medievalists.net. 2019. 'The Berber Queen Who Defied the Caliphate: Al-Kahina and the Islamic Conquest of North Africa.' Medievalists.net. December 3, 2019. www.medievalists.net/2019/12/berber-queen-al-kahina/.
70. Medievalists.net. 2019. 'The Berber Queen Who Defied the Caliphate: Al-Kahina and the Islamic Conquest of North

Africa.' Medievalists.net. December 3, 2019. www.medievalists.net/2019/12/berber-queen-al-kahina/.

71. Medievalists.net. 2019. 'The Berber Queen Who Defied the Caliphate: Al-Kahina and the Islamic Conquest of North Africa.' Medievalists.net. December 3, 2019. www.medievalists.net/2019/12/berber-queen-al-kahina/.
72. Medievalists.net. 2019. 'The Berber Queen Who Defied the Caliphate: Al-Kahina and the Islamic Conquest of North Africa.' Medievalists.net. December 3, 2019. www.medievalists.net/2019/12/berber-queen-al-kahina/.
73. Mark, Joshua J. 2018. Review of *Kahina.* World History Encyclopaedia. March 16, 2018. www.worldhistory.org/Kahina/.
74. Ushi. 2018. 'Queen of the Desert: The Amazing Story of "Jewish Khaleesi."' Museum of the Jewish People. October 14, 2018. www.anumuseum.org.il/blog/queen-desert-amazing-story-jewish-khaleesi/.
75. Ushi. 2018. 'Queen of the Desert: The Amazing Story of "Jewish Khaleesi."' Museum of the Jewish People. October 14, 2018. www.anumuseum.org.il/blog/queen-desert-amazing-story-jewish-khaleesi/.
76. Mark, Joshua J. 2018. Review of *Kahina.* World History Encyclopaedia. March 16, 2018. www.worldhistory.org/Kahina/.
77. 'Queen Kahina's Well, Bir El-Kahen, Algeria | Archive | Diarna.org.' Archive.diarna.org. www.archive.diarna.org/site/detail/public/280/.
78. Ushi. 2018. 'Queen of the Desert: The Amazing Story of "Jewish Khaleesi."' Museum of the Jewish People. October 14, 2018. www.anumuseum.org.il/blog/queen-desert-amazing-story-jewish-khaleesi/.
79. Mark, Joshua J. 2018. Review of *Kahina.* World History Encyclopaedia. March 16, 2018. www.worldhistory.org/Kahina/.
80. Mark, Joshua J. 2018. Review of *Kahina.* World History Encyclopaedia. March 16, 2018. www.worldhistory.org/Kahina/.

81. Mark, Joshua J. 2018. Review of *Kahina*. World History Encyclopaedia. March 16, 2018. www.worldhistory.org/Kahina/.
82. 'Queen Kahina's Well, Bir El-Kahen, Algeria | Archive | Diarna.org.' Archive.diarna.org. www.archive.diarna.org/site/detail/public/280/.
83. Mark, Joshua J. 2018. Review of *Kahina*. World History Encyclopaedia. March 16, 2018. www.worldhistory.org/Kahina/.
84. Mark, Joshua J. 2018. Review of *Kahina*. World History Encyclopaedia. March 16, 2018. www.worldhistory.org/Kahina/.

Chapter 7

1. Ajayi, J.F. Ade, Udo, Reuben Kenrick, Kirk-Greene, Anthony Hamilton Millard and Falola, Toyin O. 'Nigeria.' Encyclopaedia Britannica, March 18, 2024. www.britannica.com/place/Nigeria.
2. Ajayi, J.F. Ade, Udo, Reuben Kenrick, Kirk-Greene, Anthony Hamilton Millard and Falola, Toyin O. 'Nigeria.' Encyclopaedia Britannica, March 18, 2024. www.britannica.com/place/Nigeria.
3. Ajayi, J.F. Ade, Udo, Reuben Kenrick, Kirk-Greene, Anthony Hamilton Millard and Falola, Toyin O. 'Nigeria.' Encyclopaedia Britannica, March 18, 2024. www.britannica.com/place/Nigeria.
4. Ajayi, J.F. Ade, Udo, Reuben Kenrick, Kirk-Greene, Anthony Hamilton Millard and Falola, Toyin O. 'Nigeria.' Encyclopaedia Britannica, March 18, 2024. www.britannica.com/place/Nigeria.
5. Ajayi, J.F. Ade, Udo, Reuben Kenrick, Kirk-Greene, Anthony Hamilton Millard and Falola, Toyin O. 'Nigeria.' Encyclopaedia Britannica, March 18, 2024. www.britannica.com/place/Nigeria.
6. Ajayi, J.F. Ade, Udo, Reuben Kenrick, Kirk-Greene, Anthony Hamilton Millard and Falola, Toyin O. 'Nigeria.' Encyclopaedia Britannica, March 18, 2024. www.britannica.com/place/Nigeria.
7. Ajayi, J.F. Ade, Udo, Reuben Kenrick, Kirk-Greene, Anthony Hamilton Millard and Falola, Toyin O. 'Nigeria.' Encyclopaedia Britannica, March 18, 2024. www.britannica.com/place/Nigeria.

8. Ajayi, J.F. Ade, Udo, Reuben Kenrick, Kirk-Greene, Anthony Hamilton Millard and Falola, Toyin O. 'Nigeria.' Encyclopaedia Britannica, March 18, 2024. www.britannica.com/place/Nigeria.
9. Ajayi, J.F. Ade, Udo, Reuben Kenrick, Kirk-Greene, Anthony Hamilton Millard and Falola, Toyin O. 'Nigeria.' Encyclopaedia Britannica, March 18, 2024. www.britannica.com/place/Nigeria.
10. Ajayi, J.F. Ade, Udo, Reuben Kenrick, Kirk-Greene, Anthony Hamilton Millard and Falola, Toyin O. 'Nigeria.' Encyclopaedia Britannica, March 18, 2024. www.britannica.com/place/Nigeria.
11. Ajayi, J.F. Ade, Udo, Reuben Kenrick, Kirk-Greene, Anthony Hamilton Millard and Falola, Toyin O. 'Nigeria.' Encyclopaedia Britannica, March 18, 2024. www.britannica.com/place/Nigeria.
12. Ajayi, J.F. Ade, Udo, Reuben Kenrick, Kirk-Greene, Anthony Hamilton Millard and Falola, Toyin O. 'Nigeria.' Encyclopaedia Britannica, March 18, 2024. www.britannica.com/place/Nigeria.
13. Ajayi, J.F. Ade, Udo, Reuben Kenrick, Kirk-Greene, Anthony Hamilton Millard and Falola, Toyin O. 'Nigeria.' Encyclopaedia Britannica, March 18, 2024. www.britannica.com/place/Nigeria.
14. Ajayi, J.F. Ade, Udo, Reuben Kenrick, Kirk-Greene, Anthony Hamilton Millard and Falola, Toyin O. 'Nigeria.' Encyclopaedia Britannica, March 18, 2024. www.britannica.com/place/Nigeria.
15. Ajayi, J.F. Ade, Udo, Reuben Kenrick, Kirk-Greene, Anthony Hamilton Millard and Falola, Toyin O. 'Nigeria.' Encyclopaedia Britannica, March 18, 2024. www.britannica.com/place/Nigeria.
16. Ajayi, J.F. Ade, Udo, Reuben Kenrick, Kirk-Greene, Anthony Hamilton Millard and Falola, Toyin O. 'Nigeria.' Encyclopaedia Britannica, March 18, 2024. www.britannica.com/place/Nigeria.
17. Ajayi, J.F. Ade, Udo, Reuben Kenrick, Kirk-Greene, Anthony Hamilton Millard and Falola, Toyin O. 'Nigeria.' Encyclopaedia Britannica, March 18, 2024. www.britannica.com/place/Nigeria.
18. Ajayi, J.F. Ade, Udo, Reuben Kenrick, Kirk-Greene, Anthony Hamilton Millard and Falola, Toyin O. 'Nigeria.' Encyclopaedia Britannica, March 18, 2024. www.britannica.com/place/Nigeria.

19. May 24, Lauren DavidUpdated. 'Baobab Fruit: 10 Things Nutritionists Need You to Know.' The Healthy. May 24, 2021. www.thehealthy.com/nutrition/baobab-fruit/.
20. Britannica, T. Editors of Encyclopaedia. 'Tamarind.' Encyclopaedia Britannica, February 2, 2024. www.britannica.com/plant/tamarind.
21. Heuzé, V., Thiollet, H., Tran, G., Edouard, N., Lebas, F., 'African Locust Bean (Parkia Biglobosa & Parkia Filicoidea) | Feedipedia.' March 21, 2019. www.feedipedia.org/node/268.
22. Britannica, T. Editors of Encyclopaedia. 'doum nut.' Encyclopaedia Britannica, March 6, 2012. www.britannica.com/topic/doum-nut.
23. Ajayi, J.F. Ade, Udo, Reuben Kenrick, Kirk-Greene, Anthony Hamilton Millard and Falola, Toyin O. 'Nigeria.' Encyclopaedia Britannica, March 18, 2024. www.britannica.com/place/Nigeria.
24. Ajayi, J.F. Ade, Udo, Reuben Kenrick, Kirk-Greene, Anthony Hamilton Millard and Falola, Toyin O. 'Nigeria.' Encyclopaedia Britannica, March 18, 2024. www.britannica.com/place/Nigeria.
25. Ajayi, J.F. Ade, Udo, Reuben Kenrick, Kirk-Greene, Anthony Hamilton Millard and Falola, Toyin O. 'Nigeria.' Encyclopaedia Britannica, March 18, 2024. www.britannica.com/place/Nigeria.
26. Ajayi, J.F. Ade, Udo, Reuben Kenrick, Kirk-Greene, Anthony Hamilton Millard and Falola, Toyin O. 'Nigeria.' Encyclopaedia Britannica, March 18, 2024. www.britannica.com/place/Nigeria.
27. Ajayi, J.F. Ade, Udo, Reuben Kenrick, Kirk-Greene, Anthony Hamilton Millard and Falola, Toyin O. 'Nigeria.' Encyclopaedia Britannica, March 18, 2024. www.britannica.com/place/Nigeria.
28. Britannica, T. Editors of Encyclopaedia. 'Hausa.' Encyclopaedia Britannica, February 22, 2024. www.britannica.com/topic/Hausa.
29. Britannica, T. Editors of Encyclopaedia. 'Yoruba.' Encyclopaedia Britannica, January 23, 2024. www.britannica.com/topic/Yoruba.
30. Britannica, T. Editors of Encyclopaedia. 'Igbo.' Encyclopaedia Britannica, December 27, 2023. www.britannica.com/topic/Igbo.

31. Britannica, T. Editors of Encyclopaedia. 'Igbo.' Encyclopaedia Britannica, December 27, 2023. www.britannica.com/topic/Igbo.
32. Ajayi, J.F. Ade, Udo, Reuben Kenrick, Kirk-Greene, Anthony Hamilton Millard and Falola, Toyin O. 'Nigeria.' Encyclopaedia Britannica, March 18, 2024. www.britannica.com/place/Nigeria.
33. Britannica, T. Editors of Encyclopaedia. 'Zaria.' Encyclopaedia Britannica, July 20, 1998. www.britannica.com/place/Zaria-historical-kingdom-and-province-Nigeria.
34. Britannica, T. Editors of Encyclopaedia. 'Zaria.' Encyclopaedia Britannica, July 20, 1998. www.britannica.com/place/Zaria-historical-kingdom-and-province-Nigeria.
35. Britannica, T. Editors of Encyclopaedia. 'Zaria.' Encyclopaedia Britannica, July 20, 1998. www.britannica.com/place/Zaria-historical-kingdom-and-province-Nigeria.
36. Britannica, T. Editors of Encyclopaedia. 'Zaria.' Encyclopaedia Britannica, July 20, 1998. www.britannica.com/place/Zaria-historical-kingdom-and-province-Nigeria.
37. Britannica, T. Editors of Encyclopaedia. 'Zaria.' Encyclopaedia Britannica, July 20, 1998. www.britannica.com/place/Zaria-historical-kingdom-and-province-Nigeria.
38. Britannica, T. Editors of Encyclopaedia. 'Zaria.' Encyclopaedia Britannica, July 20, 1998. www.britannica.com/place/Zaria-historical-kingdom-and-province-Nigeria.
39. Britannica, T. Editors of Encyclopaedia. 'Hausa states.' Encyclopaedia Britannica, May 31, 2023. www.britannica.com/place/Hausa-states.
40. Britannica, T. Editors of Encyclopaedia. 'Nupe.' Encyclopaedia Britannica, September 16, 2015. www.britannica.com/topic/Nupe.
41. Britannica, T. Editors of Encyclopaedia. 'Jukun.' Encyclopaedia Britannica, July 20, 1998. www.britannica.com/topic/Jukun.
42. Britannica, T. Editors of Encyclopaedia. 'Zaria.' Encyclopaedia Britannica, July 20, 1998. www.britannica.com/place/Zaria-historical-kingdom-and-province-Nigeria.

43. '100 Hausa Proverbs (Karin Magana Tsantsa) - Northpad Nigeria.' 2022. Northpad.ng. March 24, 2022. www.northpad.ng/karin-magana-tsan-tsa/.
44. Merrick, Captain G. 2019. *Hausa Proverbs*. Wentworth Press.
45. Merrick, Captain G. 2019. *Hausa Proverbs*. Wentworth Press.
46. 'Amina of Zaria.' Muslim Heritage. Accessed March 21, 2024. www.muslimheritage.com/people/scholars/amina-of-zaria/.
47. *BBC News*. 'The Warrior Queen Who Led Men into Battle.' Accessed October 17, 2023. www.bbc.com/news/av/world-africa-44888718.
48. B. A., Mundelein College, and Meadville/Lombard Theological School M. Div. 2019. 'Amina - Learn about an African Warrior Queen in What Is Today Nigeria.' ThoughtCo. June 3, 2019. www.thoughtco.com/amina-queen-of-zazzua-3529742.
49. 'Amina of Zaria.' Muslim Heritage. www.muslimheritage.com/people/scholars/amina-of-zaria/.
50. Schwarz-Bart, Simone, André Schwarz-Bart, and Unesco. 2001. *In Praise of Black Women*. Madison: The University of Wisconsin Press; Houston, Tex. Page 152.
51. Schwarz-Bart, Simone, André Schwarz-Bart, and Unesco. 2001. *In Praise of Black Women*. Madison: The University of Wisconsin Press; Houston, Tex. Page 154.
52. Schwarz-Bart, Simone, André Schwarz-Bart, and Unesco. 2001. *In Praise of Black Women*. Madison: The University of Wisconsin Press; Houston, Tex. Page 158.
53. 'Who Is Queen Amina, the Warrior Queen of Zaria – Leading Ladies Africa.' August 31, 2023. www.leadingladiesafrica.org/who-is-queen-amina-the-warrior-queen-of-zaria/.
54. 'Amina of Zaria | Encyclopedia.com.' www.encyclopedia.com/history/encyclopedias-almanacs-transcripts-and-maps/amina-zaria.
55. 'Amina of Zaria | Encyclopedia.com.' www.encyclopedia.com/history/encyclopedias-almanacs-transcripts-and-maps/amina-zaria.

56. Britannica, T. Editors of Encyclopaedia. 'Zaria.' Encyclopaedia Britannica, July 20, 1998. www.britannica.com/place/Zaria-historical-kingdom-and-province-Nigeria.
57. Britannica, T. Editors of Encyclopaedia. 'Zaria.' Encyclopaedia Britannica, July 20, 1998. www.britannica.com/place/Zaria-historical-kingdom-and-province-Nigeria.
58. Britannica, T. Editors of Encyclopaedia. 'Zaria.' Encyclopaedia Britannica, July 20, 1998. www.britannica.com/place/Zaria-historical-kingdom-and-province-Nigeria.
59. Britannica, T. Editors of Encyclopaedia. 'Zaria.' Encyclopaedia Britannica, July 20, 1998. www.britannica.com/place/Zaria-historical-kingdom-and-province-Nigeria.
60. Britannica, T. Editors of Encyclopaedia. 'Zaria.' Encyclopaedia Britannica, July 20, 1998. www.britannica.com/place/Zaria-historical-kingdom-and-province-Nigeria.

Chapter 8

1. Clarence-Smith, W. Gervase and Thornton, John Kelly. 'Angola.' Encyclopaedia Britannica, March 17, 2024. www.britannica.com/place/Angola.
2. Clarence-Smith, W. Gervase and Thornton, John Kelly. 'Angola.' Encyclopaedia Britannica, March 17, 2024. www.britannica.com/place/Angola.
3. Clarence-Smith, W. Gervase and Thornton, John Kelly. 'Angola.' Encyclopaedia Britannica, March 17, 2024. www.britannica.com/place/Angola.
4. Clarence-Smith, W. Gervase and Thornton, John Kelly. 'Angola.' Encyclopaedia Britannica, March 17, 2024. www.britannica.com/place/Angola.
5. Clarence-Smith, W. Gervase and Thornton, John Kelly. 'Angola.' Encyclopaedia Britannica, March 17, 2024. www.britannica.com/place/Angola.

6. Clarence-Smith, W. Gervase and Thornton, John Kelly. 'Angola.' Encyclopaedia Britannica, March 17, 2024. www.britannica.com/place/Angola.
7. Clarence-Smith, W. Gervase and Thornton, John Kelly. 'Angola.' Encyclopaedia Britannica, March 17, 2024. www.britannica.com/place/Angola.
8. Clarence-Smith, W. Gervase and Thornton, John Kelly. 'Angola.' Encyclopaedia Britannica, March 17, 2024. www.britannica.com/place/Angola.
9. Clarence-Smith, W. Gervase and Thornton, John Kelly. 'Angola.' Encyclopaedia Britannica, March 17, 2024. www.britannica.com/place/Angola.
10. Clarence-Smith, W. Gervase and Thornton, John Kelly. 'Angola.' Encyclopaedia Britannica, March 17, 2024. www.britannica.com/place/Angola.
11. Cartwright, Mark. 2021. 'Portuguese Angola.' World History Encyclopaedia. July 12, 2021. www.worldhistory.org/Portuguese_Angola/.
12. Cartwright, Mark. 2021. 'Portuguese Angola.' World History Encyclopaedia. July 12, 2021. www.worldhistory.org/Portuguese_Angola/.
13. Cartwright, Mark. 2021. 'Portuguese Angola.' World History Encyclopaedia. July 12, 2021. www.worldhistory.org/Portuguese_Angola/.
14. Britannica, T. Editors of Encyclopaedia. 'Jesuit.' Encyclopaedia Britannica, March 13, 2024. www.britannica.com/topic/Jesuits.
15. Britannica, T. Editors of Encyclopaedia. 'Jesuit.' Encyclopaedia Britannica, March 13, 2024. www.britannica.com/topic/Jesuits.
16. Cartwright, Mark. 2022. 'Weapons of the Conquistadors.' World History Encyclopaedia. July 20, 2022. www.worldhistory.org/article/2042/weapons-of-the-conquistadors/.
17. Cartwright, Mark. 2022. 'Weapons of the Conquistadors.' World History Encyclopaedia. July 20, 2022. www.worldhistory.org/article/2042/weapons-of-the-conquistadors/.

18. Cartwright, Mark. 2022. 'Weapons of the Conquistadors.' World History Encyclopaedia. July 20, 2022. www.worldhistory.org/article/2042/weapons-of-the-conquistadors/.
19. Heywood, Linda M. 2019. *Njinga of Angola: Africa's Warrior Queen*. Cambridge, Massachusetts: Harvard University Press. Page 27.
20. Harris, John. 2023. '9 Facts about the Transatlantic Slave Trade.' HISTORY. May 2, 2023. www.history.com/news/transatlantic-slave-trade-facts.
21. Harris, John. 2023. '9 Facts about the Transatlantic Slave Trade.' HISTORY. May 2, 2023. www.history.com/news/transatlantic-slave-trade-facts.
22. Harris, John. 2023. '9 Facts about the Transatlantic Slave Trade.' HISTORY. May 2, 2023. www.history.com/news/transatlantic-slave-trade-facts.
23. Lewis, T. 'transatlantic slave trade.' Encyclopaedia Britannica, February 29, 2024. www.britannica.com/topic/transatlantic-slave-trade.
24. Harris, John. 2023. '9 Facts about the Transatlantic Slave Trade.' HISTORY. May 2, 2023. www.history.com/news/transatlantic-slave-trade-facts.
25. Harris, John. 2023. '9 Facts about the Transatlantic Slave Trade.' HISTORY. May 2, 2023. www.history.com/news/transatlantic-slave-trade-facts.
26. Harris, John. 2023. '9 Facts about the Transatlantic Slave Trade.' HISTORY. May 2, 2023. www.history.com/news/transatlantic-slave-trade-facts.
27. Harris, John. 2023. '9 Facts about the Transatlantic Slave Trade.' HISTORY. May 2, 2023. www.history.com/news/transatlantic-slave-trade-facts.
28. Magazine, Smithsonian, and Smithsonian magazine. 2016. 'The Powerful Objects from the Collections of the Smithsonian's Newest Museum.' Smithsonian Magazine. September 2016.

www.smithsonianmag.com/smithsonian-institution/powerful-objects-collections-smithsonian-museum-180960126/.

29. Jaffer, Aaron. 2017. 'Dying on Their Own Terms: Suicides Aboard Slave Ships.' www.rmg.co.uk. Royal Museums Greenwich. August 16, 2017. www.rmg.co.uk/stories/blog/curatorial/dying-on-their-own-terms-suicides-aboard-slave-ships.
30. Cleveland Clinic. 2022. 'Dysentery: Causes, Symptoms, Diagnosis & Treatment.' Cleveland Clinic. August 15, 2022. www.my.clevelandclinic.org/health/diseases/23567-dysentery.
31. History.com Editors. 2019. 'Congress Abolishes the African Slave Trade.' HISTORY. March 7, 2019. www.history.com/this-day-in-history/congress-abolishes-the-african-slave-trade.
32. Jordan, Jonathan W, and Emily Anne Jordan. 2020. *The War Queens: Extraordinary Women Who Ruled the Battlefield.* New York, Ny: Diversion Books. Page 170.
33. Jordan, Jonathan W, and Emily Anne Jordan. 2020. *The War Queens: Extraordinary Women Who Ruled the Battlefield.* New York, Ny: Diversion Books. Page 170.
34. Heywood, Linda M. 2019. *Njinga of Angola: Africa's Warrior Queen.* Cambridge, Massachusetts: Harvard University Press. Page 35
35. Heywood, Linda M. 2019. *Njinga of Angola: Africa's Warrior Queen.* Cambridge, Massachusetts: Harvard University Press. Page 14.
36. Heywood, Linda M. 2019. *Njinga of Angola: Africa's Warrior Queen.* Cambridge, Massachusetts: Harvard University Press. Page 35.
37. Heywood, Linda M. 2019. *Njinga of Angola: Africa's Warrior Queen.* Cambridge, Massachusetts: Harvard University Press. Page 37.
38. Heywood, Linda M. 2019. *Njinga of Angola: Africa's Warrior Queen.* Cambridge, Massachusetts: Harvard University Press. Page 42.

39. Jordan, Jonathan W, and Emily Anne Jordan. 2020. *The War Queens: Extraordinary Women Who Ruled the Battlefield.* New York, Ny: Diversion Books. Page 170.
40. Jordan, Jonathan W, and Emily Anne Jordan. 2020. *The War Queens: Extraordinary Women Who Ruled the Battlefield.* New York, Ny: Diversion Books. Page 170.
41. Heywood, Linda M. 2019. *Njinga of Angola: Africa's Warrior Queen.* Cambridge, Massachusetts: Harvard University Press. Page 44.
42. Heywood, Linda M. 2019. *Njinga of Angola: Africa's Warrior Queen.* Cambridge, Massachusetts: Harvard University Press. Page 45.
43. Heywood, Linda M. 2019. *Njinga of Angola: Africa's Warrior Queen.* Cambridge, Massachusetts: Harvard University Press. Page 45.
44. Heywood, Linda M. 2019. *Njinga of Angola: Africa's Warrior Queen.* Cambridge, Massachusetts: Harvard University Press. Page 45.
45. Heywood, Linda M. 2019. *Njinga of Angola: Africa's Warrior Queen.* Cambridge, Massachusetts: Harvard University Press. Page 45.
46. Jordan, Jonathan W, and Emily Anne Jordan. 2020. *The War Queens: Extraordinary Women Who Ruled the Battlefield.* New York, Ny: Diversion Books. Page 170.
47. Jordan, Jonathan W, and Emily Anne Jordan. 2020. *The War Queens: Extraordinary Women Who Ruled the Battlefield.* New York, Ny: Diversion Books. Page 172.
48. Jordan, Jonathan W, and Emily Anne Jordan. 2020. *The War Queens: Extraordinary Women Who Ruled the Battlefield.* New York, Ny: Diversion Books. Page 172.
49. Jordan, Jonathan W, and Emily Anne Jordan. 2020. *The War Queens: Extraordinary Women Who Ruled the Battlefield.* New York, Ny: Diversion Books. Page 172.

50. Jordan, Jonathan W, and Emily Anne Jordan. 2020. *The War Queens: Extraordinary Women Who Ruled the Battlefield.* New York, Ny: Diversion Books. Page 173.
51. Jordan, Jonathan W, and Emily Anne Jordan. 2020. *The War Queens: Extraordinary Women Who Ruled the Battlefield.* New York, Ny: Diversion Books. Page 173.
52. Jordan, Jonathan W, and Emily Anne Jordan. 2020. *The War Queens: Extraordinary Women Who Ruled the Battlefield.* New York, Ny: Diversion Books. Page 173.
53. Jordan, Jonathan W, and Emily Anne Jordan. 2020. *The War Queens: Extraordinary Women Who Ruled the Battlefield.* New York, Ny: Diversion Books. Page 173.
54. Jordan, Jonathan W, and Emily Anne Jordan. 2020. *The War Queens: Extraordinary Women Who Ruled the Battlefield.* New York, Ny: Diversion Books. Page 174.
55. Jordan, Jonathan W, and Emily Anne Jordan. 2020. *The War Queens: Extraordinary Women Who Ruled the Battlefield.* New York, Ny: Diversion Books. Page 174.
56. Jordan, Jonathan W, and Emily Anne Jordan. 2020. *The War Queens: Extraordinary Women Who Ruled the Battlefield.* New York, Ny: Diversion Books. Page 179.
57. Jordan, Jonathan W, and Emily Anne Jordan. 2020. *The War Queens: Extraordinary Women Who Ruled the Battlefield.* New York, Ny: Diversion Books. Page 179.
58. Jordan, Jonathan W, and Emily Anne Jordan. 2020. *The War Queens: Extraordinary Women Who Ruled the Battlefield.* New York, Ny: Diversion Books. Page 180.
59. Jordan, Jonathan W, and Emily Anne Jordan. 2020. *The War Queens: Extraordinary Women Who Ruled the Battlefield.* New York, Ny: Diversion Books. Page 181.
60. Jordan, Jonathan W, and Emily Anne Jordan. 2020. *The War Queens: Extraordinary Women Who Ruled the Battlefield.* New York, Ny: Diversion Books. Page 181.

61. Jordan, Jonathan W, and Emily Anne Jordan. 2020. *The War Queens: Extraordinary Women Who Ruled the Battlefield.* New York, Ny: Diversion Books. Page 181.
62. Jordan, Jonathan W, and Emily Anne Jordan. 2020. *The War Queens: Extraordinary Women Who Ruled the Battlefield.* New York, Ny: Diversion Books. Page 181.
63. Jordan, Jonathan W, and Emily Anne Jordan. 2020. *The War Queens: Extraordinary Women Who Ruled the Battlefield.* New York, Ny: Diversion Books. Page 183.
64. Jordan, Jonathan W, and Emily Anne Jordan. 2020. *The War Queens: Extraordinary Women Who Ruled the Battlefield.* New York, Ny: Diversion Books. Page 185.
65. Jordan, Jonathan W, and Emily Anne Jordan. 2020. *The War Queens: Extraordinary Women Who Ruled the Battlefield.* New York, Ny: Diversion Books. Page 186.
66. Jordan, Jonathan W, and Emily Anne Jordan. 2020. *The War Queens: Extraordinary Women Who Ruled the Battlefield.* New York, Ny: Diversion Books. Page 187.
67. Jordan, Jonathan W, and Emily Anne Jordan. 2020. *The War Queens: Extraordinary Women Who Ruled the Battlefield.* New York, Ny: Diversion Books. Page 187.
68. Jordan, Jonathan W, and Emily Anne Jordan. 2020. *The War Queens: Extraordinary Women Who Ruled the Battlefield.* New York, Ny: Diversion Books. Page 185.
69. Jordan, Jonathan W, and Emily Anne Jordan. 2020. *The War Queens: Extraordinary Women Who Ruled the Battlefield.* New York, Ny: Diversion Books. Page 188.
70. Jordan, Jonathan W, and Emily Anne Jordan. 2020. *The War Queens: Extraordinary Women Who Ruled the Battlefield.* New York, Ny: Diversion Books. Page 188.
71. Jordan, Jonathan W, and Emily Anne Jordan. 2020. *The War Queens: Extraordinary Women Who Ruled the Battlefield.* New York, Ny: Diversion Books. Page 189.

72. Jordan, Jonathan W, and Emily Anne Jordan. 2020. *The War Queens: Extraordinary Women Who Ruled the Battlefield.* New York, Ny: Diversion Books. Page 189.
73. Jordan, Jonathan W, and Emily Anne Jordan. 2020. *The War Queens: Extraordinary Women Who Ruled the Battlefield.* New York, Ny: Diversion Books. Page 189.
74. Jordan, Jonathan W, and Emily Anne Jordan. 2020. *The War Queens: Extraordinary Women Who Ruled the Battlefield.* New York, Ny: Diversion Books. Page 190.
75. Clarence-Smith, W. Gervase and Thornton, John Kelly. 'Angola.' Encyclopaedia Britannica, March 17, 2024. www.britannica.com/place/Angola.

Chapter 9

1. 'Geography of Madagascar.' MapsofWorld.com. www.mapsofworld.com/madagascar/geography/.
2. 'Geography of Madagascar.' MapsofWorld.com. www.mapsofworld.com/madagascar/geography/.
3. 'Geography of Madagascar.' MapsofWorld.com. www.mapsofworld.com/madagascar/geography/.
4. 'Geography of Madagascar.' MapsofWorld.com. www.mapsofworld.com/madagascar/geography/.
5. 'Geography of Madagascar.' MapsofWorld.com. www.mapsofworld.com/madagascar/geography/.
6. Covell, M. Ann, Southall, Aidan William, Dresch, Jean, Deschamps, Hubert Jules and Kent, Raymond K. 'Madagascar.' Encyclopaedia Britannica, March 19, 2024. www.britannica.com/place/Madagascar.
7. Covell, M. Ann, Southall, Aidan William, Dresch, Jean, Deschamps, Hubert Jules and Kent, Raymond K. 'Madagascar.' Encyclopaedia Britannica, March 19, 2024. www.britannica.com/place/Madagascar.

8. Covell, M. Ann, Southall, Aidan William, Dresch, Jean, Deschamps, Hubert Jules and Kent, Raymond K. 'Madagascar.' Encyclopaedia Britannica, March 19, 2024. www.britannica.com/place/Madagascar.
9. Covell, M. Ann, Southall, Aidan William, Dresch, Jean, Deschamps, Hubert Jules and Kent, Raymond K. 'Madagascar.' Encyclopaedia Britannica, March 19, 2024. www.britannica.com/place/Madagascar.
10. Covell, M. Ann, Southall, Aidan William, Dresch, Jean, Deschamps, Hubert Jules and Kent, Raymond K. 'Madagascar.' Encyclopaedia Britannica, March 19, 2024. www.britannica.com/place/Madagascar.
11. Covell, M. Ann, Southall, Aidan William, Dresch, Jean, Deschamps, Hubert Jules and Kent, Raymond K. 'Madagascar.' Encyclopaedia Britannica, March 19, 2024. www.britannica.com/place/Madagascar.
12. Edu, World History. 2022. 'Ranavalona I, Queen of Madagascar: History, Reign & Facts.' World History Edu. December 8, 2022. www.worldhistoryedu.com/ranavalona-i-queen-of-madagascar-history-reign-facts/.
13. Edu, World History. 2022. 'Ranavalona I, Queen of Madagascar: History, Reign & Facts.' World History Edu. December 8, 2022. www.worldhistoryedu.com/ranavalona-i-queen-of-madagascar-history-reign-facts/.
14. Kent, R. K., Southall, Aidan William, Dresch, Jean, Deschamps, Hubert Jules and Covell, Maureen Ann. 'Madagascar.' Encyclopaedia Britannica, March 19, 2024. www.britannica.com/place/Madagascar.
15. Arnaldo. 'Ranavalona I: "Mad Queen" of Madagascar?' Biographics. August 11, 2023. www.biographics.org/ranavalona-i-mad-queen-of-madagascar/.
16. Arnaldo. 'Ranavalona I: "Mad Queen" of Madagascar?' Biographics. August 11, 2023. www.biographics.org/ranavalona-i-mad-queen-of-madagascar/.

17. Arnaldo. 'Ranavalona I: "Mad Queen" of Madagascar?' Biographics. August 11, 2023. www.biographics.org/ranavalona-i-mad-queen-of-madagascar/.
18. Laidler, Keith. 2005. *Female Caligula*. John Wiley & Sons. Page 34.
19. Laidler, Keith. 2005. *Female Caligula*. John Wiley & Sons. Page 35.
20. Arnaldo. 2023. 'Ranavalona I: "Mad Queen" of Madagascar?' Biographics. August 11, 2023. www.biographics.org/ranavalona-i-mad-queen-of-madagascar/.
21. Whistler, Simon. 2023. Review of *Queen Ranavalona I of Madagascar*. *Biographics*. www.youtube.com/watch?v=u_JZm4-FT64.
22. Whistler, Simon. 2023. Review of *Queen Ranavalona I of Madagascar*. *Biographics*. www.youtube.com/watch?v=u_JZm4-FT64.
23. Whistler, Simon. 2023. Review of *Queen Ranavalona I of Madagascar*. *Biographics*. www.youtube.com/watch?v=u_JZm4-FT64.
24. Whistler, Simon. 2023. Review of *Queen Ranavalona I of Madagascar*. *Biographics*. www.youtube.com/watch?v=u_JZm4-FT64.
25. Laidler, Keith. 2005. *Female Caligula*. John Wiley & Sons. Page 41.
26. Whistler, Simon. 2023. Review of *Queen Ranavalona I of Madagascar*. *Biographics*. www.youtube.com/watch?v=u_JZm4-FT64.
27. Laidler, Keith. 2005. *Female Caligula*. John Wiley & Sons. Page 102.
28. Laidler, Keith. 2005. *Female Caligula*. John Wiley & Sons. Page 103.
29. Laidler, Keith. 2005. *Female Caligula*. John Wiley & Sons. Page 103.
30. Laidler, Keith. 2005. *Female Caligula*. John Wiley & Sons. Page 103.

31. Laidler, Keith. 2005. *Female Caligula*. John Wiley & Sons. Page 104.
32. Laidler, Keith. 2005. *Female Caligula*. John Wiley & Sons. Page 104.
33. Whistler, Simon. 2023. Review of *Queen Ranavalona I of Madagascar*. *Biographics*. www.youtube.com/watch?v=u_JZm4-FT64.
34. Edu, World History. 2022. 'Ranavalona I, Queen of Madagascar: History, Reign & Facts.' World History Edu. December 8, 2022. www.worldhistoryedu.com/ranavalona-i-queen-of-madagascar-history-reign-facts/.
35. Whistler, Simon. 2023. Review of *Queen Ranavalona I of Madagascar*. *Biographics*. www.youtube.com/watch?v=u_JZm4-FT64.
36. Whistler, Simon. 2023. Review of *Queen Ranavalona I of Madagascar*. *Biographics*. www.youtube.com/watch?v=u_JZm4-FT64.
37. Whistler, Simon. 2023. Review of *Queen Ranavalona I of Madagascar*. *Biographics*. www.youtube.com/watch?v=u_JZm4-FT64.
38. Whistler, Simon. 2023. Review of *Queen Ranavalona I of Madagascar*. *Biographics*. www.youtube.com/watch?v=u_JZm4-FT64.
39. Whistler, Simon. 2023. Review of *Queen Ranavalona I of Madagascar*. *Biographics*. www.youtube.com/watch?v=u_JZm4-FT64.
40. Whistler, Simon. 2023. Review of *Queen Ranavalona I of Madagascar*. *Biographics*. www.youtube.com/watch?v=u_JZm4-FT64.
41. Archives, The National. 2015. 'The National Archives - Battle of Madagascar 1845.' The National Archives Blog. November 30, 2015. www.blog.nationalarchives.gov.uk/battle-madagascar-1845/.

42. Archives, The National. 2015. 'The National Archives - Battle of Madagascar 1845.' The National Archives Blog. November 30, 2015. www.blog.nationalarchives.gov.uk/battle-madagascar-1845/.
43. Archives, The National. 2015. 'The National Archives - Battle of Madagascar 1845.' The National Archives Blog. November 30, 2015. www.blog.nationalarchives.gov.uk/battle-madagascar-1845/.
44. Archives, The National. 2015. 'The National Archives - Battle of Madagascar 1845.' The National Archives Blog. November 30, 2015. www.blog.nationalarchives.gov.uk/battle-madagascar-1845/.
45. Whistler, Simon. 2023. Review of *Queen Ranavalona I of Madagascar*. *Biographics*. www.youtube.com/watch?v=u_JZm4-FT64.
46. 'Ranavalona I, Queen of Madagascar | Encyclopedia.com.' www.encyclopedia.com/history/encyclopedias-almanacs-transcripts-and-maps/ranavalona-i-queen-madagascar.
47. Whistler, Simon. 2023. Review of *Queen Ranavalona I of Madagascar*. *Biographics*. www.youtube.com/watch?v=u_JZm4-FT64.
48. Whistler, Simon. 2023. Review of *Queen Ranavalona I of Madagascar*. *Biographics*. www.youtube.com/watch?v=u_JZm4-FT64.
49. Whistler, Simon. 2023. Review of *Queen Ranavalona I of Madagascar*. *Biographics*. www.youtube.com/watch?v=u_JZm4-FT64.
50. Whistler, Simon. 2023. Review of *Queen Ranavalona I of Madagascar*. *Biographics*. www.youtube.com/watch?v=u_JZm4-FT64.
51. Bloks, Moniek. 2017. 'Queens Regnant - Rasoherina of Madagascar.' History of Royal Women. June 27, 2017. www.historyofroyalwomen.com/rasoherina-of-madagascar/queens-regnant-rasoherina-madagascar/.

52. Bloks, Moniek. 2017. 'Queens Regnant - Rasoherina of Madagascar.' History of Royal Women. June 27, 2017. www.historyofroyalwomen.com/rasoherina-of-madagascar/queens-regnant-rasoherina-madagascar/.
53. Bloks, Moniek. 2017. 'Queens Regnant - Rasoherina of Madagascar.' History of Royal Women. June 27, 2017. www.historyofroyalwomen.com/rasoherina-of-madagascar/queens-regnant-rasoherina-madagascar/.
54. Bloks, Moniek. 2017. 'Queens Regnant - Rasoherina of Madagascar.' History of Royal Women. June 27, 2017. www.historyofroyalwomen.com/rasoherina-of-madagascar/queens-regnant-rasoherina-madagascar/.
55. Raminosa, Rasoanalimanga, Berthe. 1868. 'Ranavalona II.' Dictionary of African Christian Biography. 1868. www.dacb.org/stories/madagascar/ranavalona2/.
56. Raminosa, Rasoanalimanga, Berthe. 1868. 'Ranavalona II.' Dictionary of African Christian Biography. 1868. www.dacb.org/stories/madagascar/ranavalona2/.
57. Raminosa, Rasoanalimanga, Berthe. 1868. 'Ranavalona II.' Dictionary of African Christian Biography. 1868. www.dacb.org/stories/madagascar/ranavalona2/.
58. Raminosa, Rasoanalimanga, Berthe. 1868. 'Ranavalona II.' Dictionary of African Christian Biography. 1868. www.dacb.org/stories/madagascar/ranavalona2/.
59. Raminosa, Rasoanalimanga, Berthe. 1868. 'Ranavalona II.' Dictionary of African Christian Biography. 1868. www.dacb.org/stories/madagascar/ranavalona2/.
60. Raminosa, Rasoanalimanga, Berthe. 1868. 'Ranavalona II.' Dictionary of African Christian Biography. 1868. www.dacb.org/stories/madagascar/ranavalona2/.
61. Raminosa, Rasoanalimanga, Berthe. 1868. 'Ranavalona II.' Dictionary of African Christian Biography. 1868. www.dacb.org/stories/madagascar/ranavalona2/.

62. Davis-Marks, Isis. n.d. 'The Little-Known Story of Madagascar's Last Queen, Ranavalona III.' Smithsonian Magazine. www.smithsonianmag.com/smart-news/madagascars-extraordinary-last-queens-objects-are-sale-180976467/.
63. Davis-Marks, Isis. n.d. 'The Little-Known Story of Madagascar's Last Queen, Ranavalona III.' Smithsonian Magazine. www.smithsonianmag.com/smart-news/madagascars-extraordinary-last-queens-objects-are-sale-180976467/.
64. Davis-Marks, Isis. n.d. 'The Little-Known Story of Madagascar's Last Queen, Ranavalona III.' Smithsonian Magazine. www.smithsonianmag.com/smart-news/madagascars-extraordinary-last-queens-objects-are-sale-180976467/.
65. Davis-Marks, Isis. n.d. 'The Little-Known Story of Madagascar's Last Queen, Ranavalona III.' Smithsonian Magazine. www.smithsonianmag.com/smart-news/madagascars-extraordinary-last-queens-objects-are-sale-180976467/.

Acknowledgements

Behind this accomplishment is a team that helped make it possible. My family has dedicated so much support and encouragement throughout the writing of this book. They are the best cheer squad I could ever ask for. I dedicate this book to my husband Ben, and our wonderful children, Bella, Danielle, Jax, and Audrey. Thank you for believing in me long before I ever did. I love you.

I want to express a special thank you to my sister, Ky. She is my dedicated beta reader, offering input and useful feedback for each chapter. Ky, I cannot thank you enough for not only being my beta reader, but for every ounce of encouragement and complete honesty you gave me. To my sister-in-law, Lauren, I cannot begin to express my gratitude for all your help regarding the formatting of my photo selections. You were an integral part of the completion of this book, and I'm so grateful for you.

Thank you to the many scholars, historians, archaeologists, conservationists, and archivists who are so dedicated to their field, allowing for the women written about in this book to remain ever present in our world's history. It is because of your important work that books like mine can be written.

Bibliography

'100 Hausa Proverbs (Karin Magana Tsantsa) - Northpad Nigeria.' 2022. Northpad.ng. March 24, 2022. www.northpad.ng/karin-magana-tsan-tsa/.

'Amenhotep III and Tiye Colossal Statue.' Egymonuments.gov.eg. www.egymonuments.gov.eg/en/collections/amenhotep-iii-and-tiye-colossal-statue-6/.

'Amina of Zaria | Encyclopedia.com.' www.encyclopedia.com/history/encyclopedias-almanacs-transcripts-and-maps/amina-zaria.

'Amina of Zaria.' Muslim Heritage. Accessed March 21, 2024. www.muslimheritage.com/people/scholars/amina-of-zaria/.

'Blue Nile - New World Encyclopaedia.' www.newworldencyclopedia.org. www.newworldencyclopedia.org/entry/Blue_Nile.

'Geography of Madagascar.' MapsofWorld.com. www.mapsofworld.com/madagascar/geography/.

'History Channel Documentary - Ancient History - the Queen of Sheba.' 2017. www.youtube.com. Accessed March 10, 2024. www.youtube.com/watch?v=F9zW85DgfW4.

'Kom El-Dekka.' www.touregypt.net. Accessed March 13, 2024. www.touregypt.net/alkom.htm.

'Nubian Archers | Institute for the Study of Ancient Cultures.' www.isac.uchicago.edu/museum-exhibits/nubia/nubian-archers.

'Queen Kahina's Well, Bir El-Kahen, Algeria | Archive | Diarna.org.' Archive.diarna.org. Accessed March 17, 2024. www.archive.diarna.org/site/detail/public/280/.

'Ranavalona I, Queen of Madagascar | Encyclopedia.com.' www.encyclopedia.com/history/encyclopedias-almanacs-transcripts-and-maps/ranavalona-i-queen-madagascar.

'Ray Johnson on the Forensic Reconstruction of the "Younger Lady"| Institute for the Study of Ancient Cultures.' 2018. Isac.uchicago.edu. www.isac.uchicago.edu/article/ray-johnson-forensic-reconstruciton-younger-lady.

'Stela | British Museum.' The British Museum. www.britishmuseum.org/collection/object/Y_EA1650.

'Study Finds Skin Cream Caused Egyptian Queen's Death.' 2011. Biblical Archaeology Society. August 22, 2011. www.biblicalarchaeology.org/daily/news/study-finds-skin-cream-caused-egyptian-queens-death/.

'Temple of Awwam - AtlasIslamica.' 2021. May 24, 2021. www.atlasislamica.com/temple-of-awwam/.

'The History of Ancient Nubia | Institute for the Study of Ancient Cultures.' www.isac.uchicago.edu/museum-exhibits/history-ancient-nubiaOLD.

'The Lion Temple.' Musawwarat. Accessed March 13, 2024. www.musawwarat.com/about-musawwarat/the-lion-temple/. Koekoe, Jade. March 23, 2017. "Object in Focus: The Meroe Head of Augustus – World History et Cetera. www.etc.worldhistory.org/photos/meroe-head-augustus/.

'Who Is Queen Amina, the Warrior Queen of Zaria – Leading Ladies Africa.' August 31, 2023. www.leadingladiesafrica.org/who-is-queen-amina-the-warrior-queen-of-zaria/.

Afsaruddin, A. 'Caliphate.' Encyclopaedia Britannica, February 25, 2024. www.britannica.com/place/Caliphate.

Ajayi, J.F. Ade, Udo, Reuben Kenrick, Kirk-Greene, Anthony Hamilton Millard and Falola, Toyin O. 'Nigeria.' Encyclopaedia Britannica, March 18, 2024. www.britannica.com/place/Nigeria.

AnnaEverywhere. 2020. 'Ethiopian Food Guide: Best Ethiopian Dishes to Try.' Anna Everywhere. July 6, 2020. www.annaeverywhere.com/ethiopian-food-guide

Archives, The National. 2015. 'The National Archives - Battle of Madagascar 1845.' The National Archives Blog. November 30, 2015. www.blog.nationalarchives.gov.uk/battle-madagascar-1845/.

Arnaldo. 'Ranavalona I: "Mad Queen" of Madagascar?' Biographics. August 11, 2023. www.biographics.org/ranavalona-i-mad-queen-of-madagascar/.

B. A., Mundelein College, and Meadville/Lombard Theological School M. Div. 2019. 'Amina - Learn about an African Warrior Queen in What Is Today Nigeria.' ThoughtCo. June 3, 2019. www.thoughtco.com/amina-queen-of-zazzua-3529742.

BBC News. 'The Warrior Queen Who Led Men into Battle.' Accessed October 17, 2023. www.bbc.com/news/av/world-africa-44888718.

Bloks, Moniek. 2017. 'Queens Regnant - Rasoherina of Madagascar.' History of Royal Women. June 27, 2017. www.historyofroyalwomen.com/rasoherina-of-madagascar/queens-regnant-rasoherina-madagascar/.

Britannica, T. Editors of Encyclopaedia. 'Aghlabid dynasty.' Encyclopaedia Britannica, October 17, 2017. www.britannica.com/topic/Aghlabid-dynasty.

Britannica, T. Editors of Encyclopaedia. 'Ahmose I.' Encyclopaedia Britannica, November 8, 2017. www.britannica.com/biography/Ahmose-I.

Britannica, T. Editors of Encyclopaedia. 'Alaric.' Encyclopaedia Britannica, February 9, 2024. www.britannica.com/biography/Alaric.

Britannica, T. Editors of Encyclopaedia. 'Amarna style.' Encyclopaedia Britannica, June 28, 2013. www.britannica.com/art/Amarna-style.

Britannica, T. Editors of Encyclopaedia. 'Amenhotep I.' Encyclopaedia Britannica, February 12, 2024. www.britannica.com/biography/Amenhotep-I.

Britannica, T. Editors of Encyclopaedia. 'Blue Nile River.' Encyclopaedia Britannica, March 9, 2024. www.britannica.com/place/Blue-Nile-River.

Britannica, T. Editors of Encyclopaedia. 'Crowns of Egypt.' Encyclopaedia Britannica, October 31, 2008. www.britannica.com/topic/crowns-of-Egypt.

Britannica, T. Editors of Encyclopaedia. 'doum nut.' Encyclopaedia Britannica, March 6, 2012. www.britannica.com/topic/doum-nut.

Britannica, T. Editors of Encyclopaedia. 'Dysentery.' Encyclopaedia Britannica, February 18, 2024. www.britannica.com/science/dysentery.

Britannica, T. Editors of Encyclopaedia. 'Ea.' Encyclopaedia Britannica, March 1, 2024. www.britannica.com/topic/Ea.

Britannica, T. Editors of Encyclopaedia. 'Gaius Cornelius Gallus.' Encyclopaedia Britannica, March 5, 2024. www.britannica.com/biography/Gaius-Cornelius-Gallus.

Britannica, T. Editors of Encyclopaedia. 'Hausa states.' Encyclopaedia Britannica, May 31, 2023. www.britannica.com/place/Hausa-states.

Britannica, T. Editors of Encyclopaedia. 'Hausa.' Encyclopaedia Britannica, February 22, 2024. www.britannica.com/topic/Hausa.

Britannica, T. Editors of Encyclopaedia. 'Heb-Sed.' Encyclopaedia Britannica, June 1, 2016. www.britannica.com/topic/Heb-Sed.

Britannica, T. Editors of Encyclopaedia. 'Igbo.' Encyclopaedia Britannica, December 27, 2023. www.britannica.com/topic/Igbo.

Britannica, T. Editors of Encyclopaedia. 'Jesuit.' Encyclopaedia Britannica, March 13, 2024. www.britannica.com/topic/Jesuits.

Britannica, T. Editors of Encyclopaedia. 'Jukun.' Encyclopaedia Britannica, July 20, 1998. www.britannica.com/topic/Jukun.

Britannica, T. Editors of Encyclopaedia. 'Maʾrib.' Encyclopaedia Britannica, September 13, 2023. www.britannica.com/place/Marib.

Britannica, T. Editors of Encyclopaedia. 'Menes.' Encyclopaedia Britannica, December 17, 2020. www.britannica.com/biography/Menes.

Britannica, T. Editors of Encyclopaedia. 'Nupe.' Encyclopaedia Britannica, September 16, 2015. www.britannica.com/topic/Nupe.

Britannica, T. Editors of Encyclopaedia. 'Piye.' Encyclopaedia Britannica, January 30, 2015. www.britannica.com/biography/Piye.

Britannica, T. Editors of Encyclopaedia. 'Queen of Sheba.' Encyclopaedia Britannica, March 6, 2024. www.britannica.com/biography/Queen-of-Sheba.

Britannica, T. Editors of Encyclopaedia. 'Scurvy.' Encyclopaedia Britannica, February 19, 2024. www.britannica.com/science/scurvy.

Britannica, T. Editors of Encyclopaedia. 'Tamarind.' Encyclopaedia Britannica, February 2, 2024. www.britannica.com/plant/tamarind.

Britannica, T. Editors of Encyclopaedia. 'Thutmose I.' Encyclopaedia Britannica, April 3, 2014. www.britannica.com/biography/Thutmose-I.

Britannica, T. Editors of Encyclopaedia. 'Torah.' Encyclopaedia Britannica, March 15, 2024. www.britannica.com/topic/Torah.

Britannica, T. Editors of Encyclopaedia. 'Visigoth.' Encyclopaedia Britannica, February 20, 2024. www.britannica.com/topic/Visigoth.

Britannica, T. Editors of Encyclopaedia. 'Yoruba.' Encyclopaedia Britannica, January 23, 2024. www.britannica.com/topic/Yoruba.

Britannica, T. Editors of Encyclopaedia. 'Zaria.' Encyclopaedia Britannica, July 20, 1998. www.britannica.com/place/Zaria-historical-kingdom-and-province-Nigeria.

Britannica, T. Editors of Encyclopaedia. 'Zaria.' Encyclopaedia Britannica, July 20, 1998. www.britannica.com/place/Zaria-historical-kingdom-and-province-Nigeria.

Brown, Nicholas. Review of *The KV55 Coffin*. American Research Centre in Egypt. Department of Near Eastern Languages and Cultures, University of California, Los Angeles. The KV55 Coffin.

Cartwright, Mark. 2019. 'Cosmetics in the Ancient World.' World History Encyclopaedia. September 6, 2019. www.worldhistory.org/article/1441/cosmetics-in-the-ancient-world/.

Cartwright, Mark. 2019. 'Trade in the Ancient World.' World History Encyclopaedia. February 22, 2019. www.worldhistory.org/collection/39/trade-in-the-ancient-world/.

Cartwright, Mark. 2021. 'Portuguese Angola.' World History Encyclopaedia. July 12, 2021. www.worldhistory.org/Portuguese_Angola/.

Cartwright, Mark. 2022. 'Weapons of the Conquistadors.' World History Encyclopaedia. July 20, 2022. www.worldhistory.org/article/2042/weapons-of-the-conquistadors/.

Cassar, Claudine. 2023. 'The Nightly Journey of Khonsu - the Ancient Egyptian God of the Moon.' Anthropology Review. September 4, 2023. www.anthropologyreview.org/history/ancient-egypt/egyptian-god-of-the-moon/.

Cavazzi, Franco. 2021. 'Roman Military Tactics.' The Roman Empire. December 18, 2021. www.roman-empire.net/army/tactics/.

Clarence-Smith, W. Gervase and Thornton, John Kelly. 'Angola.' Encyclopaedia Britannica, March 17, 2024. www.britannica.com/place/Angola.

Clarence-Smith, W. Gervase and Thornton, John Kelly. 'Angola.' Encyclopaedia Britannica, March 17, 2024. www.britannica.com/place/Angola.

Cleveland Clinic. 2022. 'Dysentery: Causes, Symptoms, Diagnosis & Treatment.' Cleveland Clinic. August 15, 2022. www.my.clevelandclinic.org/health/diseases/23567-dysentery.

Communications, Office of Public Affairs &. n.d. 'Pharaoh's Unusual Feminine Appearance Suggests Two Gene Defects.' Medicine.yale.edu. www.medicine.yale.edu/news-article/pharaohs-unusual-feminine-appearance-suggests-two-gene-defects/.

Cooney, Kara, and National Geographic Society (U.S. 2018. *When Women Ruled the World: Six Queens of Egypt*. Washington, D.C.: National Geographic.

Cooney, Kara. 2015. *Woman Who Would Be King: Hatshepsut's Rise to Power in Ancient Egypt.* New York: Broadway Books.

Covell, M. Ann, Southall, Aidan William, Dresch, Jean, Deschamps, Hubert Jules and Kent, Raymond K. 'Madagascar.' Encyclopaedia Britannica, March 19, 2024. www.britannica.com/place/Madagascar.

Cox, Jessica. 2012. 'Trade and Power: The Role of Naqada as a Trading Centre in Predynastic Egypt.' *Egyptology in Australia and New Zealand 2009: Proceedings of the Conference Held in Melbourne, September 4th-6th*, January. www.academia.edu/2980599/Trade_and_Power_The_Role_of_Naqada_as_a_Trading_Centre_in_Predynastic_Egypt.

Crummey, D. Edward, Marcus, Harold G. and Mehretu, Assefa. 'Ethiopia.' Encyclopaedia Britannica, March 9, 2024. www.britannica.com/place/Ethiopia.

Davis-Marks, Isis. n.d. 'The Little-Known Story of Madagascar's Last Queen, Ranavalona III.' Smithsonian Magazine. www.smithsonianmag.com/smart-news/madagascars-extraordinary-last-queens-objects-are-sale-180976467/.

DHWTY. 2016. 'Mythical Benben Stone: The Landing Site of Egyptian God Atum.' Ancient-Origins.net. Ancient Origins. August 25, 2016. www.ancient-origins.net/artifacts-other-artifacts/mythical-benben-stone-landing-site-egyptian-god-atum-006513.

Dimitrovsky, H. Zalman and Silberman, Lou Hackett. 'Talmud and Midrash.' Encyclopaedia. Britannica, March 10, 2024. www.britannica.com/topic/Talmud.

Dodson, Aidan. 2020. *Nefertiti, Queen and Pharaoh of Egypt*. American University in Cairo Press.

Dorman, P. F. 'Akhenaten.' Encyclopaedia Britannica, February 9, 2024. www.britannica.com/biography/Akhenaten.

Dorman, Peter. 'Akhenaten - Religion of the Aton.' Encyclopaedia Britannica. www.britannica.com/biography/Akhenaten/Religion-of-the-Aton.

Drower, M. Stefana and Dorman, Peter F. 'Karnak.' Encyclopaedia Britannica, October 2, 2023. www.britannica.com/place/Karnak.

Drower, M. Stefana and Dorman, Peter F. 'Thutmose III.' Encyclopaedia Britannica, January 30, 2024. www.britannica.com/biography/Thutmose-III.

Editors at Britannica. 'Ancient Egypt - Thutmose IV.' 2019. In *Encyclopaedia Britannica*. www.britannica.com/place/ancient-Egypt/Thutmose-IV.

Editors, History com. 2009. 'Nero.' HISTORY. November 9, 2009. www.history.com/topics/ancient-rome/nero.

Editors, History com. 2019. 'Nefertiti.' HISTORY. June 7, 2019. www.history.com/topics/ancient-egypt/nefertiti.

Edu, World History. 2022. 'Ranavalona I, Queen of Madagascar: History, Reign & Facts.' World History Edu. December 8, 2022. www.worldhistoryedu.com/ranavalona-i-queen-of-madagascar-history-reign-facts/.

Flame (Leah), Working the. 2022. '14 Types of African Swords [Ancient to Modern].' Working the Flame. August 14, 2022. www.workingtheflame.com/african-swords/.

Franklin, Harper. 2020. '1830-1839 | Fashion History Timeline.' Fashionhistory.fitnyc.edu. April 3, 2020. www.fashionhistory.fitnyc.edu/1830-1839/.

Hanson, Marilee. 2022. 'Roman Weapons - English History.' English History. June 13, 2022. www.englishhistory.net/romans/roman-weapons/.

Harper Franklin. 2020. '1840-1849 | Fashion History Timeline.' Fitnyc.edu. March 26, 2020. www.fashionhistory.fitnyc.edu/1840-1849/.

Harris, John. 2023. '9 Facts about the Transatlantic Slave Trade.' HISTORY. May 2, 2023. www.history.com/news/transatlantic-slave-trade-facts.

Heuzé, V., Thiollet, H., Tran, G., Edouard, N., Lebas, F., 'African Locust Bean (Parkia Biglobosa & Parkia Filicoidea) | Feedipedia.' March 21, 2019. www.feedipedia.org/node/268.

Heywood, Linda M. 2019. *Njinga of Angola: Africa's Warrior Queen.* Cambridge, Massachusetts: Harvard University Press.

Hill, J. 2018. 'Neithhotep.' Ancient Egypt Online: Ancient Egyptian History and Art. 2018. www.ancientegyptonline.co.uk/neithhotep/.

HISTORY.COM EDITORS. 2009. 'Hatshepsut.' HISTORY. December 16, 2009. www.history.com/topics/ancient-egypt/hatshepsut.

History.com Editors. 2019. 'Congress Abolishes the African Slave Trade.' HISTORY. March 7, 2019. www.history.com/this-day-in-history/congress-abolishes-the-african-slave-trade.

History.com Editors. 2021. 'Israel.' HISTORY. May 11, 2021. www.history.com/topics/middle-east/history-of-israel

Jaffer, Aaron. 2017. 'Dying on Their Own Terms: Suicides Aboard Slave Ships.' Www.rmg.co.uk. Royal Museums Greenwich. August 16, 2017. www.rmg.co.uk/stories/blog/curatorial/dying-on-their-own-terms-suicides-aboard-slave-ships.

Jerusalem, The Hebrew University of. n.d. 'Popular Archaeology - a Sabaean Inscription on a Large Clay Jar Deciphered and Discovered Less than 300 Meters from the Site of the Jerusalem Temple.' Popular Archaeology. www.popular-archaeology.com/article/a-sabaean-inscription-on-a-large-clay-jar-deciphered-and-discovered-less-than-300-meters-from-the-site-of-the-jerusalem-temple/.

Jordan, Jonathan W, and Emily Anne Jordan. 2020. *The War Queens: Extraordinary Women Who Ruled the Battlefield.* New York, Ny: Diversion Books.

Kent, R. K., Southall, Aidan William, Dresch, Jean, Deschamps, Hubert Jules and Covell, Maureen Ann. 'Madagascar.'

Encyclopaedia Britannica, March 19, 2024. www.britannica.com/place/Madagascar.

King, Arienne. 'Dodekaschoinos.' October 5, 2017. World History Encyclopaedia. www.worldhistory.org/Dodekaschoinos/.

Klimczak, Natalia. 2017. 'Searching for the Lost Footsteps of the Scorpion Kings.' Ancient-Origins.net. Ancient Origins. February 23, 2017. www.ancient-origins.net/history-famous-people/searching-lost-footsteps-scorpion-kings-007598.

Knott, Elizabeth. 2019. 'The Amarna Letters.' Metmuseum.org. 2019. www.metmuseum.org/toah/hd/amlet/hd_amlet.htm.

Laidler, Keith. 2005. *Female Caligula*. John Wiley & Sons.

Lasserre, F. 'Strabo.' Encyclopaedia Britannica, February 8, 2019. www.britannica.com/biography/Strabo.

Lewis, T. 'Transatlantic Slave Trade.' Encyclopaedia Britannica, February 29, 2024. www.britannica.com/topic/transatlantic-slave-trade.

Life Application Study Bible. 2019. 3rd ed. Vol. NIV. Carol Stream, Illinois: Tyndale House and Zondervan. (Orig. pub. 1988.). Knox, John. 2017. 'Solomon.' World History Encyclopaedia. January 25, 2017. www.worldhistory.org/solomon/.

Magak, Adhiambo Edith. 'The One-Eyed African Queen Who Defeated the Roman Empire.' www.narratively.com/p/the-one-eyed-african-queen-who-defeated-the-roman-empire.

Magak, Adhiambo Edith. 'The One-Eyed African Queen Who Defeated the Roman Empire.' www.narratively.com/p/the-one-eyed-african-queen-who-defeated-the-roman-empire.

Magazine, Smithsonian, and Max Kutner. October 20, 2018 'Unearthing America's Lawrence of Arabia, Wendell Phillips.' Smithsonian Magazine. www.smithsonianmag.com/smithsonian-institution/unearthing-americas-lawrence-arabia-wendell-phillips-180953059/.

Magazine, Smithsonian, and Smithsonian magazine. 2016. 'The Powerful Objects from the Collections of the Smithsonian's Newest Museum.' Smithsonian Magazine. September 2016. www.

smithsonianmag.com/smithsonian-institution/powerful-objects-collections-smithsonian-museum-180960126/.

Mark, Joshua J. 2011. Review of *Tiye*. World History Encyclopaedia. July 18, 2011. www.worldhistory.org/tiye/.

Mark, Joshua J. 2016. 'Ancient Egyptian Religion.' World History Encyclopaedia. World History Encyclopaedia. January 20, 2016. www.worldhistory.org/Egyptian_Religion/.

Mark, Joshua J. 2016. Review of *Karnak*. World History Encyclopaedia. September 16, 2016. www.worldhistory.org/Karnak/.

Mark, Joshua J. 2018. 'The Kingdom of Kush.' World History Encyclopaedia. February 26, 2018. www.worldhistory.org/Kush/.

Mark, Joshua J. 2018. Review of *Kahina*. World History Encyclopaedia. March 16, 2018. www.worldhistory.org/Kahina/.

Mark, Joshua J. 2018. Review of *Kingdom of Saba*. World History Encyclopaedia. March 2, 2018. www.worldhistory.org/Kingdom_of_Saba/.

Mark, Joshua J. 2018. Review of *Queen of Sheba*. World History Encyclopaedia. March 26, 2018. www.worldhistory.org/Queen_of_Sheba/.

Mark, Joshua. 2016. 'Narmer.' World History Encyclopaedia. February 1, 2016. www.worldhistory.org/Narmer/.

Mark, Joshua. 2016. 'Neith.' WorldHistory.org. September 14, 2016. www.worldhistory.org/Neith/.

Mark, Joshua. 2016. 'Osiris.' World History Encyclopaedia. March 6, 2016. www.worldhistory.org/osiris/.

Mark, Joshua. 2017. 'Amarna Period of Egypt.' World History Encyclopaedia. August 3, 2017. www.worldhistory.org/Amarna_Period_of_Egypt/.

Mark, Joshua. 2017. 'Great Female Rulers of Ancient Egypt2017.' World History Encyclopaedia. March 29, 2017. www.worldhistory.org/article/1040/great-female-rulers-of-ancient-egypt/.

Mark, Joshua. 2017. 'Thutmose III.' World History Encyclopaedia. July 20, 2017. www.worldhistory.org/Thutmose_III/.

Mark, Joshua. 2019. 'Western Roman Empire.' World History Encyclopaedia. September 27, 2019. www.worldhistory.org/Western_Roman_Empire/.

May 24, Lauren DavidUpdated. 'Baobab Fruit: 10 Things Nutritionists Need You to Know.' The Healthy. May 24, 2021. www.thehealthy.com/nutrition/baobab-fruit/.

Medievalists.net. 2019. 'The Berber Queen Who Defied the Caliphate: Al-Kahina and the Islamic Conquest of North Africa.' Medievalists.net. December 3, 2019. www.medievalists.net/2019/12/berber-queen-al-kahina/.

Merrick, Captain G. 2019. *Hausa Proverbs*. Wentworth Press.

Moll, Michele. 2011. 'Burial Practices at Naqada.' Archaeology of Ancient Egypt. July 14, 2011. www.anthropology.msu.edu/egyptian-archaeology/2011/07/14/burial-practices-at-naqada/.

Mora, Kai. 2022. 'The Nubian Queen Who Fought Back Caesar's Army.' HISTORY. March 23, 2022. www.history.com/news/nubian-queen-amanirenas-roman-army.

NatGeoUK. 2021. 'These Pharaohs' Private Letters Expose How Politics Worked 3,300 Years Ago.' National Geographic. January 8, 2021. www.nationalgeographic.co.uk/history-and-civilisation/2021/01/.

Oakes, Lorna, and Lucia Gahlin. 2022. *The Illustrated Encyclopaedia of Ancient Egypt: An Illustrated Reference to the Myths, Religions, Pyramids and Temples of the Land of the Pharaohs*. Edited by Helena Sudell. Cambridgeshire: Anness Publishing Limited.

Raminosa, Rasoanalimanga, Berthe. 1868. 'Ranavalona II.' Dictionary of African Christian Biography. 1868. www.dacb.org/stories/madagascar/ranavalona2/.

Room, and Hamilton Lugar. 'National African Language Resource Centre (NALRC).' www.nalrc.indiana.edu/doc/brochures/tamazight.pdf.

Room, and Hamilton Lugar. n.d. 'National African Language Resource Centre (NALRC).' www.nalrc.indiana.edu/doc/brochures/tamazight.pdf.

Ryckmans, J. 'Arabian religion.' Encyclopaedia Britannica, January 19, 2024. www.britannica.com/topic/Arabian-religion.

Salo Wittmayer Baron, and Haim Zalman Dimitrovsky. 2018. 'Judaism | History, Beliefs, & Facts.' In *Encyclopedialike Britannica*. www.britannica.com/topic/Judaism.

Schimmel, A., Mahdi, Muhsin S., and Rahman, Fazlur. 'Islam.' Encyclopaedia Britannica, March 15, 2024. www.britannica.com/topic/Islam.

Schwarz-Bart, Simone, André Schwarz-Bart, and Unesco. 2001. *In Praise of Black Women*. Madison: The University of Wisconsin Press; Houston, Tex.

Schwarz-Bart, Simone, André Schwarz-Bart, Rose-Myriam Réjouis, Val Vinokur, Stephanie Daval, and Stephanie K Turner. 2001. *In Praise of Black Women*. Madison, Wi: The University of Wisconsin Press.

Serjeant, R. Bertram, Ghul, Mahmud Ali, Ochsenwald, William L. and Beeston, Alfred Felix L. 'History of Arabia.' Encyclopaedia Britannica, April 30, 2020. www.britannica.com/topic/history-of-Arabia-31558.

Smith, Cathy Anne. 2019. 'Akhenaten and Nefertiti's Children | World History.' September 20, 2019. www.worldhistory.us/ancient-history/ancient-egypt/akhenaten-and-nefertitis-children.php.

Smith, Cathy Anne. 'Mutemwiya and the Divine Birth of Amenhotep III | World History.' www.worldhistory.us/ancient-history/ancient-egypt/mutemwiya-and-the-divine-birth-of-amenhotep-iii.php.

Spence, Kate. 2011. 'BBC - History - Ancient History in Depth: Akhenaten and the Amarna Period.' Bbc.co.uk. 2011. www.bbc.co.uk/history/ancient/egyptians/akhenaten_01.shtml.

Stevens, Anna. Review of *Akhenaten, Nefertiti & Aten: From Many Gods to One*. American Research Center in Egypt. University of Cambridge & Monash University. www.arce.org/resource/akhenaten-nefertiti-aten-many-gods-one.

Team, Editorial. 2018. 'Dihya, Queen of the Berbers | African History | ThinkAfrica.' Think Africa. November 14, 2018. www.thinkafrica.net/dihya-kahina/.

The British Museum, 'Ancient Nubia and the Kingdom of Kush, an introduction,' in *Smarthistory,* March 9, 2021, www.smarthistory.org/ancient-nubia-kingdom-kush-intro/.

The British Museum. 'Ancient Nubia and the Kingdom of Kush, an Introduction (Article).' Khan Academy. Accessed March 13, 2024. www.khanacademy.org/humanities/ancient-art-civilizations/egypt-art/x7e914f5b:kingdom-of-kush/a/ancient-nubia-and-the-kingdom-of-kush.

Tyldesley, J. 'Nefertiti.' Encyclopaedia Britannica, February 25, 2024. www.britannica.com/biography/Nefertiti.

Tyldesley, Joyce A. 2005. *Nefertiti: Egypt's Sun Queen*. London; New York: Penguin.

Ushi. 2018. 'Queen of the Desert: The Amazing Story of "Jewish Khaleesi."' Museum of the Jewish People. October 14, 2018. www.anumuseum.org.il/blog/queen-desert-amazing-story-jewish-khaleesi/.

Vaughan, D. 'scorched-earth policy.' Encyclopaedia Britannica, March 8, 2024. www.britannica.com/topic/scorched-earth-policy.

Wallis, A. 2020. *The Kebra Nagast*. 2020. Metmuseum.org. 2020. www.metmuseum.org/art/collection/search/465954.

Whistler, Simon. 2023. Review of *Queen Ranavalona I of Madagascar*. *Biographics*. www.youtube.com/watch?v=u_JZm4-FT64.

White, Shelby, and Leon Levy. 2018. 'Amun Sanctuary – Jebel Barkal (Sudan).' Harvard.edu. Program for Archaeological Publications. 2018. www.whitelevy.fas.harvard.edu/amun-sanctuary-%E2%80%93-jebel-barkal-sudan.

Wilford, John Noble. 2007. 'Tooth May Have Solved Mummy Mystery.' *The New York Times*, June 27, 2007, sec. World. www.nytimes.com/2007/06/27/world/middleeast/27mummy.html

World Health Organization. 2009. 'Influenza.' www.who.int. www.who.int/europe/news-room/fact-sheets/item/influenza.

World Health Organization. 2013. 'Malaria.' www.who.int. www.who.int/europe/news-room/fact-sheets/item/malaria.

World Health Organization. 2022. 'Smallpox.' www.who.int. World Health Organization. 2022. www.who.int/health-topics/smallpox#tab=tab_1.

World Health Organization. 2023. 'Measles and Rubella EURO.' www.who.int. www.who.int/europe/health-topics/measles#tab=tab_1.

World History Edu. 2020. 'Khonsu: Ancient Egyptian God of the Moon and Time.' World History Edu. October 21, 2020. www.worldhistoryedu.com/khonsu-ancient-egyptian-god-of-the-moon-and-time/.

World History Edu. 2021. 'Ahmose I: History, Accomplishments and Facts.' World History Edu. October 13, 2021. www.worldhistoryedu.com/ahmose-i-history-accomplishments-and-facts/.

World History Edu. 2021. 'Neith – Origins, Family, Meaning, Symbols & Powers.' World History Edu. March 25, 2021. www.worldhistoryedu.com/neith-origins-family-meaning-symbols-powers/.

World History Edu. 2022. 'Neithhotep: History, Facts, & Achievements.' World History Edu. April 15, 2022. www.worldhistoryedu.com/neithhotep-history-facts-achievements/.

Zaimeche, S., Sutton, Keith, Brown, L. Carl and Chanderli, Abdel Kader. 'Algeria.' Encyclopaedia Britannica, March 13, 2024. www.britannica.com/place/Algeria.

Index